150 MOVIES
YOU SHOULD ˄ SEE
DIE BEFORE YOU

150 MOVIES
YOU SHOULD ∧ SEE
DIE BEFORE YOU

Steve Miller

Avon, Massachusetts

Copyright © 2010 by F+W Media, Inc.
All rights reserved.
This book, or parts thereof, may not be reproduced in any
form without permission from the publisher; exceptions are
made for brief excerpts used in published reviews.

Published by
Adams Media, a division of F+W Media, Inc.
57 Littlefield Street, Avon, MA 02322. U.S.A.
www.adamsmedia.com

ISBN 10: 1-4405-0362-1
ISBN 13: 978-1-4405-0362-7
eISBN 10: 1-4405-0902-6
eISBN 13: 978-1-4405-0902-5

Printed in the United States of America.

10 9 8 7 6 5 4 3 2 1

Library of Congress Cataloging-in-Publication Data
is available from the publisher.

Movie title film strip art © istockphoto / korhankaracan
Vertical film strip art and table of contents film strip art © istockphoto / begur
Thumbs-down art © istockphoto / kkonkle
Movie clapboard © istockphoto / browndogstudios

This book is available at quantity discounts for bulk purchases.
For information, please call 1-800-289-0963.

Acknowledgments

I may be having fun at the expense of their movies in this book, but it wouldn't exist if not for some filmmakers who have made bad movies for which I have genuine affection. My deep gratitude for all the entertainment to Charles Band, Mario Bava, Uwe Boll, Roger Corman, Kerry Douglas Dye, John Johnson, Sam Katzman, Lloyd Kaufman, Henry Towers, Ted V. Mikels, Dan Wascavage, and Edward D. Wood, Jr.

I also want to extend a big thank you to my editor, Peter Archer. This would have been a very different book without his invaluable input.

Dedication

To Dan, Lars, Jesper, Vibeke, Loie, Jeff, Michelle, Miranda, Greg, Shaun, and Kate—as well as anyone I may be forgetting—who, over the past thirty years, repeatedly sat down to watch bad movies with me. (And I offer apologies for the times I had to trick you.)

CONTENTS

Chapter Eleven.
Mysteries of the Orient

Chapter Twelve.
Independent Oddities

INTRODUCTION

From when I was in my early teens, about the time we were the first family in our neighborhood to have a VCR, I've had a strange fascination with what People of Taste call "bad movies." Whether it's weak plots or just nonsensical storylines; whether it's acting on the level of a bad high school play; whether it's special effects created in someone's kitchen with a Mixmaster and a bottle of ketchup; whether it's technical incompetence on the part of some or all members of the crew; or whether it's a mind-shattering combination of all of the above, there is something magical about bad movies. Something that makes them worth the sometimes considerable effort to sit through.

After watching and reviewing thousands of movies that even the most charitable reviewer would describe as "pathetic," I've concluded that the reason we keep coming back to bad movies and the people who make them—because, as you will see, there are filmmakers whose long lists of credits don't contain a single good movie—is because for every minute of film time that is completely unwatchable, there are ten that are full of creative insanity that the makers of mainstream movies wouldn't dare to put on screen.

We, the lovers of bad movies, dig through the piles of trash, looking for those shining gems of pure cinematic magic. We prefer that quest over the blandness and uniformity of the "good movie" and its adherence to standards determined by convention and critical fiat.

Despite the derogatory things I say about the films in this book, I have great respect for the men and women who created them. A lot of work goes into filming even the worst movies. Movie making is hard, time-consuming labor, no matter what role the professional plays in its creation. The act of finishing a film and getting it before an audience is worthy of respect—particularly in the fifties and sixties, when many of these movies were made, a time when movie-making was even more backbreaking than today.

Although the movies in this book are uniformly awful, I number some of them among my all-time favorites. *1941*, *The Black Cat*, *Dead Alive*, *Hideous*, and *Mask of Fu Manchu* are but a few of the dozen or so films in this book that I recommend to anyone who has trashy taste—like me. In fact, in spite of this book's title, I suspect that someone out there will find every one of these films a guilty pleasure. (Except, possibly, for the films discussed in Chapter 15. These movies were probably included in the CIA's arsenal of "harsh interrogation techniques.")

So though my critical alarm bells go off when a bad movie hits the screen, I have to confess that often the film finds a visceral response. My respect for a movie doubles when the film is entertaining . . . even if that entertainment may be of a different kind than its creators intended.

In particular, I want to express special gratitude to the people who worked on more than one of the movies discussed in this book, be they filmmakers or actors. Often I seek out work by these people, no matter how bad their films are by critical standards.

If you want to share your opinion on a film discussed in this book, please visit my website at *www.moviesyoushouldnotsee.com*. I enjoy hearing what other aficionados of trash movies have to say about them, and even more I love recommendations for what I should see next.

I hope to get to know you all through the wonders of computer technology!

CHAPTER ONE

EXHIBITS IN THE BAD MOVIE MUSEUM

If you ask a film buff to name five bad movies, at least one of the following is likely to be on his or her list. Some are "so bad they're good," while others are, well, just plain bad.

BATTLEFIELD EARTH: A SAGA OF THE YEAR 3000
Franchise Pictures/Morgan Creek Productions/Warner Bros., 2000

PRODUCERS Jonathan D. Krane, Ellie Samaha, and John Travolta
WRITERS Corey Mandell and J. D. Shapiro (based on a novel by L. Ron Hubbard)
DIRECTOR Roger Christian
STARS John Travolta (*Terl*), Barry Pepper (*Jonnie Goodboy Tyler*), and Forest Whitaker (*Ker*)

For 1,000 years, the monstrous aliens known as Psychlos have ruled Earth, plundering its natural resources and slowly driving humanity ever closer to extinction. Now, the arrogance and greed of embittered Psychlo security chief Terl (Travolta) and the unbreakable spirit of a young man named Jonnie Goodboy Tyler (Pepper) will clash and give humanity one last chance for survival. It's the Final Battle, and one species will live while another will die.

Why It Sucks

Battlefield Earth is very much like the L. Ron Hubbard novel it's based on. It's *waaaay* too long, and the longer it drags on, the more ridiculous it becomes. The only way to get through this film is to park your brain at the door, because the story starts out silly and by the time the climactic battle rolls around it's galloped all the way into drooling blather. Even the battle scenes can't help the movie get over trying to stretch 70 minutes of moderate excitement into 120 minutes. And the whole thing is punctuated by bad special-effect shots, characters running about aimlessly, and John Travolta in dreadlocks.

Thumbs Down Rating: 🖓🖓🖓

The Crappies

The Worst Acting Award goes to . . . John Travolta, for the bizarre, pseudo-British, ever-shifting accent that poses a serious challenge to Madonna in the Worst Fake Accent Ever competition. (Is this what Psychlos sound like in English?)

And the Worst Writing Logic Award goes to . . . Corey Mandell and J. D. Shapiro, with a nod to L. Ron Hubbard for the original novel. The U.S. Army base at Fort Hood has flight simulators and Harrier fighter planes that after 1,000 years of disuse are functioning and filled with useable fuel? Uh huh.

They Really Said It!

Terl: Kill all man-animals!

Betcha Didn't Know

» The film was intended to be the first of two, but plans for the sequel were scrapped following its poor performance.

» *Battlefield Earth* was reported to have cost $73 million to make, but only grossed some $22 million at the U.S. box office. In truth, the film only cost $44 million, but production company

Franchise Pictures inflated the budget in an attempt to defraud investors. They were successfully sued, ordered to pay $121 million in damages, and went bankrupt.

 Trivia Quiz

What tagline was often used during the movie's promotion?

A: It's the Year 3000 and Humans Are the Endangered Species.

B: From the Mind of Sci-Fi Legend L. Ron Hubbard

C: Go for the Gold on Battlefield Earth!

D: Prepare to Go Psychlo

Answer: D. Prepare to Go Psychlo. (Other taglines for the film were "Prepare for Battle" and "Take Back the Planet.")

BRIDE OF THE MONSTER (AKA *"BRIDE OF THE ATOM"*)
Rolling M. Productions, 1955

PRODUCER Edward D. Wood Jr.

WRITER Edward D. Wood Jr.

DIRECTOR Edward D. Wood Jr.

STARS Bela Lugosi (*Dr. Eric Vornoff*), Loretta King (*Janet Lawton*), Tor Johnson (*Lobo*), Tony McCoy (*Lt. Dick Craig*), Harvey B. Dunn (*Capt. Tom Robbins*), Paul Marco (*Officer Kelton*), and George Becwar (*Prof. Vladimir Strowski*)

A mad scientist (Lugosi) captures those who venture too close to his dilapidated house and subjects them to weird experiments intended to create a new race of radioactive supermen. When he captures a nosy female tabloid reporter (King), can it be long before his simpleminded assistant (Johnson) falls in love with her?

Why It Sucks

Ed Wood is sometimes characterized as the worst director who ever lived, and *Bride of the Monster* is the quintessential Ed Wood movie. It's full of strange characters badly acted, situations that are minimally explained, sets that are shoddily made . . . almost everything about it is supremely dreadful. The film reaches its nadir when Bela Lugosi is turned into an atomic monster via the use of platform shoes (yes, you read that correctly). (Tor Johnson looks sort of like Shrek, but Wood couldn't help that.)

Thumbs Down Rating: 👎 👎

The Crappies

The Weirdest Character Award goes to . . . The bird-loving police captain Harvey Dunn, who is more interested in discussing his pet exotic birds than the murders and missing-person cases.

And the Lamest Prop Award goes to . . . The atomic-monster-making contraption in Dr. Vornoff's lab, key components of which are darkroom equipment and the metal salad bowl worn on the head of those subjected to Dr. Vornoff's evil experiments.

They Really Said It!

Janet: When did I tell you my name?

Dr. Vornoff: You didn't. But since you were unconscious, I took the liberty of looking into your purse.

Betcha Didn't Know

» This was Edward D. Wood Jr.'s only financially successful film.

» Wood Jr. vowed *Bride of the Monster* would return Bela Lugosi to the star status he had lost as a result of bad career choices and drug abuse. It was perhaps a blessing in disguise that Lugosi passed away less than a year after the film's release.

 ### Trivia Quiz
In what movie did Bela Lugosi play God (literally)?

A: *The Ten Commandments* (1956)

B: *His Girl Friday* (1940)

C: *Glen or Glenda?* (1953)

D: *The Devil Bat* (1940)

Answer: C. *Glen or Glenda?* Bela Lugosi appears as one of several narrators featured in one of the most jumbled and confusing movies ever made. His character is named "The Scientist" in the script, but the character is clearly intended to be God.

CREATURE WITH THE ATOM BRAIN
Clover Productions, 1955

PRODUCER Sam Katzman

WRITER Curt Siodmak

DIRECTOR Edward L. Cahn

STARS Richard Denning (*Dr. Chet Walker*), S. John Launer (*Capt. Dave Harris*), Gregory Gaye (*Dr. Wilhelm Steigg*), Michael Granger (*Frank Buchanan*), and Angela Stevens (*Joyce Walker*)

When police scientist Dr. Chet Walker (Denning) discovers that dead men are walking the streets of a California town, killing law enforcers and gangsters alike, it is only the first glimpse into a nightmarish case that will bring him face to face with impervious zombies created by Nazi science and the power of the atom in order to sate the vengeance of an exiled gang lord (Granger).

Why It Sucks

In the 1950s, people believed "the power of the atom can do anything." Scientists smoked pipes and wore white coats to show how moral and reliable they were, while their wives stayed at home and looked pretty. This movie features all these things, overlaid by a storyline about corpses reanimated by nuclear-powered brains and nervous systems (which goes to show that the power of the atom can do some nasty things along the way). It's an example of dusty old sci-fi conventions that seem stale by today's criteria and that even by the standards of the 1950s were pretty awful.

Thumbs Down Rating: 👎

The Crappies

The Most Ignorant of Laws of Physics and Modern Technology Award goes to . . . Writer Curt Siodmak and director Edward L. Cahn for depicting Air Force jets flying very, very slooooowly over an urban area while searching for radioactivity.

And the Shoulda Thought This Through Award goes to . . . The character of Frank Buchanan (Granger), who financed the "atomic zombies" project but had no contingency plans when things started to go sideways. Makes you wonder how he made enough money to back the crackpot scientist in the first place.

They Really Said It!

Dr. Chet Walker: There seems to be some sort of definite pattern. Can't put my finger on it, but I do know that Hennessey and McGraw were killed for a reason.

Joyce Walker: Well, it's all right then?

Dr. Chet Walker: Well, for a while. I don't think they've gotten around to indiscriminate killings yet.

Betcha Didn't Know

» This is the first film to use squibs to simulate gunshot wounds.

» Screenwriter Curt Siodmack left Germany for the United States in 1937 after the Nazis came to power.

Exhibits in the Bad Movie Museum

 Trivia Quiz

What is a "squib"?

A: An animated effect added in post-production to simulate blood-spatter.

B: A tiny explosive attached to an actor or prop and used to simulate bullet impacts.

C: Movie biz slang for the person who supervises firearms on-set.

D: A special effects technician who throws tiny capsules at actors to make it appear they've been shot during a scene.

Answer: B. The originals were used to separate coal from rocks in mining. They were later adapted for use on stage or in films, often covered with packs of stage blood or other materials to simulate bullet strikes.

PRODUCERS David DeFalco and Michael Feichtner (executive producers), Charles Band, Kirk Edward Hansen, and Vlad Paunescu (producers)

WRITERS Benjamin Carr (script) and Charles Band (story)

DIRECTOR Charles Band

STARS Jerry O'Donnell (*Detective Kantor*), Jacqueline Lovell (*Sheila*), Tracie May (*Belinda Yost*), Rhonda Griffin (*Elvina*), Mel Johnson Jr. (*Napoleon Lazar*), and Michael Citriniti (*Dr. Lorca*)

Two rival collectors of preserved fetuses and other "medical oddities" (Citriniti and Johnson) and their staffs are trapped inside a house. Also present: a bizarre mutant who has reanimated a collection of deformed fetuses and turned them into tiny killing machines.

Why It Sucks

Well, for starters, it's a movie about reanimated malformed fetuses that turn a house into a death trap! It's got performers who are in overacting hyperdrive, chewing up the scenery and playing as if to the back of a very large theater. Just when you think the film can't get any more twisted . . . it does!

Thumbs Down Rating: 👎

The Crappies

The Lamest Death Award goes to . . . Rhonda Griffin (as Elvina), the dumb blond who gets a dumber death when she trips, falls, and dies, tumbling onto broken glass. Watch out next time you drop a glass on the kitchen floor!

And the Bad Feng Shui Award goes to . . . Writers Charles Band and Benjamin Carr for dreaming up a house where a feature of the living room is a pit full of acid.

They Really Said It!

Napoleon Lazar (to Sheila, who is dressed in hiking boots, shorts, and a gorilla mask): And what are you doing walking around like that, with no top on?

Sheila: I'm free, I'm proud, I'm woman!

Betcha Didn't Know

» Deformed fetuses (or "medical oddities," as they are referred to in *Hideous!*) displayed in glass jars used to be among the most popular attractions at carnival sideshows.

» Charles Band brought Dr. Lorca back in the 2010 film *Demonic Toys 2: Personal Demons*. Apparently, he too escaped from the acid pit. Sadly, topless Sheila is nowhere to be seen in that movie.

Trivia Quiz

What term was typically used to describe the "medical oddities" displayed in glass jars in sideshows?

A: Little Dead Things

B: Hideous Deformities

C: Pickled Punks

D: Bathed Babies

Answer: C. Pickled Punks. In the 1960s, laws finally caught up with the unsavory practices of sideshow carnies, and exhibitors of the fetuses were driven out of business.

TROLL 2
Filmirage, 1990

PRODUCERS David Hills and Brenda Norris

WRITERS Rosella Drudi and Drake Floyd

DIRECTOR Drake Floyd

STARS Michael Stephenson (*Josh*), Robert Ormsby (*Grandpa Seth*), George Hardy (*Michael*), Connie MacFarland (*Holly*), Margo Prey (Diana), Deborah Reed (*Creedence Leonore Gielgud*), Jason Wright (*Elliot*), and Darren Ewing (*Arnold*)

Little Josh (Stephenson) and the ghost of his dead grandpa (Ormsby) are the only two who know the hideous secret of the tiny town where Josh's family is spending their vacation. Can Josh convince the adults (Hardy and Prey) and his older sister (Mac-Farland) of the truth before they become goblin chow?

Why It Sucks

This flick displays every shade of bad you can think of. The pacing is erratic and always off, racing through parts that could have used a little more time (like the final fight against the goblins) and dragging through parts that should have been quick (like shopping trips). Parts that were supposed to be scary are hilarious (the flesh-eating goblins are vegetarians), and the parts that were supposed to be funny or dramatic are just strange. Oh, and the "clever" parts are just stupid. (Nilbog, the town where the family is vacationing, is "goblin" spelled backward!)

Thumbs Down Rating: 👎👎👎👎👎

The Crappies

The Worst Picture Award goes to . . . David Hills and Brenda Norris for producing and Rosella Drudi and Drake Floyd for writing and directing a movie titled *Troll 2* that features no trolls. Not one. Not even one of those spikey-haired Norwegian dolls.

And the Most Shocking Misuse of Magical Time Distortion Award goes to . . . Little Josh (played by Michael Stephenson). When his magical undead grandpa manages to stop time for a few seconds, Josh pees on the poisoned food the goblins are using to turn humans into vegetables, thus stopping his family from eating it. Yuck!!!!

They Really Said It!

Holly: If my father discovers you here, he'll cut off your little nuts and eat them.

Betcha Didn't Know

» Morgan, Utah, the town that served as Nilbog in the film, played host to a festival in June of 2008 that celebrated *Troll 2*.

» David Hills is one of the seventy (verified) pseudonyms for the late, multitalented Italian writer/director/producer/composer cinematographer/pornographer Joe D'Amato. (Joe D'Amato is itself a pseudonym, as he was born Arestide Massaccesi.)

 Trivia Quiz

How do the flesh-eating goblins in *Troll 2* manage to keep true to their vegetarian diets?

A: They eat tofu, the substance that alchemists sought after for centuries, because it can be transformed into any conceivable food item.

B: Fish, and lots of it.

C: They eat fillet of soul.

D: They turn people into plants then reduce them to a Cream of Wheat–like substance.

Answer: D. They turn people into plants, then reduce them to a Cream of Wheat–like substance. And no, it still doesn't make sense after you've seen the movie.

CHAPTER TWO

BIG BUDGET BOMBS

Sometimes, even the best idea doesn't click with the audience. Sometimes, a film was just too expensive and the investment couldn't be recovered. And then there are films that fail because they deserve to.

THE BLACK DAHLIA
Universal Pictures/Millennium Films, 2006

PRODUCERS Rudy Cohen, Moshe Diamant, Avi Lerner, and Art Linson

WRITERS Josh Friedman (script), James Ellroy (novel)

DIRECTOR Brian De Palma

STARS Josh Hartnett (*Bucky Bleichert*), Aaron Eckhart (*Lee Blanchard*), Scarlett Johansson (*Kay Lake*), Mia Kirshner (*Elizabeth Short*), and Hilary Swank (*Madeleine Linscott*)

A publicity-hungry police detective (Eckhart) arranges to have himself and his younger partner (Hartnett) assigned to the grisly murder of a would-be actress (Kirshner). As one detective starts to mysteriously come unglued, the other uncovers not only dark secrets relating to the dead actress, but to his partner as well.

Why It Sucks

Does it seem weird that the Black Dahlia murder, one of the most well-known scandals in Hollywood history *and the title of the freakin' film* is relegated to a minor tangent in this movie? The story moves randomly from plot to subplot, while director De Palma swings widely between cinematic tones and styles, from film noir to documentary. Not a single shot in the film lasts more than ten seconds, and all the quick edits and jumps accomplish nothing other than to provide insight into what it must be like to suffer from Attention Deficit Disorder.

Thumbs Down Rating: 🐾🐾🐾🐾

The Crappies

The Worst Actor Award goes to . . . Josh Hartnett for the role of Bucky Bleichert. The character's such a weepy crybaby that you feel embarrassed for him.

And the Worst Director Award goes to . . . Brian De Palma for having such inability to command a proper tone that he can't even make footage from a supposed screen test of Elizabeth Short believable.

They Really Said It!

Bucky Bleichert: The basic rules of homicide applied: Nothing stays buried forever. Corpses. Ghosts. Nothing stays buried forever. Nothing.

Betcha Didn't Know

» The film had an estimated budget of $50 million, but it only grossed around $23 million during its American theatrical run.
» Brian De Palma also directed the 2007 flop *Redacted*. It cost $5 million to make, but barely made $64,000 during its theatrical run in the United States.

Trivia Quiz

What celebrity did Los Angeles authorities investigate as a suspect in the murder of Elizabeth Short?

A: Orson Welles

B: Alfred Hitchcock

C: Woody Guthrie

D: Boris Karloff

Answer: C: Woody Guthrie. The folk singer was, according to the Los Angeles district attorney's files on the case, briefly a suspect due to sexually explicit letters he sent to a woman in Northern California.

THE CONQUEROR (AKA *"CONQUEROR OF THE DESERT"*)

RKO Radio Pictures, 1956

PRODUCERS Dick Powell and Howard Hughes

WRITER Oscar Millard

DIRECTOR Dick Powell

STARS John Wayne (*Temujin, Genghis Khan*), Susan Hayward (*Bortai*), Agnes Moorhead (*Hunlun*), Pedro Armendáriz *(Jamuga)*, and Ted de Corsia (*Kumlek*)

Mongolian warlord Temujin (Wayne) must do battle against the rival tribe that killed his father, fight with the red-haired Tartar prisoner Bortai (Hayward) whom he captured in a raid and has vowed to make his wife, and deal with intrigues in his inner circle. Enemies of every type stand arrayed against him as he fights his way to a place in history as the legendary Genghis Khan.

Why It Sucks

Few bad movies look as good as *The Conqueror*. It's got great costumes, brilliant colors, and the tale of a great warlord. But sometimes it takes only one thing to turn a film from a triumph to a turkey, and someone in central casting who must have been drunk, high, or both, decided to star John Wayne as Genghis

Big Budget Bombs

Khan. That's right. *John Wayne!* Few movies have such a dramatic mix of the spectacular with the absolutely atrocious as this one.

Thumbs Down Rating: 👎👎👎

The Crappies

The Worst Acting Award goes to . . . John Wayne as Temujin. No contest. Not even a question. What were they thinking?

And the Worst Picture Award goes to . . . Howard Hughes and Dick Powell for making a movie about a cool subject, and researching Genghis Khan about as badly as one of those Italian Hercules films—at ten times the cost.

They Really Said It!

(To get the full effect, close your eyes and imagine John Wayne saying it.) *Temujin:* While I live, while my blood burns hot, your daughter is not safe in her tent.

Betcha Didn't Know

» The movie was shot downwind from where the United States conducted above-ground atomic weapons tests. Rumor has it the cast and crew developed cancer at three times higher than the average among the general population.

» Financier Howard Hughes felt so guilty about the cast and crew being exposed to radioactivity that he reportedly spent $12 million to acquire every existing print of the film.

Trivia Quiz

What famous movie detective did John Wayne turn down the opportunity to play?

A: Bulldog Drummond

B: Sam Spade

C: Nero Wolfe

D: "Dirty" Harry Callahan

Answer: D. "Dirty" Harry Callahan. Wayne was offered but turned down the role of hard-bitten Inspector Harry Callahan, which eventually became one of Clint Eastwood's signature roles.

HEAVEN'S GATE

United Artists, 1980

PRODUCERS Denis O'Dell, Charles Okun, Wayne Reynolds (executive producers), Joann Carelli (producer)

WRITER Michael Cimino

DIRECTOR Michael Cimino

STARS Kris Kristofferson (*James Averill*), Isabelle Huppert (*Ella Watson*), Christopher Walken (*Nathan D. Champion*), Jeff Bridges (*John Bridges*), and Sam Waterston (*Frank Canton*)

When a wealthy and powerful rancher's association hires killers to wipe out settlers in Johnson County, Wyoming, the Harvard-educated and privileged-by-birth county sheriff (Kristofferson) stands against his own class to protect them.

Why It Sucks

Infamous as the film that destroyed United Artists, this movie is the definition of bloated. Filled with irrelevant scenes and characters, the film is torture to sit through (the original cut shown to the studio was five and a half hours long). During production, Cimino built and rebuilt sets and took retakes of retakes of retakes. The final budget of $40 million, followed by the film's collapse at the box office, crushed the studio founded by Charlie Chaplin and D. W. Griffith, contributing to its sale to MGM.

Thumbs Down Rating: 🦃🦃🦃🦃

The Crappies

The Worst Auteur Award goes to . . . Michael Cimino for forcing the audience to sit through scene after scene that goes on endlessly while adding nothing to the story. Special mention also goes to Cimino for managing to shoot *fifty* takes of Kris Kristofferson brandishing a bullwhip.

And the Special Bailout Award for Worst Business Sense goes to . . . The producers of *Heaven's Gate* and United Artist executives for not putting on the brakes sooner.

They Really Said It!

John Bridges: It's getting dangerous to be poor in this country.

Betcha Didn't Know

» The original budget Cimino presented to executives was just over $2 million. The film cost a total of $42 million and took in less than $3 million at the box office.

» French actress Isabelle Huppert was hired for the role of Ella Watson, a Wyoming madam, despite her poor English. Cimino said her accent "would add to the richness of the soundtrack."

Trivia Quiz

Who said of *Heaven's Gate*: "I enjoy the film each time I see it more and more."

A: Michael Cimino

B: Jeff Bridges

C: Sam Waterston

D: Isabelle Huppert

Answer: B. Jeff Bridges, as quoted in Mark Cousin's 2002 book *Scene By Scene: Film Actors and Directors Discuss Their Work*.

HOWARD THE DUCK
Lucasfilm/Universal Pictures, 1986

PRODUCERS George Lucas (executive producer) and Gloria Katz (producer)

WRITERS William Huyck and Gloria Katz (script), Steve Gerber (characters)

DIRECTOR William Huyck

STARS Lea Thompson (*Beverly Switzler*), Chip Zien (*voice of Howard T. Duck*), Jeffrey Jones (*Dr. Walter Jenning*), Tim Robbins (*Phil Blumburtt*), and Ed Gale (*Howard T. Duck*)

When Howard T. Duck (Gale/Zien) is teleported to Earth from his home planet, this human-sized, talking bird must find out how to

17

live in a new world. And while he's adjusting, he must also thwart an alien invasion.

Why It Sucks

It could have been so damn good! This is one of many tragic examples of Hollywood paying lots of money for a creative property and then completely missing the point. *Howard the Duck*, the comic book created by the great Steve Gerber for Marvel Comics, was full of great satire and dark humor. *None* of that made it into the film adaptation. Nor did any of the series' ongoing subtext of isolation and alienation. Instead we get shallow comedy and an even shallower plot.

Thumbs Down Rating: 🦃🦃🦃

The Crappies

The Award for Worst Production Management goes to . . . Gloria Katz and George Lucas, for spending time and money on an animatronic duck suit, as if that were the answer to the film's script problems.

And the Award for Worst Animation goes to . . . The animators of the alien overlords, who did stop motion so badly that we feel like we're watching an outtake of a Ray Harryhausen film (though even Harryhausen's rejected bits were undoubtedly better animation than what we see here).

They Really Said It!

Howard T. Duck: "If God had wanted us to fly, he wouldn't have taken away our wings."

Betcha Didn't Know

» The film cost over $30 million dollars (some sources estimate as high as $37 million) but only grossed some $5.1 million during its theatrical run.
» Howard the Duck creator Steve Gerber engaged Marvel in a bitter legal battle over the rights to the character.

HUDSON HAWK

TriStar Pictures and Silver Pictures, 1991

PRODUCERS Robert Kraft (executive producer), Joel Silver (producer)

WRITERS Steven E. de Souza and Daniel Waters (script), Bruce Willis and Robert Kraft (story)

DIRECTOR Michael Lehmann

STARS Bruce Willis (*Hudson Hawk*), Danny Aiello (*Tommy "Five-Tone" Messina*), Andie MacDowell (*Anna Baragli*), Richard E. Grant (*Darwin Mayflower*), Sandra Bernhard (*Minerva Mayflower*), and James Coburn (*George Kaplan*)

On the day once-renowned cat-burglar Hudson Hawk (Willis) is released from prison, he is forced to help a pair of crazed billionaires (Bernhard and Grant) and a renegade CIA operative (Coburn) retrieve the hidden pieces of Leonardo Da Vinci's greatest invention: a device that will turn any metal into gold. All Hudson wants to do is go straight . . . or at least get a good cup of cappuccino.

Why It Sucks

The actors reportedly had a good time making this movie, but the audience sure doesn't have a good time watching it. The jokes often turn on obscure film buff references—which probably struck the writers as hilarious but to us sound lame. The film's

19

Big Budget Bombs

pacing and tone swing from frenetic slapstick to slow-moving black comedy, to a simple-minded action movie spoof. Bruce Willis spends so much time mugging at the camera that you expect to hear rim shots.

Thumbs Down Rating: 👎 👎 👎

The Crappies
The Worst Writing Award goes to . . . Steven E. de Souza and Daniel Waters for alluding to (though not, thank God, showing) Sandra Bernhard, Richard Grant, and Leonardo de Vinci naked and eating sushi in the back of a limo. California rolls will never taste the same again.

And the Worst Acting Award goes to . . . Bruce Willis. The guy can do comedy—as *Moonlighting* proved—but in this movie he confuses being funny with overacting.

They Really Said It!
Darwin Mayflower: History, tradition, culture are not concepts. These are trophies I keep in my den as paperweights!

Betcha Didn't Know
» George Kaplan, the CIA agent played by James Coburn, is also the name of the spy everyone is hunting in Hitchcock's *North By Northwest* (1959).

» The film cost around $65 million to make but barely made $17 million during its theatrical run in the United States.

 Trivia Quiz
What was the premise of the television series *Moonlighting*?
A: A police detective works nights as a stand-up comedian.
B: A stand-up comedian works as a private detective on the side.
C: A golf pro hunts werewolves during every full moon.
D: A detective agency is run by a former model and a wise-cracking tough guy.

(Willis starred as the tough guy, David Addison.)
Answer: D. A detective agency run by a former model and a wise-cracking tough guy.

ISHTAR
Columbia Pictures, 1987

PRODUCER Warren Beatty

WRITER Elaine May

DIRECTOR Elaine May

STARS Warren Beatty (*Lyle Rogers*), Dustin Hoffman (*Chuck Clarke*), Charles Grodin (*Jim Harrison*), and Isabelle Ajani (*Shirra Assel*)

A pair of wannabe singer/songwriters (Beatty and Hoffman) is booked by their indifferent agent for a gig in a civil-war torn area of North Africa. They are soon ignorantly bumbling their way through the schemes of vicious dictators, coldhearted CIA operatives, and rebel forces looking for divine signs that their revolution will be successful.

Why It Sucks

Some "comedies" are painful to watch because the main characters are so damn . . . *dumb*. The idiocy and naiveté on display from Beatty and Hoffman goes beyond comedic knuckleheadedness (remember Abbott and Costello?) and into stupidity so deep viewers can't help but feel embarrassed for them. The financial crater this movie created virtually assured that they'd never appear together in a film again.

Thumbs Down Rating: 🦃🦃🦃

The Crapples

The Worst Writing Award goes to . . . Elaine May, the punchlines for whose jokes can be sighted several miles away.

And the Worst Director Award goes to . . . Also Elaine May for constantly disrupting the film's comedic flow with heavy-handed speeches about friendship, hanging onto dreams, and the evils of American imperialism. Really. In a comedy.

They Really Said It!

Lyrics from a song by Rogers & Clarke: Telling the truth can be dangerous business. / Honest and popular don't go hand in hand. / If you admit that you can play the accordion, / No one'll hire you in a rock 'n' roll band.

Betcha Didn't Know

» Elaine May worked obsessively on editing the film and only turned it over to the studio after she was threatened with legal action.

» *Ishtar* had an estimated budget of $55 million but only made $12.7 million during its American theatrical run.

 Trivia Quiz

What was Warren Beatty's only movie during the 1990s that wasn't a financial disaster?

A: *Dick Tracy* (1990)

B: *Bugsy* (1991)

C: *Love Affair* (1994)

D: *Bulworth* (1998)

Answer: A. *Dick Tracy* had a budget of $47 million and earned almost $104 million during its American theatrical run.

SAHARA
Paramount Pictures/Bristol Bay Productions, 2005

PRODUCERS Gus Gustawes, William J. Immerman, Matthew McConaughey, and Vicky Dee Rock (executive producers), Stephanie Austin, Howard Baldwin, Karen Baldwin, and Mace Neufeld (producers)

WRITERS Thomas Dean Donnelly, Joshua Oppenheimer, John C. Richards, and James V. Hart (script), Clive Cussler (novel)

DIRECTOR Breck Eisner

STARS Matthew McConaughey (*Dirk Pitt*), Steve Zahn (*Al Giordino*), Penélope Cruz (*Eva Rojas*), Lambert Wilson (*Yves Massarde*), and William H. Macy (*Jim Sandecker*)

Big Budget Bombs

Professional salvagers and adventurers (McConaughey, Zahn, and Macy) are on the trail of an American Civil War–era ironclad that vanished with millions of dollars worth of Confederate gold coins aboard. Evidence points to its final resting place deep within the wastelands of the Sahara desert.

Why It Sucks

Sahara could have been a turn-off-your-brain-and-enjoy-the-ride movie in the Indiana Jones mode. After all, that's the kind of novels Clive Cussler writes. Instead, the movie's saddled with a halfhearted political message (why do directors *do* that?). If that weren't bad enough there's the add-water-and-stir romance between McConaughey and Cruz's characters.

Thumbs Down Rating: 👎

The Crappies

The Worst Actress Award goes to . . . Penélope Cruz for being about as annoying and shrewish as possible. She even makes you forget how gorgeous she is.

And the Take the Money and Run Award goes to . . . Author Clive Cussler, who, after selling the rights to adapt his characters to film, immediately badmouthed *Sahara*. Dude, it's Hollywood. What did you think they were going to do with it?

They Really Said It!

General Kazim: Don't worry. It's Africa. Nobody cares about Africa.

Betcha Didn't Know

» *Sahara* reportedly cost $160 million to make but only made some $70 million during its theatrical run.

» Clive Cussler was paid $10 million for the rights to adapt the movie.

Trivia Quiz

What other movie based on a Clive Cussler novel detailed the adventures of Dirk Pitt and his associates?

A: *Dirk Pitt and Blackbeard's Treasure* (1994)

B: *Raise the Titanic* (1980)

C: *Hell and High Water* (1954)

D: *The Deep* (1977)

Answer: B. *Raise the Titanic* (1980). While Clive Cussler's novels may have been bestsellers, the films based upon them have been financial disasters. ITC spent $36 million to make the film but it only made some $14 million between theatrical screenings and home video rentals.

THE SPIRIT

Odd Lot Entertainment/Lions Gate Entertainment, 2008

PRODUCERS Michael Burns, Bill Lischak, Steven Maier, and Benjamin Melniker (executive producers), Deborah Del Prete, Gigi Pritzker, and Michael E. Uslan (producers)

WRITERS Frank Miller (script) and Will Eisner (characters, original comic book series)

DIRECTOR Frank Miller

STARS Gabriel Macht (*The Spirit/Denny Colt*), Samuel L. Jackson (*The Octopus*), Eva Mendes (*Sand Saref*), Scarlett Johannson (*Dr. Silken Floss*), Louis Lombardi (*Pathos/Ethos/Logos*), Dan Lauria (*Commisioner Dolan*), Stana Katic (*Officer Morgenstern*), and Paz Vega (*Plaster of Paris*)

The mysterious protector of Central City, the Spirit (Macht) squares off against the villainous Octopus (Jackson) over the secret behind the Spirit's powers and the key to world domination. But will triumph mean defeat for the Spirit? Has his long-lost childhood sweetheart, Sand Saref (Mendes), really joined forces with the Octopus?

Why It Sucks

Frank Miller claims to be a huge fan of comic book genius Will Eisner. Why then did he choose to write an adaptation of Eisner's signature creation that gutted it of its signature charm? Miller's convinced he can improve on a masterpiece by tearing it apart and rebuilding it in his own image. *The Spirit* is an empty shell of a movie that rehashes, poorly, the visual approach and writing style of Miller's *Sin City*.

Thumbs Down Rating: 🦃🦃🦃🦃

The Crappies

The Worst Script Award goes to . . . Frank Miller for combining three of Eisner's best and most complex characters—master criminal Sand Saref, black widow con-artist P'Gell, and international jewel thief Silk Satin—into one single, beautiful dame in a skimpy dress.

Big Budget Bombs

And the Worst Actor Award goes to . . . Samuel L. Jackson for his portrayal of the Octopus. Over the top is putting it mildly. He makes Jack Nicholson's Joker look like a model of restraint.

They Really Said It!

The Octopus: Free-range chickens with their big brown ugly-ass eggs. They piss me off. Every time I think about those big brown eggs they piss. Me. Off.

Betcha Didn't Know

» *The Spirit* was the lead feature in a weekly comic book supplement produced by Eisner's art studio between 1940 and 1952.

» The film made roughly $20 million during its U.S. theatrical run, but it had an estimated production cost of $35 million.

 Trivia Quiz

In *The Spirit* movie, Ellen Dolan is a physician. What does she do in the comic book series?

A: Dilettante and later mayor of Central City

B: Headmistress at a private school for girls

C: Dilettante and later a secret agent for the United States government

D: Accountant for the IRS

Answer: A. Dilettante and later mayor of Central City. For the first years of the series, Ellen Dolan tried a range of careers, including private investigator. At the end of an extended story arc, she became mayor.

CHAPTER THREE
CREAKY CLASSICS

The term "classic" implies a movie will transcend the moment of its creation and still hold appeal years after its creation. Marketers and reviewers, especially in the entertainment business, tend to use—and overuse—the oxymoronic phrase "instant classic." It is to them that I dedicate this chapter.

BLACK DRAGONS
Banner Productions, 1942

PRODUCERS Jack Dietz and Sam Katzman

WRITERS Harvey Gates (screenplay), Robert Kehoe (story)

DIRECTOR William Nigh

STARS Bela Lugosi (*Dr. Melcher/Colomb*), Clayton Moore (*Dick Martin*), Joan Barclay (*Alice Saunders*), George Pembroke (*Dr. William Saunders*), and Irving Mitchell (*John Van Dyke*)

As America gears up to fight the Japanese during World War II, a group of wealthy Fifth Columnists finalize their plans to sabotage the war effort from the top down. However, they share a secret far deeper and more sinister. Why is the mysterious Mr. Colomb (Lugosi) murdering them, one by one? Is Colomb an American patriot, or is he a threat more sinister than even the enemy agents?

Why It Sucks

Back in the 1940s, Hollywood was cranking out war propaganda, and some of it was actually pretty good filmmaking. *Black Dragons*, sadly, isn't. A sloppy, badly constructed script manages to snuff out every spark that could have set this movie on fire. The ideas the filmmakers had aren't too bad; but evidently William Nigh was so worried about enemy sabotage that he forgot how to direct a movie.

Thumbs Down Rating: 👎👎👎👎👎

The Crappies

The Worst Script Award goes to . . . Harvey Gates for a script in which Bela Lugosi's character can apparently vanish into thin air when at risk of discovery and capture.

And the Worst Director Award goes to . . . William Nigh for letting Lugosi chew up the scenery and not even giving him a decent supporting cast.

They Really Said It!

Amos Hanlin: "A busy man has very little time to engage in feminine emotions."

Betcha Didn't Know

» The Black Dragon Society was a real-world, ultranationalist Japanese organization founded in 1901. From the 1920s to the 1940s, it assisted the Japanese Imperial Army in espionage, psychological warfare campaigns, and in the distribution of propaganda materials. It operated its own spy school and dispatched espionage agents throughout the world. (Unlike this movie, however, there is no record of the society using plastic surgery to transform short Japanese men into tall Caucasian men.)

 Trivia Quiz
What was the first movie in which William Nigh directed Bela Lugosi?

A: *The Ghost and the Guest*
B: *Mystery Liner*
C: *Monte Carlo Nights*
D: *The Mysterious Mr. Wong*

Answer: D. *The Mysterious Mr. Wong* (1934). Bela Lugosi stars as Mr. Wong, a Chinese crime lord seeking ultimate power through the mystical Twelve Coins of Confucius, and only a wisecracking reporter (Wallace Ford) can stop him.

CREATURE FROM THE BLACK LAGOON
Universal International Pictures, 1954

PRODUCER William Alland

WRITERS Harry Essex and Arthur A. Ross (script), Maurice Zimm (story)

DIRECTOR Jack Arnold

STARS Richard Carlson (*Dr. David Reed*), Julie Adams (*Kay Lawrence*), Antonio Moreno (*Carl Maia*), Richard Denning (*Dr. Mark Williams*), and Nestor Paiva (*Capt. Lucas*)

A group of scientists travel into the Amazon jungle to retrieve an unusual fossil, but instead they find themselves battling a very-much-alive amphibious humanoid.

Why It Sucks

Sometimes a movie's so bad you root for the monster. If the so-called scientists in this movie behaved a little more like, oh, I don't know, *scientists* instead of 1920s big-game hunters, they might learn the creature's intelligent. More intelligent than them, anyway, though that's not saying much. I mean, look at it from the creature's point of view: Wouldn't you be angry with interlopers

Creaky Classics

29

who keep shooting sharp sticks and shining blinding lights at you? Someone needed to ask, "What would Margaret Mead do?"

Thumbs Down Rating: 👎👎

The Crappies

The Ugly American Award goes to . . . The main human characters for being unsympathetic, stupid, or both.

And the Worst Picture Award goes to . . . Producer William Alland for a film that was creepy and politically incorrect even in 1954.

They Really Said It!

Lucas: I can tell you something about this place. The boys around here call it "The Black Lagoon"; a paradise. Only they say nobody has ever come back to prove it

Creaky Classics

Betcha Didn't Know

» This was the first 3D feature produced by Universal Studios. It was made in attempt to replicate the financial success that Warner Bros. enjoyed with its 1953 3D film *House of Wax*.

» The Creature (or "Gill Man") is considered by many critics to be the last of the great monsters created at Universal Pictures, although some might argue that the Graboids from the *Tremors* series have taken that title. The latter were also featured in two fairly decent movies, two semi-watchable ones, and a television series of dubious quality. The Creature was only in one watchable film and a couple awful sequels.

Trivia Quiz

In what country is the Black Lagoon located?

A: Brazil

B: Mexico

C: Paraguay

D: Argentina

Answer: A. Brazil, along the Amazon River. Despite this, in one of the first scenes there is a large sign reading in Spanish "Instituto de Investigaciones Biológicas." The official language in Brazil is Portuguese.

THE MASK OF FU MANCHU
MGM, 1932

PRODUCER Irving G. Thalberg

WRITERS Irene Kuhn, Edgar Allan Woolf, and John Willard (script), Sax Rohmer (story)

DIRECTORS Charles Brabin and Charles Vidor

STARS Boris Karloff (*Fu Manchu*), Myrna Loy (*Fah Lo See*), Lewis Stone (*Sir Denis Nayland Smith*), Charles Starrett (*Terrence Granville*), Jean Hersholt (*Von Berg*), and Karen Morley (*Sheila Barton*)

Sir Nayland Smith (Stone) and an international group of archaeologists led by Professor Von Berg (Hersholt) square off against evil genius Fu Manchu (Karloff) and his diabolical daughter Fah

Creaky Classics

Lo See (Loy) in an effort to stop Fu Manchu's latest scheme to conquer the world.

Why It Sucks

Despite the fact that this is one of the best cinematic uses of Sax Rohmer's characters, it's marred by incredible racism. Even in 1932 this was pretty over the top, and by today's hypersensitive standards it makes this a very hard film to watch. This is despite the mix of weird science, bizarre torture-traps, supernatural hokum, savage natives lusting for a white girl to be sacrificed to dark gods, and, of course, Fu Manchu being thwarted with his own superweapon on the edge of his victory.

Thumbs Down Rating: 👎

The Crappies

The Worst Makeup Award goes to . . . Boris Karloff's Fu Manchu makeup. Apparently, the director and producer wanted to make so sure that we understood the Asians are *alien* that they made him look like a Martian.

And the Worst Actor Award goes to . . . Charles Starrett for portraying a macho hero so dull that it's impossible to understand why Fah Lo See, Fu Manchu's sadistic daughter, doesn't get tired of him. Maybe horniness trumps boredom.

They Really Said It!

Fah Lo See: He is not entirely unhandsome, is he, my father?
Fu Manchu: For a white man, no.

Betcha Didn't Know

» Although best remembered for playing witty high-society women like Nora Charles in the Thin Man series, Myrna Loy spent her early career playing exotic femmes fatales. Fah Lo See in this movie was her final turn as a villainous female.

» During the 1940s, Boris Karloff brought another fictional Chinese character from the printed page to the silver screen, the San Francisco-born detective James Lee Wong.

Trivia Quiz

Which of these actors has *not* played Fu Manchu on film?

A: Peter Sellers

B: Nicholas Cage

C: James Wong

D: Christopher Lee

Answer: C. James Wong, the only Asian actor on the list.

RED DAWN
United Artists, 1984

PRODUCERS Sidney Beckerman (executive producer), Barry Beckerman and Buzz Feitshans (producers)

WRITERS Kevin Reynolds (story), Kevin Reynolds and John Milius (script)

DIRECTOR John Milius

STARS Patrick Swayze (*Jed*), Charlie Sheen (*Matt*), C. Thomas Howell (*Robert*), Jennifer Grey (*Toni*), Lea Thompson (*Erica*), Darren Dalton (*Daryl*), Harry Dean Stanton (*Mr. Eckert*), and Powers Boothe (*Col. Andy Tanner*)

A group of teens band together to fight the Russian and Cuban troops who have occupied their small town as the United States is invaded during World War III.

Why It Sucks

This movie is a survivalists' wet dream. It's not the big armies that matter in a Cold War conflict between the Soviets and the United States. It's a bunch of armed high-school students in Colorado. Even accepting the film as a product of its time, this is the kind of movie that you enjoy if you're holed up in a compound on a mountaintop in Idaho, waiting to fend off the agents of the New World Order.

Creaky Classics

33

Thumbs Down Rating: 🖕🖕

The Crappies

The Worst Picture Award goes to . . . Barry Beckerman and Buzz Feitshans for a film so essentially silly that today it looks like something dragged out of a time capsule.

And the Worst Picture Award goes to . . . Lea Thompson for a playing a quintessential thick-skulled, nonessential female—which probably says something about the filmmakers' attitudes toward women in general.

They Really Said It!

Erica: You American?

Col. Andy Tanner: Red-blooded.

Erica: What's the capital of Texas.

Col. Andy Tanner: Austin

Erica: Wrong, Commie! It's Houston!

Betcha Didn't Know

» This was Charlie Sheen's first screen appearance, and the first major film role for Jennifer Grey.

» This was the first film released with a PG-13 rating.

Trivia Quiz

What real-world documents inspired the storyline of the film, according to John Milius?

A: Speeches by President Ronald Reagan

B: Memoirs of French and Danish WWII freedom fighters

C: A report by the CIA and Army War College

D: The writings of Nostradamus

Answer: C. A report by the CIA and Army War College. In the early 1980s, the CIA and the Army War College released a study that described a possible invasion through Mexico by Soviet and Cuban troops.

TRAPPED BY TELEVISION
(AKA *"CAPTURED BY TELEVISION"*)
Columbia Pictures, 1936

PRODUCER Ben Pivar

WRITERS Harold Buchman and Lee Loeb (script), Sherman L. Lowe and Al Martin (story)

DIRECTOR Del Lord

STARS Mary Astor (*Roberta "Bobby" Blake*), Nat Pendleton (*Rocky O'Neil*), Lyle Talbot (*Fred Dennis*), Joyce Compton (*Mae Collins*), Robert Strange (*Standish*), Thurston Hall (*John Curtis*), Henry Mollison (*Thornton*), and Wyrley Birch (*Paul Turner*)

A tech-loving bill collector (Pendleton) decides to help an inventor (Talbot) promote the perfect television broadcasting/receiving device. Unfortunately, a group of violent techno-thieves are scheming to sell another type of television system, and they won't allow our hero and his roguish helpers to spoil their payday.

Why It Sucks

I suppose when television was new, some executive thought this was a great idea. Now, when my cellphone can handle what the broadcast camera in the film does, the movie is hopelessly dated.

Thumbs Down Rating: 👎👎

The Crappies

The Worst Actor Award goes to . . . Lyle Talbot for being a scientist so unconvincing you'd be nervous about trusting him to turn on the overhead light in the laboratory.

And the Special Award for a Vision of the Future goes to . . . Harold Buchman, Lee Loeb, Sherman Lowe, Al Martin, and Del Lord for having the perspicacity to show a flat-screen TV sixty-five years before they were actually available to the public.

They Really Said It!

Rocky: Ain't that marvelous? Did I ever tell you that science wuz my hobby?

Betcha Didn't Know

» Bela Lugosi also starred in a television-themed thriller in 1936. Titled *Death by Television*, the plot revolves around an inventor who dies under mysterious circumstances while demonstrating his new television broadcast method. One of Lugosi's more obscure films, it survives only in mangled and damaged prints.

» Mary Astor started her show business career after her father pushed her into signing up for a beauty pagent. She went on to appear in many successful films, such as *The Maltese Falcon* and her Oscar-winning performance in *The Great Lie*.

 Trivia Quiz

In what movies did Mary Astor appear alongside celebrated leading man William Powell?

A: *The Bright Shawl* (1923) and *The Kennel Murder Case* (1933)

B: *Map of the World* (1931) and *The Maltese Falcon* (1941)

C: *The Girl Who Had Everything* (1953) and *Grumpy Old Men* (1993)

D: *The Thin Man* (1934) and *Blonde Fever* (1944)

Answer: A. *The Bright Shawl* (1923) and *The Kennel Murder Case* (1933). *The Bright Shawl* involved gun-running in Cuba. In *The Kennel Murder Case*, Powell appears as private detective Philo Vance and Astor is a suspect in a baffling locked-room murder mystery.

ZOMBIES ON BROADWAY
(AKA *"LOONIES ON BROADWAY"*)
RKO Radio Pictures, 1945

PRODUCERS Sid Rogell (executive producer) and Benjamin Stoloff (producer)

WRITERS Lawrence Kimble (script), Robert Faber and Charles Newman (story)

DIRECTOR Gordon Douglas

STARS Wally Brown (*Jerry Miles*), Alan Carney (*Mike Streger*), Sheldon Leonard (*Ace Miller*), Bela Lugosi (*Dr. Paul Renault*), Anne Jeffreys (*Jean LeDance*), and Darby Jones (*Kolaga, the zombie*)

A pair of bumbling promoters (Brown and Carney) travel to the voodoo-haunted San Sebastian Island to find a real zombie for the opening night of a racketeer's new night club, the Zombie Hut.

Why It Sucks

Maybe the 1940s, with Fascism, the atomic bomb, and everything, just wasn't a good decade for comedy. In the years since it was made, *Zombies on Broadway* has had all its punch zapped out of it as if it had been attacked by, well, zombies. It was intended as a spoof of *I Walked with a Zombie*, a film practically no one remembers. Then there's the awful job the film's makeup artists did on the poor schmoe who plays the zombie. Incidentally, he's a zombie of the non–flesh-eating variety. They were standard before George Romero made *Night of the Living Dead.*

Thumbs Down Rating: 🎀 🎀 🎀 🎀

The Crappies

The Worst Acting Award goes to . . . Wally Brown and Alan Carney for performances that will make viewers wonder why they aren't watching the real Abbott and Costello instead of a studio-manufactured knockoff.

And the Worst Script Award goes to . . . Lawrence Kimble for writing a film so tightly connected with then-contemporary pop culture references that it is an antique *Disaster Movie.*

They Really Said It!

Jerry: How will we know a zombie if we see one?

Jean: If you see a corpse walking around—that's a zombie.

Betcha Didn't Know

» Actor Darby Jones and calypso singer Sir Lancelot play identical roles in this film and *I Walked with a Zombie.*

» This is one of three movies where Bela Lugosi got to show his talent for comedic acting.

 Trivia Quiz

In what series of zombie movies are zombies created via a scientifically developed chemical?

A: *Night of the Living Dead*

B: *Return of the Living Dead*

C: *White Zombie*

D: *Dead Alive*

Answer: B. *Return of the Living Dead.* The chemical Tri-Oxin turns people into unstoppable killing machines that crave the taste of human brains.

CHAPTER FOUR
FREAKY FAMILIES

When you're mad or unhappy with your relatives and/or family situation, you might find solace in watching the films talked about in this chapter. They will remind you that no matter how strange your family is, there's always one that's worse.

AMITYVILLE DOLLHOUSE
Promark Entertainment Group, 1996

PRODUCERS David Newlon (executive producer), Zane W. Levitt, Steve White, and Mark Yellen (producers)

WRITER Joshua Michael Stern

DIRECTOR Steve White

STARS Robin Thomas (*Bill Martin*), Starr Andreeff (*Claire Martin*), Allen Cutler (*Todd Martin*), Rachel Duncan (*Jessica Martin*), Jarrett Lennon (*Jimmy Martin*), Franc Ross (*Tobias*), and Lisa Robin Kelly (*Dana*)

Somewhere in the American southwest, a family moves into a newly constructed home. An old shack was left standing on the property, and within is found a dollhouse—an evil, haunted dollhouse built in the image of the infamous Amityville House. The youngest child starts playing with the dollhouse . . .

Why It Sucks

Don't bother asking why someone built a dollhouse replica of a place on Long Island. And don't ask how it ended up in a shack in the desert, or how it became filled with *eeeeevil*—the writer and director barely gave any thought to the subjects. The film's story is rendered even less scary by the fact that no one seems particularly distressed by the weird developments . . . at least not until the home's fireplace becomes a gateway to Hell.

Thumbs Down Rating: 🦃🦃🦃

The Crappies

The Worst Script Award goes to . . . Joshua Michael Stern for writing in the monumental fact that family friend Tobias just happens to be a demon hunter in his spare time.

And the Worst Director Award goes to . . . Steve White for a horror movie so illogical that the audience keeps looking around to make sure it hasn't fallen down a rabbit hole.

They Really Said It!

Kelly: For some reason, I feel right at home in this house.

Betcha Didn't Know

» This direct-to-video movie was the seventh and final sequel to *The Amityville Horror* (1979), and the fourth to feature a cursed object that was somehow tenuously connected to the haunted house in the original film. (The mysterious dollhouse in this film was certainly the weirdest exploration of this idea.)

» Director Steve White was a producer on three of the previous Amityville Horror sequels, *Amityville: The Evil Escapes* (1989), *Amityville 1992* (1992), and *Amityville: A New Generation* (1993).

In another of the sequels to *The Amityville Horror*, what ordinary object was cursed?

A: A lamp

B: A door

C: A couch

D: A water heater

Answer: A. A lamp. No, really. In *Amityville: The Evil Escapes*, nasty spirits hitch a ride in a lamp that is moved from the original Amityville house to a home on the West Coast. Spooky things ensue.

THE CORPSE VANISHES
(AKA *"THE CASE OF THE MISSING BRIDES"*)
Banner Productions/Monogram Pictures, 1942

PRODUCERS Jack Dietz and Sam Katzman

WRITERS Harvey Gates (script), Sam Robins and Gerald Schnitzer (story)

DIRECTOR Wallace Fox

STARS Luana Walters (*Patricia Hunter*), Bela Lugosi (*Prof. Lorenz*), Angelo Rossitto (*Toby*), and Elizabeth Russell (*Countess Lorenz*)

Certifiable madman and scientific genius Professor Lorenz (Lugosi) places beautiful, virgin brides into deathlike states at the altar and drains fluids from them to keep his wife (Russell) looking youthful. But when society columnist and wanna-be hardnosed reporter Patricia Hunter (Walters) pays him a visit at his isolated home, the professor's fountain of youth is threatened. . . .

Why It Sucks

Talk about your crazy houses. *The Corpse Vanishes* might be just a standard mad-scientist-versus-plucky-girl-reporter lightweight horror movie . . . except for the bizarre group of characters that make up Lorenz's household. From Lorenz's wife (who sleeps in a coffin for no apparent reason) to the housekeeper

Freaky Families

41

(a doom-saying withered old hag), her bestial son (who likes fondling the comatose brides Lorenz brings home), to her midget son (who serves as valet, butler, and Lorenz's chief henchman), to Lorenz himself, this is the weirdest group this side of those freakish hillbillies from *Texas Chainsaw Massacre*.

Thumbs Down Rating: 🎭🎭🎭

The Crappies

The Worst Actress Award goes to . . . Luana Walters for playing Patricia Hunter, Plucky Girl Reporter, with near complete blandness. *And the Worst Director Award goes to* . . . Wallace Fox for creating a bizarre tone to the film and then failing to keep it up.

They Really Said It!

Patricia Hunter: Oh, professor, do you also make a habit of collecting coffins?
Professor Lorenz: Why, yes, in a manner of speaking. I find a coffin much more comfortable than a bed.

Betcha Didn't Know

» Angelo Rossitto, the actor who portrayed Dr. Lorenz's freaky midget assistant, had a successful career that spanned sixty years. Along the way, he costarred with Bela Lugosi in three horror films and one comedy.

» Whenever Bela Lugosi appeared as a married man in a film, he, his wife, or both were invariably insane or murderous.

 Trivia Quiz

According to legend, what historical figure retained her youth by bathing in the blood of virgins?

A: Countess Elizabeth Báthory
B: Countess Carmilla Karnstein
C: Queen Elizabeth I of England
D: Queen Cleopatra of Egypt

Answer: A. Elizabeth Báthory was found guilty of killing eighty young girls and was bricked into a room in her castle in 1611 CE. There is no evidence that she actually bathed in blood in an attempt to maintain her youth.

Freaky Families

THE HOUSE ON SKULL MOUNTAIN
Chocolate Chip & Pinto, 1974

PRODUCERS Joe R. Hartsfield (executive producer), Tom Boutross and Ray Storey (producers)

WRITER Mildred Pares

DIRECTOR Ron Honthaner

STARS Victor French (*Dr. Andrew Cunningham*), Janee Michelle (*Lorena Christophe*), Jean Duran (*Thomas Pettione*), Mike Evans (*Phillipe Wilette*), Ella Woods (*Louette*), and Xernona Clayton (*Harriet Johnson*)

Four distant relatives of a recently deceased voodoo queen (Clayton, Evans, French, and Michelle) are summoned to her house. They then start dying under mysterious circumstances.

Why It Sucks

The House on Skull Mountain is such a failure at an African-American–oriented horror film that Blacula wouldn't be caught dead in it. It may star African Americans, but it doesn't have any horror, a decent story, or a reason to watch it. The filmmakers tried to mix the seventies tradition of Blaxploitation films with the classic "dark old house" thrillers of the 1930s, but they created a disaster.

Thumbs Down Rating: 🖓🖓🖓🖓🖓

The Crappies

The Worst Actor Award goes to . . . Mike Evans for his portrayal of an obnoxious, drunken, horny black man. The character is so repulsive that theater audiences probably cheered at his death scene. *And the Worst Script Award goes to* . . . Mildred Pares for a script that doesn't even make an attempt at explaining why the butler did it. (Yes, in this movie the butler really *did* do it!)

They Really Said It!

Phillippe: See, you done got yourself all upset cuz you went to the funeral.
Lorena: Ah, what a shame. You missed it.

Freaky Families

43

Phillippe: Yeah, yeah, cuz don't go to these funerals, you understand. I can't stand to see a woman cry, especially when she's fine. And you is fine.

Betcha Didn't Know

» Victor French was a successful television actor and director, who worked on dozens of episodes of *Gunsmoke*, *Little House on the Prairie* and a number of other long-running series, both behind and in front of the camera.

» Mike Evans is most famous for his role in the television series *Good Times*. He retired from show business after finishing this movie and went into real estate.

 Trivia Quiz

Which of these is *not* a title of a Blaxploitation horror movie from the 1970s?

A: *Blacula*

B: *Blackenstein*

C: *Brother Jekyll and Massah Hyde*

D: *Black Werewolf*

Answer: C. *Brother Jekyll and Massah Hyde. Blacula, Blackenstein, and Black Werewolf* were released in 1972, 1973, and 1974 respectively. *Black Werewolf* is better known under the title of *The Beast Must Die.*

LADY FRANKENSTEIN
(AKA *"DAUGHTER OF FRANKENSTEIN"*)
Condor International Productions, 1971

Freaky Families

PRODUCERS Umberto Borsato, Hurbert Case, Gioele Centanni, Harry Cushing, Egidio Gelso, Jules Kenton, and Mel Welles

WRITERS Umberto Borsato, Edward Di Lorenzo, Egidio Gelso, Aureliano Luppi, and Dick Randall (script), Mel Welles (story). Based on the characters from Mary Shelley's novel.

DIRECTORS Mel Welles and Aureliano Luppi

STARS Sara Bay (*Tania Frankenstein*), Joseph Cotten (*Baron Frankenstein*), Paul Muller (*Dr. Charles Marshall*), Mickey Hargitay (*Capt. Harris*), and Paul Whiteman (*the Creature*)

Tania Frankenstein (Bay) proves psychopathy is an inherited trait when she continues and perfects her dead father's work in reanimation and monster making . . . by creating her perfect mate, using the body of a hunky (but retarded) handyman, and the brain of her father's former assistant (Muller).

Why It Sucks

This is one of the sleaziest twists on the Frankenstein story ever presented. It also features one of the most disturbing sex scenes on film, when Tania Frankenstein has an orgasm as her lover is being murdered beneath her.

Tania Frankenstein not only creates a monster that looks like the retarded country cousin of Troma Entertainment's Toxic Avenger, but she is one of the most twisted members of that already disturbed family to ever grace the silver screen.

Thumbs Down Rating:

The Crappies

The Worst Script Award goes to . . . Umberto Borsato for writing the character of Captain Harris like a bad version of Columbo who does nothing but waste time and space in the movie.

And the Monster-on-the-Cheap Award goes to . . . Costume Designer Maurice Nichols for bringing us a creature that looks like the backwoodsmen from *Deliverance* had a baby with the mutant cannibals from *The Hills Have Eyes*.

They Really Said It!

Tania: You don't need to kill him! He thinks he killed you! Now he can be controlled!

Betcha Didn't Know

» Sara Bay's true name is Rosalba Neri, an Italian actress who started her film career at the age of fifteen.

» Mickey Hargitay was a bodybuilder and fitness expert before he turned to acting. He is the father of Mariska Hargitay, star of the long-running TV series *Law and Order: Special Victims Unit.*

 Trivia Quiz
Which of these actors has not played Dr. Frankenstein?

A: Raul Julia

B: Donald Pleasence

C: Udo Kier

D: Christopher Lee

Answer: D. Christopher Lee appeared as the Creature in *The Curse of Frankenstein* (1957) but never as the doctor.

CHAPTER FIVE

GORY, GORIER, GORIEST

Gorehounds, this chapter is for you. Everyone else might use it as a guide to what movies you want to put the kibosh on at the rental store. More than half of these movies are made by Italians. I don't know if it has something to do with the color of spaghetti sauce. (The Japanese have been trying to steal away that honor in the past ten to fifteen years, but they still have a long way to go.)

CANNIBAL HOLOCAUST
United Artists, 1980

PRODUCERS Franco Di Nunzio and Franco Palaggi

WRITER Gianfranco Clerici

DIRECTOR Ruggero Deodato

STARS Robert Kerman (*Harold Monroe*), Francesca Ciardi (*Faye Daniels*), Carl Gabriel Yorke (*Alan Yates*), Perry Pirkanen (*Jack Anders*), and Luca Giorgio Barbareschi (*Mark Tomaso*)

Professor Harold Monroe (Kerman) agrees to lead a search-and-rescue party into the Amazon jungle to determine the fate of a missing documentary crew. When he recovers their footage what he discovers is beyond imagination.

Why It Sucks

This sort of thing makes "torture porn" films like *Saw* seem like Cannes Film Festival winners. This film about vicious European/American explorers being massacred in hideous ways is probably the best of the worst, but that still means it's damn disgusting —more so by the filmmakers' attempts at realism.

Thumbs Down Rating: 🤙🤙🤙

The Crappies

The "I Didn't Mean That" Award goes to . . . Writer Gianfranco Clerici and director Ruggero Deodato for accidentally creating a fillm that can be interpreted as a condemnation of Mondo documentarians and their habit of staging events to make their films more interesting.

And the Worst Director Award goes to . . . Ruggero Deodato for actually having live animals tortured to death on camera, just to make a crappy horror movie.

They Really Said It!

Harold Monroe: I've seen the rest of the material. You haven't. You haven't seen the stuff that even your own editors didn't have the stomach to put together, and if you had, you wouldn't hesitate but to agree with me.

Betcha Didn't Know

» The film is so realistic that Italian authorities arrested director Ruggero Deodato shortly after its release and put him on trial for murder.
» The film was rated X for violence when it was first released, and it remains banned in several countries.

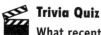

Trivia Quiz

What recent gore-fest movie did Ruggero Deodato have a cameo appearance in?

A: *Final Destination* (2000)

B: *The Texas Chainsaw Massacre* (2003 remake)

C: *Saw III* (2006)

D: *Hostel: Part II* (2007)

Answer: D. *Hostel: Part II.* Ruggero Deodato plays a patron of the cannibal hostel and is seen chewing on a leg.

CEMETERY MAN (AKA *"DEMONS '95"*)
Audiofilm, 1994

PRODUCERS Conchita Airoldi (executive producer), Heinz Bibo, Tilde Corsi, Giovanni Romoli, and Michele Soavi (producers)

WRITERS Gianni Romoli (script), Tiziano Sclavi (original novel)

DIRECTOR Michele Soavi

STARS Rupert Everett (*Francesco Dellamorte*), Anna Falchi (*She*), François Hadji-Lazaro (*Gnahgi*), Mickey Knox (*Marshall Straniero*), Fabiana Formica (*Valentina Scanarotti*), and Katja Anton (*Claudio's girlfriend*)

Francesco Dellamorte (Everett), caretaker of a small-town cemetery, spends the days burying the deceased, and his nights fighting them when they rise as flesh-eating zombies. But when he and his assistant (Hadji-Lazaro) meet the loves of their lives (Falchi and Formica, respectively), only to see them turned into undead residents of the cemetery, things really start to get bad.

Why It Sucks

Cemetery Man could have been a nice little surreal horror comedy. (What says comedy like flesh-eating zombies?) But it far too often *draaaaaaags*, as the director plays with interesting visuals and struggles to capture the feel of the Tiziano Sclavi story on which it's based. For all the great imagery, gore, violence, nudity, and bizarre sex, the film turns out to be . . . boring.

Gory, Gorier, Goriest

49

Thumbs Down Rating: 🔻🔻

The Crappies

The Worst Writer Award goes to . . . Screen writer Gianni Romoli and novelist Tiziano Sclavi in a shared effort for coming up with an ending so nonsensical that even the most generous-minded viewer will be left feeling cheated.

And the Worst Director Award goes to . . . Michele Soavi for getting so wrapped up playing with the camera that he forgot to keep the story moving. We're torn between wondering if there ever will be another crazy zombie attack and looking at Anna Falchi's naked body.

They Really Said It!

Francesco Dellamorte: You're supposed to be setting a good example. Now, will you get back in your coffin immediately!

Betcha Didn't Know

» The appearance of Rupert Everett's character, Dellamorte, purposefully echoes the look of Dylan Dog, a character in a popular Italian comic book series. That series was created by Tiziano Sclavi, the author of the novel *Cemetery Man* was based on.

» Despite the alternate title *Demons '95*, this film has nothing to do with with the 1984 gore fest *Demons*, which is covered later in this chapter.

 Trivia Quiz

What literary character has Rupert Everett *not* portrayed onscreen?

A: Sherlock Holmes

B: Oberon

C: Solomon Kane

D: Lancelot

Answer: C. Solomon Kane. Everett played Lancelot in the 1985 made-for-television movie Arthur the King; Oberon in a 1999 version of A Midsummer Night's Dream; and Sherlock Holmes in the 2004 television movie Sherlock Holmes and the Case of the Silk Stocking.

DEAD ALIVE (AKA *"BRAINDEAD"*)
WingNut Films, 1991 and Trimark Pictures, 1992

PRODUCER Jim Booth

WRITERS Stephen Sinclair, Frances Walsh, and Peter Jackson (script), Stephen Sinclair (story)

DIRECTOR Peter Jackson

STARS Timothy Balme (*Lionel Cosgrove*), Diana Peñalver (*Paquita Maria Sanchez*), Elizabeth Moody (*Mum*), and Ian Watkin (*Uncle Les*)

Lionel (Balme) is a gentle, kindhearted young man who is suffering under the thumb of an abusive, evil mother (Moody). When he falls in love with Paquita (Peñalver), a young gypsy girl who works in the local town market, it looks like things might get better for him. But then his mom is bitten by a Sumatran rat monkey . . . and it all goes to hell from there.

Why It Sucks

Peter Jackson, who later found something else to do with his time (like the J. R. R. Tolkien movies), loves this sort of thing. The film brims with cartoony gore and craziness that's rarely been equaled in any medium. But Jackson can't stop himself from introducing character after character after character, dragging down the movie.

Thumbs Down Rating: 👎👎

The Crappies

The Worst Script Award goes to . . . Stephen Sinclair, Frances Walsh, and Peter Jackson for not knowing when enough is enough. *And the Worst Use of Gardening Tools Award goes to* . . . Peter Jackson for showing that a lawn mower can be used as an offensive weapon.

They Really Said It!

Father McGruder: I kick arse for the Lord!

Gory, Gorier, Goriest

Betcha Didn't Know

» This film is considered to be the bloodiest movie made (in terms of the number of gallons of stage blood used during filming).

» Peter Jackson returned to horror films (sort of) with *The Lovely Bones* in 2010.

 Trivia Quiz

The rat monkeys to blame for the zombie plague in *Dead Alive* were illegally imported from Skull Island. Who is the most famous expatriate from that faraway place?

A: Godzilla

B: Dr. Moreau

C: King Kong

D: The Phantom

Answer: C. King Kong, Jackson, a long-time fan of the original 1933 film, revisited Skull Island in 2005 when he directed a remake.

DEEP RED (AKA "THE HATCHET MURDERS")
Rizzoli Films/Seda Spettacoli, 1975

PRODUCERS Claudio Argento (executive producer) and Salvatore Argento (producer)

WRITERS Bernadino Zapponi (script), Dario Argento (story)

DIRECTOR Dario Argento

STARS David Hemmings (*Marcus Daly*), Daria Nicolodi (*Gianna Brezzi*), and Gabriele Lavia (*Carlo*)

Pianist Marcus Daly (Hemmings) witnesses the brutal murder of a famous psychic, and then teams up with Gianna Brezzi, a feisty woman reporter (Nicolodi) to find the killer. Soon, they find themselves stalked by the deadly, seemingly omniscient murderer who is willing to end numerous lives to protect his or her dark secrets.

Why It Sucks

Deep Red is part slasher flick and part murder mystery, but it is so sloppily written that even if your standards are low you'll want to throw something at the screen. The characters are afflicted with unbelievable stupidity. What's more, the writer/director seems to think the viewers are equally low-browed. Argento worked on the principle that if if he threw enough violence and gore onto the screen, no one would notice the lazy writing.

Thumbs Down Rating: 👎👎👎

The Crappies
The Worst Writing Award goes to . . . Dario Argento for inane dialogue and worse plotting. Sometimes gore just isn't enough.
And the Worst Actor Award goes to . . . David Hemmings for sleepwalking through most of the picture. Of course, he might have been trying to convey the fact that on more than one occasion his character acts like he was dropped on his head as a baby.

They Really Said It!
Marcus: Gianna, there's someone in the house absolutely trying to kill me!

Betcha Didn't Know
» The R-rated version widely released in the United States is 98 minutes long, while the full version is unrated with a run time of 128 minutes. The version titled *The Hatchet Murders* is the shorter, rated version.
» Despite an additional thirty minutes of screen time, the unrated version does nothing to fix the plot lapse mentioned above, not to mention the several other blunders the film contains.

 Trivia Quiz
Which of the following actresses received her first major screen role in a Dario Argento film?
A: Jennifer Connelley
B: Uma Thurman
C: Milla Jovovich
D: Diane Lane

Answer: A. Jennifer Connelley, who starred in the 1985 Argento-written/directed supernatural thrilled *Phenomena*. She portrays a girl who can psychically communicate with insects.

DEMONS
DACFILM, 1985

PRODUCER Dario Argento

WRITERS Dardano Saccheti (story), Dario Argento, Lamberto Bava, and Franco Ferrini (script)

DIRECTOR Lamberto Bava

STARS Urbano Barberini (*George*), Bobby Rhodes (*Tony*), Natasha Hovey (*Cheryl*), Fiore Argento (*Hannah*), Karl Zinni (*Ken*), Genretta Giancarlo (*Rosemary*), Nicoletta Elmi (*Ingrid*), and Paola Cozzo (*Kathy*)

The audience at a screening of a horror movie is sealed in the theater and one by one transformed into the hideous creatures featured in the film.

Why It Sucks

Evidently the director of this occasionally scary movie decided that story was an optional extra and what the audience needed was a string of transformations and violent murders to be satisfied. The focus is on gore effects, and the ending doesn't fit with anything that happens earlier in the film, compounding the feeling of blood-drenched chaos. Any viewer watching for more than gore will quickly feel his patience running thin.

Thumbs Down Rating: 🐾🐾🐾

The Crappies

The Special Recognition for Most Nonsensical Apocalypse Award goes to . . . Somehow, by the end of the movie, the world is overrun with demons. So why was it necessary to trap the characters in the theater?

And the Worst Director Award goes to . . . Lamberto Bava for carrying on his father's tradition of making films that feature some great visual set pieces but that have halfbaked, awful scripts.

They Really Said It!

Tony: We got to stop it I tell you, we got to stop the damn movie!

Betcha Didn't Know

» Lamberto Bava cites this as his favorite out of the thirty-four films he has directed.

» Lamberto Bava is a third-generation Italian filmmaker. His grandfather, Eugenio Bava, was a cameraman and trailblazing effects artist during the early days of cinema, and his father, Mario Bava, was a prolific cinematographer, director, special-effects artist, and writer.

 Trivia Quiz

How did Lamberto Bava gain his first directorial experience?

A: He took over as director on *A Shot in the Dark* after Blake Edwards quit the film

B: His father, director Mario Bava, pretended to be ill during the filming of *Shock* so Lamberto had the opportunity to direct a few scenes.

C: He bet Dario Argento that he could script the gore scenes for *Demons* in less than a week. He won the bet and got to direct the film.

D: His father, Mario Bava, was a good friend of Dario Argento and asked Argento to give Lamberto a chance to direct *Inferno*.

Answer: B. His father pretended to be ill, so his son could direct some scenes.

THE MACHINE GIRL
Fever Dreams, 2008

PRODUCERS John Sirabella (executive producer), Yoshinori Chiba, Yoko Hayama, and Satoshi Nakamura (producers)

WRITER Noboru Iguchi

DIRECTOR Noboru Iguchi

STARS Minase Yashiro (*Ami Hyuga*), Asami (*Miki*), Honoka (*Violet Kimura*), Kentarô Shimazu (*Ryûji Kimura*), and Nobuhiro Nishihara (*Sho Kimura*)

When her brother and his best friend are murdered by the spoiled sons of corrupt cops and the local ninja and yakuza clans, a high-school girl (Yashiro) goes on a gory, revenge-driven murder-spree. After the yakuza hacks off her left arm, a creative mechanic/gunsmith replaces it with a custom-made machine gun.

Why It Sucks

The Machine Girl crams all the elements of Japanese action films and cartoons into it: cute high-school girls kicking butt in their school uniform, yakuza, ninja, a quest for righteous revenge. Then it adds moral bankruptcy, depravity, dismemberment, murder, and geysers of blood. It will gross you out if you're well-adjusted but will amuse if you're deeply twisted.

Thumbs Down Rating: 👎👎

The Crappies

The Worst Acting Award goes to . . . Asami for her one-note performance as a vengeance hungry mother. Like most other one-named performers, she can't act worth a damn.

And the Worst Auteur Award goes to . . . Noboru Iguchi for depressing nihilism. The main character's machine gun arm shoots enough rounds in a second to cause a human body to evaporate into a fine red mist. And if that doesn't do it for you, a knife is thrust through the top of a character's head and another is killed when nails are pounded into his face.

They Really Said It!

Ami: Violence doesn't solve anything.

Betcha Didn't Know

» Asami began her career in porn films, but she has graduated to horror and gory action films.
» Ami isn't the first movie character to replace a severed limb with a firearm; Ash of Sam Raimi's *Evil Dead* movies did it first.

Gory, Gorier, Goriest

RE-ANIMATOR
Empire Pictures, 1985

PRODUCERS Michael Avery and Bruce William Curtis (executive producers), Brian Yunza (producer)

WRITERS Dennis Paoli, William Norris, and Stuart Gordon (script), H. P. Lovecraft (original short stories)

DIRECTOR Stuart Gordon

STARS Jeffrey Combs (*Herbert West*), Bruce Abbott (*Dan Cain*), Barbara Crampton (*Megan Halsey*), David Gale (*Dr. Carl Hill*), and Robert Sampson (*Dean Alan Halsey*)

Dan's new roommate and fellow third-year med student, Herbert West (Combs) draws him into his bizarre (and kinda-sorta successful) experiments in reanimating dead bodies. Many Very Bad Things result.

Why It Sucks

It's got a character named Herbert West who has invented a formula that reanimates the dead. And it takes place in a town called Arkham. Beyond that, the movie ignores the great H. P. Lovecraft story with the same title. There is, however, much insane pointless violence and sick sexual references.

Gory, Gorier, Goriest

57

Thumbs Down Rating: 👎👎

The Crappies
The Worst Auteur Award goes to . . . Director/co-scripter Stuart Gordon for making a movie that is wildly inconsistent in tone, swinging from deadly serious to over-the-top comedic.

And the Special Award for Worst Visual Pun Ever . . . Director/co-scripter Stuart Gordon for combining the naked Barbara Crampton and a severed reanimated head in a single scene, taking the phrase "give head" to unnerving extremes.

They Really Said It!
Dan Cain: He's dead?
Herbert West: Not anymore.

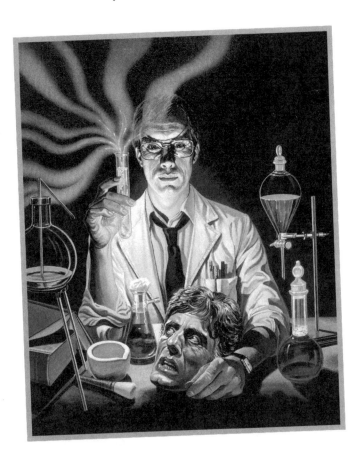

Betcha Didn't Know

» Herbert West was a minor character in the script and all through production. It wasn't until editing that the film took a different shape and he became the central figure.

» Director Stuart Gordon had a great deal of experience directing plays, but this was his first movie.

 Trivia Quiz

What was Herbert West's fate in the original H. P. Lovecraft story?

A: He was reanimated by his own serum

B: He became governor of Massachusetts

C: He was eaten by Cthulhu

D: He was dismembered and carried off by subjects of his experiments

Answer: D. In a fate that was foreshadowed in the first paragraph of the tale, West was dragged into the darkness by vengeful reanimated corpses.

THE RUINS
Spyglass Entertainment, 2008

PRODUCERS Gary Barber, Roger Birnbaum, Trish Hoffman, and Ben Stiller (executive producer), Chris Bender, Stuart Cornfeld, and Jeremy Kramer (producers)

WRITER Scott B. Smith

DIRECTOR Carter Smith

STARS Jonathan Tucker (*Jeff*), Jena Malone (*Amy*), Laura Ramsey (*Stacy*), Shawn Ashmore (*Eric*), Joe Anderson (*Mathias*), Dimitri Baveas (*Dimitri*), and Sergio Calderón (*Lead Mayan*)

A group of college-aged tourists (Anderson, Ashmore, Malone, Ramsey, and Tucker) are trapped atop an unmapped Mayan ruin by angry natives. They soon discover that what lives in the ruin is far more horrific than the murderous jungle dwellers.

Why It Sucks

The Ruins manages to be a suspense film with no suspense, a paint-by-the-numbers horror film. At the same time it dips its fingers into the "torture porn" subgenre for no good reason other than the director seems to have been bored. The only surprise comes from the nature of the monster dwelling in the ruined structure—hardly worth wading through the film for.

Thumbs Down Rating: 👎👎👎👎

The Crappies

The Worst Actor Award goes to . . . Joe Anderson for Mathias, a character who starts as vaguely sinister (for no reason) and finishes as hapless and slightly stupid.

And the Worst Picture Award goes to . . . The gaggle of producers behind this picture for making it absolutely, 100 percent predictable from beginning to end.

They Really Said It!

Jeff: Four Americans on vacation don't just disappear!

Betcha Didn't Know

» Only one character is actually killed by the monster in the film.
» Comedian Ben Stiller became involved with this film because he is a good friend of screenwriter/novelist Scott B. Smith.

Trivia Quiz

Although set in Mexico, what country and area was the film actually shot in?

A: United States, Florida

B: Spain, Catalonia

C: France, East Pyrenees

D: Australia, Queensland

Answer: D. Australia, Queensland. The interiors of the "ruins" were sets built at Warner Brothers' Movieworld, also in Queensland.

Gory, Gorier, Goriest

THE STREET FIGHTER
Toei Company/New Line Cinema, 1974

PRODUCER Uncredited

WRITERS Kôji Takada and Motohiro Torii

DIRECTOR Shigehiro Ozawa

STARS Sonny Chiba (*Terry Tsurugi*), Goichi Yamada (*Rakuda Zhang*), Yutaka Nakajima (*Sarai Hammett*), Akira Shion (*Liang Dong-Yi*), and Tony Cetera (*Abdul Jadot*)

When an antisocial martial-artist-for-hire (Chiba) turns down a yakuza contract to kidnap the heiress of an oil-based financial empire (Nakajima), he discovers they'd rather kill him than risk him revealing their plans.

Why It Sucks

Story? What story? *The Street Fighter* is plot-light and violence-heavy, with just enough explantion to move us from one extreme act of violence to another. Of course, the scene where Chiba rips off the nuts of a would-be rapist redeems the movie to a large degree.

The Crappies

The Worst Writing Award goes to . . . Kôji Takada and Motohiro Torii for a story so thin it's likely to give viewers papercuts.

And the Worst Acting Award goes to . . . Sonny Chiba for the outrageous faces he makes during fight scenes. Only the Master of Funny Face Fu, Bruce Lee himself, could look more ridiculous while kicking ass.

They Really Said It!

Terry Tsurugi: Tell that bitch who sent you how sorry I am I can no longer be her friend.

Betcha Didn't Know

» This is the first movie to be rated X by the MPAA based on violence alone. When New Line released a home video version,

Gory, Gorier, Goriest

the studio edited the gory martial arts scenes heavily to get an R rating.

» Sonny Chiba started a martial arts organization geared toward teaching

 Trivia Quiz

How many minutes of film were cut to earn *The Street Fighter's* R rating?

A: 4 minutes

B: 8 minutes

C: 16 minutes

D: 32 minutes

Answer: C. 16 minutes. The most widely available DVD versions of the film run 91 minutes.

SUSPIRIA
Seda Spettacoli, 1977

PRODUCERS Salvatore Argento (executive producer) and Claudio Argento (producer)

WRITERS Dario Argento and Daria Nicolodi

DIRECTOR Dario Argento

STARS Jessica Harper (*Suzy Banyon*), Stefania Casini (*Sara*), Joan Bennett (*Madame Blanc*), and Udo Keir (*Dr. Frank Mandel*)

Suzy Banyon (Harper) comes to study at a prestigious German dance academy, but instead is drawn into the murderous and deadly web of secrets that exist within its walls. Is there a killer on the loose in the school, or is it the spirit of its founder—a reported witch—who has returned from the depths of Hell?

Why It Sucks

When *Suspiria* is over, you won't be asking, "Is that all the gore he's got?" but rather, "Is that all the story there is?" Star Jessica Harper's deer-in-the-headlights performance is decent, and the

Gory, Gorier, Goriest

death scenes are brutal and creative—one character is killed by a roomful of barbed wire. But everything in the film is badly explained and every sympathetic character in the film suffers from Stupid Character Syndrome.

Thumbs Down Rating: 🦃🦃🦃

The Crappies

The Worst Script Award goes to . . . Dario Argento and Daria Nicolodi. The film's producer ordered them to change the setting from a boarding school for small children to a dance academy for young women, because he was uncomfortable with children being brutally murdered onscreen. Argento and Nicolodi made the change but didn't bother to rewrite the characters, who now come across as adults with the minds of children.

And the Worst Director Award goes to . . . Dario Argento for making a visually impressive film, but completely forgetting that characters and story matter, too.

They Really Said It!

Dr. Frank Mandel: Bad luck isn't brought by broken mirrors, but by broken minds.

Betcha Didn't Know

» Nearly four minutes was cut from the film to gain an R rating in the United States.

» Dario Argento is the father of actress Asia Argento, and many of his films were produced by his father or sons. Filmmaking is truly a family business for the Argentos.

Trivia Quiz

Aside from a character in *Suspiria*, who is Pat Hingle?

A: An American stage and film actor who appeared in four Batman movies.

B: A cartoon character used to sell Pringle Potato Chips.

C: The inventor of the Technicolor process.

D: Dario Argento's girlfriend in 1977 (and future wife).

THE TRAVELER

Black Boot Productions, 2006

PRODUCER Jonathan R. Skocik

WRITER Jonathan R. Skocik

DIRECTOR Jonathan R. Skocik

STARS Jonathan R. Skocik (*Alan Chesterson*), Shawn Burke (*the Traveler*), Melanie D'Alessandro (*Suzan Chesterson*), Erica Highberg (*Linda Clarke*), David L. Penn (*Dan Strife*), and Megan Hartley (*voice of Susan*)

Seven people are trapped in an abandoned house by a supernatural force. An immortal man with monstrous strength (Burke) appears and forces them to torture each other to death.

Why It Sucks

Well, it's got wooden acting and clunky dialogue. But the real problem is that the torture effects are so literal that this movie's unwatchable for many viewers. "Highlights" include teeth being shattered with a hammer and chisel. On the other hand, the film's low budget keeps both characters and viewers trapped in the torture rooms with no sense of movie fantasy or comic relief.

Thumbs Down Rating: 👎👎

The Crappies

The Worst Script Award goes to . . . Jonathan R. Skocik for dialogue that in most cases can be charitably described as "tinny."

And the Worst Director Award goes to . . . Jonathan R. Skocik for failing to recognize that some of his effects were beyond his meager budget (and pretty insane), such as when the Traveler grows a new head after his original is cut off.

They Really Said It!

The Traveler: Let's play a little game.

Gory, Gorier, Goriest

Betcha Didn't Know

» Linda Clarke is the only performer with any acting credits other than this film, She continues to appear in low-budget horror films, with eight credits to her name as of this writing.

» The movie was Jonathan R. Skocik's only solo effort to date.

Trivia Quiz

Which of the following featured two Oscar Award–winners in the roles of torturer and torturee?

A: *A Bucket of Blood* (1959)

B: *Last House on the Left* (2009)

C: *Marathon Man* (1976)

D: *The Evil of Frankenstein* (1964)

Answer: C. In *Marathon Man* Laurence Olivier plays a sadistic Nazi who tortured Dustin Hoffman, an innocent bystander caught in an international conspiracy.

URBAN FLESH: REBIRTH EDITION
Helltimate Studios, 2007

PRODUCERS Jeff Grenier and Alexandre Michaud

WRITERS Jeff Grenier and Alexandre Michaud

DIRECTOR Alexandre Michaud

STARS Martin Dubreuil (*Kane*), Mireille Leveque (*Samantha*), Marie-Ève Petit (*Sally*), K. M. Lavigne (*Inspector Blake*), Anthony Pereira (*Zack*), and Marc Vaillancourt (*Ygor*)

Four thrill-killers (Dubreuil, Petit, Pereira, and Vaillancourt) prowl a Canadian city by night in search of victims to kill . . . and eat raw. As a homicide detective (Lavigne) closes in on them, he and his wife (Leveque) are added to the menu.

Why It Sucks

If you're looking for terrifying and gory violence, this is a film for you. Time and again, it goes beyond anything you can imagine. Of course, it you like that sort of stuff, then that's a strong point

Gory, Gorier, Goriest

of the film. What isn't, however, is the way the blood-splattered urban cannibals can wander city streets unnoticed. Or the way the film just sort of dribbles off into the credits at the point where it feels as if it's about to reach a climax.

Thumbs Down Rating: 👎👎

The Crappies

The Special Award for Exceptional Achievement in Operating Nanny States goes to . . . England, Germany, and Alexandre Michaud's homeland of Canada for banning this film when Michaud starting selling the original cut of the film through mail-order catalogs in 1999.

And the Worst Auteur Award goes to . . . Coproducer/Cowriter/Director Alexandre Michaud for failing to recognize that this movie should not end in midaction with the fate of the final surviving protagonist and the villains completely unknown.

They Really Said It!

Zack: My name is Oblivion.

Betcha Didn't Know

» Although filmed in 1997, the movie took Michaud two years to edit, working in his spare time. The original version wasn't released until 1999.

» According to Michaud, the 2007 release of the film is ten minutes shorter than the original cut. However, if it's any comfort to gore freaks, no blood was left on the cutting-room floor.

 Trivia Quiz
Which of these movie madmen is a cannibal?

A: Harvey Dent

B: Hannibal Lecter

C: Richard Vollin

D: Michael Myers

Gory, Gorier, Goriest

Answer: B. Hannibal Lecter, featured in *Manhunter* (1986), *Red Dragon* (a 2002 remake of *Manhunter*), *Silence of the Lambs* (1991), and *Hannibal* (2001).

CHAPTER SIX

HAPPY HOLIDAYS!

Want to put a damper on the Christmas spirit or pull the cinematic equivalent of an April Fool's joke? Maybe the films in this chapter can be helpful.

APRIL FOOL'S DAY
Paramount Pictures/Hometown Films, 1986

PRODUCER Frank Mancuso Jr.

WRITER Danilo Bach

DIRECTOR Fred Walton

STARS Deborah Foreman (*Muffy/Buffy St. John*), Ken Olandt (*Rob Ferris*), Pat Barlow (*Clara*), Deborah Goodrich (*Nikki Beshears*), Jay Baker (*Harvey "Hal" Edison*), Griffin O'Neal (*Skip St. John*), Leah King Pinset (*Nan Youngblood*), Amy Steel (*Kit Graham*), Clayton Rohner (*Chaz Vyshinski*), and Thomas F. Wilson (*Arch Cummings*)

Muffy St. John (Foreman) invites several of her good friends from college to spend the weekend of April 1 partying at her isolated family home. Fun turns to fear when the guests start to fall victim to a murderer.

Why It Sucks

This is such a weird film: a murderer-free murder mystery in which there's no murder and a slasher film that's almost violence-free. In fact, the entire movie is a cheat, revealed in a twist ending that pissed off a lot of fans of the genre. Once we know the ending, it becomes obvious that the writers and director have been manipulating the audience and laughing at us for being stupid enough to take them seriously. Ultimately, the joke's on them, since the logic of some scenes collapses once the twist is revealed.

Thumbs Down Rating: 👎

The Crappies

The Worst Script Award goes to . . . Writer Danilo Bach for a screenplay that almost seems like a fusion of an Agatha Christie–style "cozy" mystery and a slasher flick, but which is undermined by lazily created suspense that in retrospect make no sense.
And the Worst Director Award goes to . . . Director Fred Walton for his inability to smooth over the weak parts in Bach's script. Perversely, he seems to take pleasure in enhancing them.

They Really Said It!

Kit: Muffy hasn't been in an institution for three years. She's been at Vassar.

Betcha Didn't Know!

» Amy Steel also appeared in *Friday the 13th, Part II*. She played the only targeted victim who survived.
» Frank Mancuso Jr. produced *Friday the 13th* parts 2 through 7. He also served as executive producer on *Friday the 13th: The Series* for all three seasons.

Trivia Quiz
What critical and box-office failure did Frank Mancuso Jr. produce in 2007?

A: *I Know Who Killed Me*

B: *Endangered Species*

C: *Limbo*

D: *Umbilical*

Answer: A. *I Know Who Killed Me*, which cost $12 million to make and took in only $9 million worldwide, was supposed to be a comeback vehicle for Lindsay Lohan. Her performance was an embarrassment, and her career has continued to nose downward.

MY BLOODY VALENTINE
Paramount Pictures/Famous Players/CFDC/Secret Films, 1981

PRODUCERS Lawrence Nesis (executive producer), John Dunning, André Link, and Stephen Miller (producers)

WRITERS John Beaird (script), Stephen Miller (story)

DIRECTOR George Mihalka

STARS Paul Kelman (*Jessie "T. J." Hanniger*), Neil Affleck (*Alex Palmer*), Lori Hallier (*Sarah*), Don Francks (*Chief Jake Newby*), and Peter Cowper (*the Miner/Harry Warden*)

A bunch of young miners and their girlfriends throwing a Valentine's Day party are stalked and killed by a psychotic miner bent on avenging a decades-old tragedy.

Why It Sucks

Want to kill the romantic mood on Valentine's Day? Convince that special someone to cuddle up on the sofa, turn the lights down low, pop open a bottle of champagne, and watch *this* movie with you! Nothing says love like a gasmask-wearing maniac massacring young lovers. There's also the fact that the only reason the story plot holds together is that the police chief in town is dumber than Barney Fife after a lobotomy.

There's more than one way
to lose your heart...

MY BLOODY VALENTINE

Thumbs Down Rating: 👎 👎

The Crappies

The Worst Editing Award goes to . . . Whoever butchered the film to ensure an R rating. Several attacks and displays of gore seem truncated, and many edits are so rough they are distracting. The scene where the Miner hoists a victim onto a hook is among the worst.

And the Worst Costume Design goes to . . . Whoever came up with the idea for the Miner. As creepy as he looks—dressed in old-fashioned mining gear—his getup does raise the question of how he manages to sneak up on his victims in his clomping work boots and with that light shining on his helmet.

Happy Holidays!

They Really Said It!

Tommy: Chief, listen to me. You have to go to the mine! We were having a party and Harry Warden started killing everybody!

Betcha Didn't Know

» *My Bloody Valentine* cost an estimated $2 million to make and earned $5 million during its theatrical run in the United States. Nonetheless, Paramount, the main financial backer, considered the film a financial failure. Shows what you have to do to make a hit!

» A 3D remake was released in 2009 as part of the revival of 3D movies.

 Trivia Quiz

What was the working title of this film?

A: *Pick Me as Your Valentine*

B: *The Secret*

C: *Mine, Mine, Mine*

D: *Tunnels of Blood*

Answer: B. *The Secret.* The film was made under a working title to prevent others from stealing the idea of a slasher film that used Valentine's Day as a hook.

SANTA CLAUS CONQUERS THE MARTIANS
Jalor Productions, 1964

PRODUCERS Joseph E. Levine (executive producer) and Paul L. Jacobson (producer)

WRITERS Glenville Mareth (script), Paul L. Jacobson (story)

DIRECTOR Nicholas Webster

STARS John Call (*Santa Claus*), Leonard Hicks (*Kimar*), Vincent Beck (*Voldar*), Victor Stiles (*Billy*), Donna Conforti (*Betty*), Bill McCutcheon (*Dropo*), Chris Month (*Bomar*), and Pia Zadora (*Girmar*)

When Martians kidnap Santa Claus (Call) and bring him to Mars so that he can give joy and toys to their depressed children, conservative elements in Martian society plot his assassination.

Why It Sucks

Well, the idea *sounded* good to some movie executive: Santa being kidnapped by grumpy, evil Martians who ultimately are converted to goodness by his cheerful kindness and generosity. That's one that even a cynic like me can smile about. However, the execution of that idea in this film . . . sigh.

The sets are painfully cheap, the script is brain-numbingly stupid, and while I never would have suspected that a movie involving both Santa and Martians could be boring, this movie manages to be just that.

Thumbs Down Rating: 🎀 🎀 🎀 🎀

The Crappies

The Worst Costuming Award goes to . . . Voldar's magnificent mustache, undoubtedly one of the Twelve Wonders of Mars.

And the Worst Family Film Award goes to . . . Paul L. Jacobson for producing a film that might fascinate a newborn infant for ten seconds, but is likely to bore anyone over the age of sentience. (And when it comes to younger children, it may well be child abuse to subject them to it.)

They Really Said It!

Voldar: All this trouble over a fat little man in a red suit.

Betcha Didn't Know

» Santa Claus is known as *Joulupukki* in Finland (and probably also on Mars).

» Lou Harry wrote a novelization of *Santa Clause Conquers the Martians* that was published in hardcover in 2005 and that came with a DVD of the movie bound in.

 Trivia Quiz

Which of these actors has not played Santa Claus onscreen?

A: Paul Giamatti

B: Charles Durning

C: Tim Allen

D: Raymond Burr

Answer: D. Raymond Burr, although the *Perry Mason* episode titled "The Case of the Pathetic Patient," costarred Percy Helton, who was the drunken Santa Claus in the 1947 version of *Miracle on 34th Street.*

SATAN'S LITTLE HELPER
Intrinsic Value Films, 2004

PRODUCERS Carl Tostevin (executive producer), Jeff Lieberman, Mickey McDonough, Isen Robbins, and Aimee Schoof (producers)

WRITER Jeff Lieberman

DIRECTOR Jeff Lieberman

STARS Alexander Brickel (*Dougie Whooly*), Amanda Plummer (*Merrill Whooly*), Katheryn Winnick (*Jenna Whooly*), Stephen Graham (*Alex Martin*), and Joshua Annex (*Satan Man*)

A masked killer goes on a Halloween killing spree, assisted by Dougie (Brickel), a young boy who is unable to tell reality from his favorite computer game.

Why It Sucks

In this poster child for a weak script, *every* character suffers from Stupid Character Syndrome so that the film can run past half an hour. The character of Dougie has got to be some sort of cinematic milestone in permissive parenting. That kid's inability to distinguish between reality and fantasy is so over the top that he sounds like a young male version of Paula Abdul. Only the way Katheryn Winnick fills out her costume makes it possible to sit through this film.

Thumbs Down Rating: 👎👎👎👎

The Crappies

The Worst Script Award goes to . . . Jeff Lieberman for creating the character of Dougie. (On the other hand, one has to admire child actor Alexander Brickel, who carries the movie and creates one of cinema's greatest—albeit unintentional—villains.)

And the Worst Actress Award goes to . . . Amanda Plummer's twin sister for passing herself off as Amanda Plummer. She doesn't have her sister's acting chops so . . . . Oh, wait! That *is* Amanda Plummer in this film and *she can* give performances as uninteresting as her portrayal of Dougie's mom. Admittedly it's a nothing role, but she does even less.

They Really Said It!

Jenna Whooly: That man was Alex's father . . . and Jesus is Satan!

Betcha Didn't Know

» Jeff Lieberman wrote the script for children's fantasy film *Neverending Story III*.
» Portraying Dougie is so far the only starring role for Alexander Brickel.

Which of the following characters is not a cinematic masked mass-murderer?

A: Leslie Vernon

B: Jason Vorhees

C: Freddy Krueger

D: Michael Myers

Answer: C. Freddy Krueger didn't wear a mask, and after he became a dream-haunting spirit, he didn't need one.

SILENT NIGHT, BLOODY NIGHT (AKA *"DEATH HOUSE"* AND *"NIGHT OF THE DARK FULL MOON"*)
Armor Films/Cannon Productions, 1974

PRODUCERS Ami Artzi and Jeffrey Konvitz

WRITERS Jeffrey Konvitz, Ira Teller, and Theodore Gershuny

DIRECTOR Theodore Gershuny

STARS Mary Woronov (*Diane Adams*), James Patterson (*Jeffrey Butler*), Patrick O'Neal (*John Carter*), Walter Abel (*Mayor Adams*), Astrid Heeren (*Ingrid*), and John Carradine (*Charlie Towman*)

When Jeffrey (Patterson) tries to sell the mansion he inherited from his grandfather, a past believed to be dead and buried returns to haunt the living with a bloody vengeance.

Why It Sucks

Silent Night, Bloody Night manages to disappoint on every level. First off, it's not really Christmas themed. Second, it's not even a slasher flick, despite what some marketers try to make it out to be. Then there's the fact the movie is told in flashback, so we already know that the main character survives.

Thumbs Down Rating: 🎬🎬🎬

Happy Holidays!

The Crappies

The Special Worst Plot Convenience Recognition Award goes to . . . Jeffrey Konvitz, Ira Teller, and Theodore Gershuny for the scene where Jeffrey borrows his attorney's car for no reason other than the plot needed it away from the house.

And the Worst Director Award goes to . . . Theodore Gershuny for starting the film with a scene that sets the rest of it up as a flashback and thus undermines a great deal of the suspense.

They Really Said It!

Jeffrey Butler: His hands. Someone cut off his hands.

Betcha Didn't Know

» No distributor would take on this movie until Lloyd Kaufman of Troma Films picked it up.

» The film's working title was *Zora*, although no one in the film is named that and the word is not used throughout the movie.

 Trivia Quiz

What Christmas classic was a failure at the box office when it was first released?

A: *It's A Wonderful Life* (1946)

B: *A Christmas Story* (1983)

C: *Christmas in Connecticut* (1945)

D: *White Christmas* (1954)

Answer: A. *It's a Wonderful Life* cost $3.7 million to make (an astronomical figure for movies in the 1940s) but took in only $3.3 million at the box office.

CHAPTER SEVEN:

INAUSPICIOUS BEGINNINGS

You were once young and you were once inexperienced. Most of us see time wipe away our youthful endeavors, leaving the works we produce later in life, when we've figured out what to do and how to do it. But actors' and directors' early efforts remain, fixed in place and available for all to see on DVDs available on the bargain shelf.

BAD TASTE
WingNut Films/New Zealand Film Commission, 1987

PRODUCER Peter Jackson

WRITER Peter Jackson

DIRECTOR Peter Jackson

STARS Peter Jackson (*Derek/Robert*), Terry Potter (*Ozzy*), Pete O'Herne (*Barry*), Craig Smith (*Giles*), Mike Minett (*Frank*), Doug Wren (*Lord Crumb*), and Peter Vere-Jones (*Lord Crumb's Voice*)

An alien fast-food conglomerate wants to turn humanity into the latest novelty item on their menu . . . and only a team of half-witted government agents can save us!

Why It Sucks

Bad Taste is the perfect title for this film. This may not be the goriest movie ever made, but it is certainly one of the most disgusting. You'll find yourself alternatively laughing at some repulsive slapstick violence (two aliens are dismembered and have their heads crushed while trying to kill one of our heroes with sledgehammers) and squirming at some pure gross-out scenes (a character puts a bit of stray brain matter back inside his cracked-open skull), but you'll never be bored.

Thumbs Down Rating: 👎👎

The Crappies

The Worst Script Award goes to . . . Peter Jackson, who at this point in his career had a tin ear for dialogue.
And the Before There Was South Park Award goes to . . . Peter Jackson for cramming more sophomoric gross-outs into a movie than any sane person can imagine.

They Really Said It!

Barry: We're a government department, not a paramilitary unit.
Derek: Yeah, the Astro Investigation and Defense Service!
Ozzy: Wish we'd change the name.

Betcha Didn't Know

» Peter Jackson shot this, his first directorial effort, over a four-year period, filming scenes whenever time and money was available.
» Doug Wren, the actor who played Lord Crumb, died during production, which is why another actor provided the character's voice.

Trivia Quiz

Bad Taste takes place on October 31. What is remarkable about that day?

A: It's the day famous British explorer Jack Harkness landed in New Zealand.

B: It's Peter Jackson's birthday.

C: It's Black Sheep Day, a New Zealand holiday.

D: It's a joke; October only has thirty days.

Answer: B. Peter Jackson was born October 31, 1961, on New Zealand's North Island in the small town of Pukerua Bay.

THE BLOODY BROOD
Julian Roffman Productions, 1959

PRODUCER Julian Roffman

WRITERS Ben Kerner and Elwood Ullman (script), Anne Howard Bailey (story)

DIRECTOR Julian Roffman

STARS Peter Falk (*Nico*), Jack Betts (*Cliff*), Barbara Lord (*Ellie*), Robert Christie (*Detective McLeod*), and Ron Hartmann (*Francis*)

A drug-dealing small-time hood (Falk), enamored with the beatnik lifestyle and nihilism, murders a messenger boy as a piece of performance art. However, he didn't count on the boy's brother (Betts), who begins an investigation.

Why It Sucks

It's *so* close to being a decent film. It tries to show balance in regards to the beatniks and their subculture. Further, we've got Peter Falk in his first starring role and his prerumpled overcoat days actually managing to mumble his way into a fairly decent portrayal as a bad guy. How dare they hide a halfway decent film behind a title like that?! *Sooo* close!

Thumbs Down Rating:

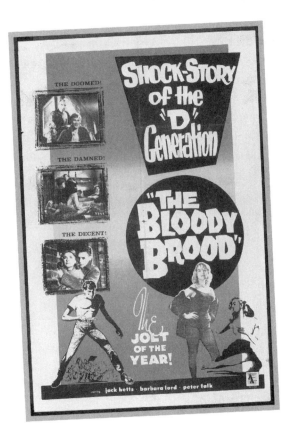

The Crappies

The Worst Actor Award goes to . . . Jack Betts for taking a pure-hearted hero who was already scripted as bland and turning him into something that looks as if he's on loan from *Attack of the Zombies.*

And the Dustbin of History Special Achievement Award goes to . . . Producer/Director Julian Roffman for making a film that gives modern audiences a chance to experience beatniks as they were. The fifty years that has gone by makes beatniks look even goofier than they did in the 1950s. (Hands up anyone who remembers the character Maynard G. Krebs from *The Many Loves of Dobie Gillis.*)

They Really Said It!

Nico: First they spend millions developing toothpaste to stop cavities, then they spend billions on bigger and better ways to blow us all to bits.

Betcha Didn't Know

» These were the first starring film roles for Peter Falk and Barbara Lord, both of whom had appeared in supporting parts on television programs previously.

» The coining of the term "beatnik" has been attributed to two different individuals. Some sources say it was first used by *San Francisco Chronicle* columnist Herb Caen in April of 1958, while others attribute it to film producer Sam Katzman, around the same time.

Trivia Quiz

What star of *The Bloody Brood* is a parent of comedian and voice actor Patrick Warburton?

A: Peter Falk

B: Barbara Lord

C: Ron Hartmann

D: Jack Betts

Answer: B. Barbara Lord married Dr. Jack Warburton in 1961 and mostly retired from acting. Patrick Warburton is the oldest of her four children.

CANNIBAL: THE MUSICAL
(AKA "ALFERD PACKER: THE MUSICAL")
Avenging Conscience, 1993

PRODUCERS Alexandra Kelly, Andrew Kemler, Jason McHugh (executive producers), Ian Hardin, Jason McHugh, Trey Parker, and Matt Stone (producers)

WRITER Trey Parker

DIRECTOR Trey Parker

STARS Juan Schwartz (*Alferd Packer*), Dian Bachar (*George Noon*), Jason McHugh (*Frank Miller*), Matt Stone (*James Humphries*), Ian Hardin (*Shannon Bell*), Jon Hegel (*Isreal Swan*), Toddy Walters (*Polly Pry*)

The lone survivor of an ill-fated mining expedition (Schwartz) tells how his hunger for gold led him to eat human flesh in this all-singing, all-dancing, all cannibalism musical extravaganza!

Why It Sucks

Yikes! This first feature film by co-creator of *South Park* Trey Parker was definitely a sign of things to come. It's a musical—that's right, a *musical*—about stranded prospectors who resort to cannibalism to survive. It's based on a real-world tragedy, and it's got several catchy tunes that will stick in your head for days after watching it, even if you try to remove them with a fondue fork. As for the "story," . . . well, Parker went on to create *South Park*, where you can see a lot of the same problems on display.

Thumbs Down Rating: 👎

The Crappies

The Worst Director Award goes to . . . Trey Parker for making a movie that almost loses its comedic momentum because he couldn't figure out how to end some scenes and pads others.
The Special Recognition for Advancing Minorities in Film Award goes to . . . Trey Parker for creating the Nihonjin Indian tribe, which consisted entirely of Japanese actors and extras.

They Really Said It!

Alferd Packer: Yeah, I hid in Wyoming for a while. I should have let them kill me.
Polly Pry: Why?
Alferd Packer: You ever been to Wyoming?

Betcha Didn't Know

» The Nihonjin tribe was played by Japanese exchange students attending the University of Colorado at Boulder. The chief of the tribe was played by Masao Maki, a restaurant owner from Boulder, Colorado.
» Trey Parker plays Alferd Packer, although he is credited as Juan Schwartz. This is a subtle joke, as Juan Schwartz is a variation of the name Packer lived under while hiding from the law after the cannibal accusations were leveled against him.

What is Alferd Packer known for?

A: Discovering the Grand Canyon

B: Inventing the Spork

C: First person tried and convicted for cannibalism in the United States, and the only convicted cannibal from Colorado

D: Coining the phrase, "It tastes like chicken."

Answer: C. Alferd Packer was convicted of manslaughter in 1886 and sentenced to forty years in prison. He was paroled in 1901, went to work as a security guard at the *Denver Post*, and died in 1907.

DEMENTIA 13
(AKA *"THE HAUNTED AND THE HUNTED"*)
Filmgroup Productions, 1963

PRODUCER Roger Corman

WRITERS Francis Coppola and Jack Hill

DIRECTOR Francis Coppola

STARS Luana Anders (*Louise Haloran*), William Campbell (*Richard Haloran*), Patrick Magee (*Justin Caleb*), Mary Mitchel (*Kane*), Bart Patton (*Billy Haloran*), and Ethne Dunne (*Lady Haloran*)

After her husband dies of a heart attack, Louise (Anders) covers up his death and enacts a scheme to gain the trust of her mentally unstable mother-in-law. Her plan is working well . . . until a crazed ax murderer shows up.

Why It Sucks

The only reason any serious critic would be found in the same room with this film is because it was made by Francis Ford Coppola while he was a gofer/assistant director for low-budget movie mogul Roger Corman. Sadly, it's mostly a snoozer. Every scene drags its feet before it gets going and hangs around long after the viewer wants to end his or her misery with a shotgun.

Thumbs Down Rating: 🖓 🖓 🖓

The Crappies

The Worst Auteuer Award goes to . . . Francis Coppola for creating a movie that was so lame after its second cut that the producer hired a second writer (and ghost director) in an attempt to pump up the excitement.

And the Worst Actress Award goes to . . . Ethne Dunne as Lady Haloran for playing a part that needed to have a touch of the sinister but instead turning in a performance that makes Tipper Gore look like Lady Gaga.

They Really Said It!

Kane: Sometimes I think you see me as a Christmas tree ornament.

Betcha Didn't Know

» This was the directorial and scripting debut of Francis Ford Coppola, in a time before he became a sensation so huge that only three names could properly describe him.

» The film was shot simultaneously with *The Young Racers*, another Roger Corman production, using many of the same actors, locations, and leftover budget dollars.

 Trivia Quiz

What iconic horror character has not been featured in a film produced or directed by Francis Ford Coppola?

A: Dracula

B: Frankenstein's monster

C: The Invisible Man

D: Dr. Jekyll/Mr. Hyde

Answer: C. Coppola directed films about Dracula (1992) and Frankenstein (1994) and was the executive producer of a television version of *Dr. Jekyll and Mr. Hyde* (1999).

HANGMEN

Cinema Sciences Corporation, 1987

PRODUCERS Robert J. Anderson (executive producer), J. Christian Ingvordson, Steven W. Kaman, and Richard R. Washburn (producers)

WRITERS J. Christian Ingvordson and Steven Kaman

DIRECTOR J. Christian Ingvordson

STARS Rick Washburn (*Rob Greene*), Keith Bogart (*Danny Greene*), Jake LaMotta (*Moe Boone*), and Sandra Bullock (*Lisa Edwards*)

When renegade CIA operatives target a government agent (Washburn) and his teenaged son (Bogart) for death, they find their brutality is exceeded only by that of the Vietnam veterans who rally to defend their old comrade.

Why It Sucks

Hangmen is a turkey on every level. Bad photography (marked by *waaay* too many extreme close-ups and dull long shots); lame action scenes that overuse slow motion and lots of blood-spurting squibs; a script so nonsensical that even the filmmakers couldn't keep track of what was supposed to be going on; and dialogue that is exceeded in its horribleness only by the acting of those delivering it.

Thumbs Down Rating: 👎👎👎👎

The Crappies

The Worst Director Award goes to . . . J. Christian Ingvordson for making a movie with a story less interesting than a stamp collection, and so free of internal consistency that you wonder if anyone bothered to read it before shooting.

And the Worst Acting Award goes to . . . Sandra Bullock for overdoing a Brooklyn accent to a degree that would lead viewers to conclude that she's from Flatbush by way of Waycross, Georgia.

They Really Said It!

Moe: Beat it, cheese dick.

Betcha Didn't Know

» This is Sandra Bullock's first film appearance. The really amazing thing is that she had a career after this movie.

» This was J. Christian Ingvordson's second film, and he has written, directed and produced over twenty movies since.

 Trivia Quiz

What attempted 1980s revival of a 1970s sci-fi television franchise was Sandra Bullock part of?

A: *The Six Million Dollar Man/Bionic Woman*

B: *Space: 1999*

C: *Battlestar Galactica*

D: *Kolchak: The Night Stalker*

Answer: A. *The Six Million Dollar Man/Bionic Woman*. Bullock appeared as a bionically enhanced sidekick to Jamie Sommers and Steve Austin. The television series never got off the ground.

KISS DADDY GOODNIGHT
Beast of Eden Productions, 1987

PRODUCERS Maureen O'Brien and William Ripka

WRITERS Michael Gabrieli and Peter Ily Huemer

DIRECTOR Peter Ily Huemer

STARS Uma Thurman (*Laura*), Paul Dillon (*Sid*), Paul Richards (*William*), and Steve Buscemi (*Johnny*)

Laura (Thurman) is a teenaged model who augments her meager earnings by picking up wealthy men, drugging them, and then stealing and selling valuable art objects from their homes. It's a nice living until she becomes the love object of a crazy old man (Richards) who will stop at nothing to make her his.

Inauspicious Beginnings

Why It Sucks

What a mind-numbingly dull film with which to introduce Uma Thurman! While the characters and acting are appropriate for a film-noir movie, the glacial pace and unfocused story aren't. Throughout, Sid wanders around the city in a pointless subplot. Halfway through the movie, the director decides the audience might like a little suspense. But that's over quickly, and we're back to Sid's efforts to start a new rock band.

Thumbs Down Rating: 🎬🎬🎬🎬

The Crappies

The Worst Actress Award goes to . . . Uma Thurman. It seems a bit harsh, but she's completely unsuitable for the role.

And the Worst Director Award goes to . . . Peter Ily Huemer. Are we *really* interested in Sid's band? Of course not! So stop for wasting so much time on pointless subplots!

They Really Said It!

William: That's *Dr. Zhivago*, a pretentious little gem that was all the rage while we were living in Italy.

Betcha Didn't Know

» This was the first film role for eighteen-year-old Uma Thurman, and her audition was reportedly the first one she had ever been on.

» The film is the second of the only two English-language films directed by Austrian-born Peter Ily Huemer.

 Trivia Quiz

For what film did Uma Thurman win an Academy Award nomination?

A: *Kiss Daddy Goodnight* (1987)

B: *The Adventures of Baron Munchausen* (1988)

C: *Pulp Fiction* (1994)

D: *Batman & Robin* (1997)

Answer: C. *Pulp Fiction* not only netted Thurman a Best Supporting Actress nomination but it revived her slumping career.

RETURN TO HORROR HIGH
Balcor Film Investors, 1987

PRODUCERS Greg H. Sims (executive producer) and Mark Lisson (producer)

WRITERS Bill Froehlich, Dana Escalante, Mark Lisson, and Greg H. Sims

DIRECTOR Bill Froehlich

STARS Lori Lethin (*Callie Cassidy/Sarah Walker/Susan*), Brendan Hughes (*Steven Blake*), Richard Brestoff (*Arthur Lyman Kastleman*), Maureen McCormick (*Officer Tyler*), Pepper Martin (*Chief Deyner*), Alex Rocco (*Harry Sleerik*), Scott Jacoby (*Josh Forbes*), Al Fann (*Amos*), Andy Romano (*Principal Kastleman*), and George Clooney (*Oliver*)

The cast and crew of a low-budget slasher film being shot at the high school where a series of real mutilation murders took place years ago are brutally murdered one by one when the killer returns and infiltrates the production.

Why It Sucks

The narrative threads of this low-budget spoof of slasher films are more tangled than the cocaine-fueled fever dreams of Quentin Tarantino. As the end credits start to roll, we sit and wonder if this was a movie about real killings or a movie within a movie based on real-life killers. Or . . . well, you get the idea.

Thumbs Down Rating: 👎👎👎

The Crappies

The Worst Actor Award goes to . . . Brendan Hughes for playing about as boring a leading man as possible without actually casting Al Gore.

And the Worst Director Award goes to . . . Bill Froehlich for failing to keep the chaos in line. Would it have been *that* hard to hold a couple more script conferences?

They Really Said It!

Josh Forbes: There will be no exploding tit shot!

Betcha Didn't Know

» *Predator: The Concert* would have been George Clooney's first movie credit, but, although filmed in 1983, that film wasn't released until 1987, shortly after *Return to Horror High.*

» The black cloak and mask of the insane murderer in this film bears a striking resemblance to the costume of the killer in the far more successful horror spoof *Scream* (1996).

 Trivia Quiz

What is the cheer shouted by the ghostly cheerleader in the original preview for *Return to Horror High*?

A: Killer to the left, killer to the right! Sit down, stand up! Fright! Fright! Fright!

B: Let's get physical, let's get mean! Let's get physical and stab them, stab them, till they scream!

C: Close that D, Dot that I, shred that E . . . Die! Die! Die!

D: There was no ghostly cheerleader in the preview for *Return to Horror High.*

Answer: A. Yes, really!

TEN FINGERS OF DEATH
(AKA "MASTER WITH CRACKED FINGERS," "SNAKE FIST FIGHTER," AND "LITTLE TIGER OF CANTON")
21st Century Film Corporation, 1971

PRODUCERS Lee Long Koan and Dick Randall

WRITER Sun Liu

DIRECTOR Mu Zhu

STARS Jackie Chan (*Jackie*), Siu Tien Yuen (*Old Master*), Casanova Wong (*Big Boss*), and Kwok Choi Hon (*Little Frog*)

Jackie (Chan) has secretly studied martial arts under the tutelage of an eccentric master (Yuen). Now, he must use his skills to defeat a vicious band of extortionists and avenge his father's death.

Why It Sucks

An unintentionally creepy scene where a dirty old man commands a little boy to take off his pants while they're alone in the dark forest . . . this is a high point of the movie? Yes, that's the *high* point! Not to mention the director's clumsy attempts to hide the fact that star Jackie Chan was not available to finish it.

Thumbs Down Rating: 🖓🖓🖓🖓

The Crappies

The Worst Picture Award goes to . . . Lee Long Koan for failing to realize hiring a stand-in for Jackie Chan was silly.

And the Worst Director Award goes to . . . Mu Zhu for his total ineptitude at masking the Jackie Chan stand-in during the second half of the movie.

They Really Said It!

Jackie: You killed him. You are responsible for his death.

Betcha Didn't Know

» Before this film was finished, production closed down when the producer reportedly stole the payroll and skipped town, leaving the actors and crew unpaid. After Jackie Chan became a full-blown movie star, the film was completed with footage lifted from *Drunken Master.* Although a few of the original actors appeared in additional scenes, Chan did not take part in the completion of the film.

» The film is scored entirely with music taken from other sources, including *Popeye the Sailor* cartoons.

 Trivia Quiz

What was Jackie Chan's first job in show business?

A: Assistant to filmmaker Godfrey Ho.

B: Playing Gamera, the amazing flying Japanese turtle monster.

C: A member of the touring Peking Opera Company, as a member of the Seven Little Fortunes troupe.

D: Bruce Lee's stunt-double during the filming of *Enter the Dragon.*

Answer: C. Chan joined Seven Little Fortunes after excelling in martial arts and singing while studying at the China Drama Academy.

CHAPTER EIGHT

IT SEEMED LIKE A GOOD IDEA AT THE TIME

The films in this chapter are noteworthy for the big names and big budgets involved. They are films that *should* have been successful based on the track records of the people involved. But, somehow, something went terribly wrong.

1941
Universal Pictures/Columbia Pictures, 1979

PRODUCERS John Milius (executive producer), Buzz Feitshans (producer)

WRITERS Bob Gale, Robert Zemeckis (script), and Bob Gale, Robert Zemeckis, and John Milius (story)

DIRECTOR Steven Spielberg

STARS Dan Aykroyd (*Sgt. Frank Tree*), John Belushi (*Capt. Wild Bill Kelso*), Treat Williams (*Cpl. Chuck "Stetch" Sitarski*), Toshirô Mifune (*Cmdr. Mitamura*), Tim Matheson (*Capt. Loomis Birkhead*), Bobby Di Ciccio (*Wally Stephens*), Nancy Allen (*Donna Stratton*), Slim Pickens (*Hollis "Holly" Wood*), Robert Stack (*Maj. Gen. Joseph W. Stilwell*), Ned

Beatty (*Ward Douglas*), Lorraine Gary (*Joan Douglas*), and Christopher Lee (*Capt. Wolfgang von Kleinschmidt*)

Shortly after the Japanese attack on Pearl Harbor in 1941, an incompetent Japanese U-boat crew squares off against equally incompetent American military and civil defense forces, while downtown Los Angeles is in the grips of a jitterbug brawl.

Why It Sucks

Before popping in the DVD of this movie, put your brain in neutral and inject a couple of beers into your bloodstream. Even with those precautions, the film's two-hour running time is likely to leave you exhausted. One thing's for sure: You won't remember much of it.

Thumbs Down Rating: 👎

The Crappies

The Worst Picture Award goes to . . . Producers John Milius and Buzz Fleitshans, with additional recognition to director Steven Speilberg, for their total lack of restraint.

The Best Accidental Stunt Man Award goes to . . . John Belushi, for a hilarious prat-fall while climbing out of a fighter plane. The slip-and-fall gag wasn't in the script, as he really did slip and fall.

They Really Said It!

Hollis "Holly" Wood: You won't get shit out of me. I've been constipated all week!

Betcha Didn't Know

» This film was Steven Spielberg's first financial flop. It cost an estimated $35 million to make, but only earned a little over $31 million during its initial American theatrical run.
» To my lasting regret, John Wayne turned down the role of Major-General Stilwell. He also asked that Spielberg cut all scenes featuring Stilwell, because he felt they were unpatriotic and insulting to war veterans.

Which was *not* a true historical event that the scriptwriters drew from for inspiration?

A: The Zoot Suit Riots of 1943, in which Hispanic zoot-suiters and military personnel engaged in a massive brawl in Los Angeles

B: The shelling by a Japanese submarine of a refinery on the coast of California

C: The Japanese invasion of Mexico in 1942

D: A decision to place anti-aircraft guns in the front yards of private homes in Maine

Answer: C. The Japanese did *not* invade Mexico in 1942, but everything else on the list really happened.

BALLISTIC: ECKS VS. SEVER

Franchise Pictures/Chris Lee Productions, 2002

PRODUCERS Tarak Ben Ammar, Oliver Hengst, Tracee Stanley, and Andrew Stevens (executive producers), Kaos, Chris Lee, and Ellie Samaha (producers)

WRITER Alan McElroy

DIRECTOR Kaos

STARS Antonio Banderas (*Jeremiah Ecks*), Lucy Liu (*Sever*), Gregg Henry (*Robert Gant/Clark*), Ray Park (*A. J. Ross*), and Talisa Soto (*Vinn/ Rayne*)

Ex-U.S. government agents (Banderas and Liu) must overcome their tortured pasts and current animosity for each other to defeat a common enemy (Henry) who has acquired the ultimate in robotic assassination tools.

Why It Sucks

Someone in the studio offices thought the title was a good idea. Unfortuately, it has nothing to do with the plot of the film. This isn't the story of Ecks and Sever fighting each other. It's about

It Seemed Like a Good Idea at the Time

93

them *teaming up* against a mutual enemy. What passes for the story drags viewers through chaotic and messily staged action set pieces. On the other hand, what do you expect from a director named Kaos?

Thumbs Down Rating: 🦃 🦃 🦃 🦃

The Crappies

The Special Reading Is Fundamental Award goes to . . . Antonia Banderas and Lucy Liu for apparently not reading the script before choosing to star in this miserable picture.

And the Worst Director Award goes to . . . Kaos for allowing his attention deficit disorder to ruin the film. Not even action scenes are allowed to play out with a consistent visual tone or flow.

They Really Said It!

Ecks: Where did you get all this ordinance?

Sever: Some women buy shoes.

Betcha Didn't Know

» The film cost $70 million to make, but only brought in $14 million during its very brief U.S. theatrical run. It didn't fare that much better on DVD.

» The 2001 Gameboy Advance first-person shooter game *Ecks vs. Sever* was based on an early version of the film's script, not the other way around.

 Trivia Quiz

Who was the first internationally renowned American-born Chinese-American actress?

A: Lotus Long (born 1909)

B: Anna May Wong (born 1905)

C: Nancy Kwan (born 1939)

D: Lucy Liu (born 1968)

Answer: B. Anna May Wong enjoyed a career throughout Europe and Asia, though she struggled against racism in the United States.

It Seemed Like a Good Idea at the Time

BATMAN & ROBIN
Warner Bros./PolyGram Pictures, 1997

PRODUCERS Benjamin Melniker and Michael E. Uslan (executive producers), Peter Macgregor-Scott (producer)

WRITERS Avika Goldsman (script), Bob Kane (original Batman character)

DIRECTOR Joel Schumacher

STARS George Clooney (*Batman/Bruce Wayne*), Chris O'Donnell (*Robin/ Dick Grayson*), Alicia Silverstone (*Batgirl/Barbara Wilson*), Arnold Schwarzenegger (*Mr. Freeze/Dr. Victor Fries*), and Uma Thurman (*Poison Ivy/Dr. Pamela Isley*)

Gotham City's dynamic duo, Batman and Robin (Clooney and O'Donnell) struggle to keep their partnership intact as the city faces the evil Mr. Freeze (Schwarzenegger) and Poison Ivy (Thurman).

Why It Sucks

The silliest, worst, and last Batman movie from the 1990s, this film is so campy that it makes the classic 1966 *Batman* movie with Adam West look like an episode of Masterpiece Theater. The story is nonsensical, the jokes are lame, and everyone looks embarrassed. General opinion is that this movie killed the Batman franchise until the release of *Batman Begins* in 2005.

Thumbs Down Rating: 🥾🥾🥾🥾

The Crappies

The Worst Costume Design Award goes to . . . Ingrid Ferrin for making Batman, Robin, and every other costumed character in the film look even more ludicrous than the average comic book. The only exception is Uma Thurman's sexy Poison Ivy outfit.

And the Worst Director Award goes to . . . Joel Schumacher for overloading the flim with action set pieces, the worst of which is a hockey match with a diamond as the puck that culminates in a motorcycle chase.

They Really Said It!

Batgirl: Chicks like you give women a bad name.

Betcha Didn't Know

» The film had a budget of $125 million, but only made $105 million domestically. The first film in the series, 1989's *Batman*, had a budget of $35 million and earned $251 million during its original U.S. theatrical run.

» A fifth Batman movie was planned, but this one's poor financial performance and even worse reception by fans and critics caused its cancellation.

 Trivia Quiz

Which of the following actors did director Joel Schumacher not consider for the role of Mr. Freeze?

A: Hulk Hogan

B: Anthony Hopkins

C: Sylvester Stallone

D: Richard Kiel

Answer: D. Richard Kiel, best known for playing Jaws, the near-indestructible foe of James Bond, was not, alas, one of Schumacher's choices for Mr. Freeze. If Schwarzenegger had turned down the role, Stallone was next in line.

CATWOMAN
Warner Bros./Village Roadshow/DiNovi Pictures, 2004

PRODUCERS Bruce Berman, Michael Fottrell, Robert Kirby, Benjamin Melniker, and Michael E. Uslan (executive producers), Denise Di Novi and Edward L. McDonnell (producers)

WRITERS Theresa Rebeck, John Brancato, and Michael Ferris (story), John Brancato, Michael Ferris, and John Rogers (script), Bob Kane (original Catwoman character)

DIRECTOR Pitof

STARS Halle Berry (*Patience Phillips/Catwoman*), Sharon Stone (*Laurel Hedare*), and Benjamin Bratt (*Tom Lone*)

Through a twist of fate, a shy woman (Berry) gains personality-bending superpowers and becomes Catwoman.

It Seemed Like a Good Idea at the Time

Why It Sucks

The biggest mystery about this film is why Halle Berry agreed to star in it after winning an Oscar and appearing in the superior superhero film *The X-Men*. Even more surprising is that Warner Bros. would treat one of its own properties so badly in what's been called "the worst superhero film ever made."

Thumbs Down Rating:

The Crappies

The Worst Actress Award goes to . . . Halle Berry for giving a performance that barely manages to be sexy. And it's *Halle Berry*, for God's sake!

And the Worst Director Award goes to . . . Pitof for displaying disregard for production continuity so sloppy that costumes change in the middle of fights, hairstyles change during the trip from a restaurant to a bedroom, and helmets appear and disappear.

They Really Said It!

Catwoman: You saved my life, Midnight. But somebody killed me and I've got to find out who and why.

Betcha Didn't Know

» After Michelle Pfeiffer declined to repeat her role from *Batman Returns*, Ashley Judd was the first choice to play Catwoman. After she also declined, Halle Berry was cast.

» The film cost around $100 million to make, but only earned some $71 million at box offices worldwide (and just $40 million in the United States).

 Trivia Quiz
For what film did Halle Berry win an Academy Award?

A: *Die Another Day* (2002)

B: *Gothika* (2003)

C: *Monster's Ball* (2001)

D: *Swordfish* (2001)

It Seemed Like a Good Idea at the Time

Answer: C. In *Monster's Ball* Berry portrayed Leticia Musgrove, wife of an executed criminal.

CITY HEAT

The Malpaso Company/Deliverance Productions, 1984

PRODUCER Fritz Manes

WRITERS Sam O. Brown and Joseph Stinson

DIRECTOR Richard Benjamin

STARS Burt Reynolds (*Mike Murphy*), Clint Eastwood (*Lt. Speer*), Jane Alexander (*Addy*), Richard Roundtree (*Dehl Swift*), Madeline Kahn (*Caroline Howley*), Rip Torn (*Primo Pitt*), and Irene Cara (*Ginny Lee*)

When his partner is murdered, P.I. Mike Murphy (Reynolds) is left trying to figure out who killed him and what scam he was running against Kansas City's biggest gangsters. To do so, he must work with his former best friend and now bitterest enemy (Eastwood).

Why It Sucks

How can a detective movie set in the 1930s and featuring excellent performers like Burt Reynolds and Clint Eastwood fail? Well, because someone apparently didn't recognize that no matter how big the stars, a film still needs, oh, I don't know, a good *script*. Instead, we have a convoluted story, flashes of absurdist humor that are out of place, and every actor but Burt Reynolds is underused.

Thumbs Down Rating: 👎 👎

The Crappies

The Special Award for Worst Preview goes to . . . The editors who created a preview that consists of random fragments of the film's jokes and punchlines in a random order.

And the Worst Acting Award goes to . . . Clint Eastwood for giving one of the worst performances of his career, a surprising fact since he had a large degree of control over the film and how it turned out.

They Really Said It!

Speer: And just what were you going to do after the bomb went off?

Betcha Didn't Know

» The writer credited as Sam O. Brown is actually Blake Edwards, creator of the Pink Panther film series. Edwards reportedly left the project following creative differences with Eastwood.

» This was one of two films produced and partially funded by Burt Reynolds's production company, Deliverance Productions. (The other was the 1981 film *Sharkey's Machine*.)

 Trivia Quiz

Which actor turned down the role of Han Solo in *Star Wars*?

A: Clint Eastwood

B: Burt Reynolds

C: Richard Roundtree

D: Rip Torn

Answer: B. Burt Reynolds also turned down the role that won Jack Nicholson an Oscar in *Terms of Endearment*, Kevin Klein's role in *Soap Dish*, and the role Bruce Willis landed in the *Die Hard* franchise, as well as an offer to take over James Bond after Sean Connery quit.

THE LOVE GURU

Paramount Pictures/Spyglass Entertainment/Michael De Luca Productions, 2008

PRODUCERS Gary Barber and Roger Birnbaum (executive producers), Mike Myers, Michael De Luca, and Donald J. Lee Jr. (producers)

WRITERS Mike Myers and Graham Gordy

DIRECTOR Marco Schnabel

STARS Mike Myers (*Guru Pitka/young Pitka/teenage Pitak/Maurice/ himself*), Jessica Alba (*Jane Bullard*), Romany Malco (*Darren Roanoke*), Manu Narayan (*Rajneesh*), Justin Timberlake (*Jacques "Le Coq" Grande*), Verne Troyer (*Coach Punch Cherkov*), and Stephen Colbert (*Jay Kell*)

Guru Pitka (Myers), a new-age, self-help sensation, is approached by the owner of a hockey team (Alba) to help her resolve relationship problems that are keeping her star player (Malco) from performing properly on the ice.

Why It Sucks

There isn't a single joke in the film that doesn't feel forced. Myers is so in love with his own humor that he repeats them, draining what little amusement the film may have contained. Worse, Myers's Guru Pitka character is slimy and obnoxious, constantly chuckling at his own jokes. By the end of the movie, you want to take a shower.

Thumbs Down Rating: 👎👎👎👎👎

The Crappies

The Worst Actor Award goes to . . . Michael Myers for Guru Pitka, a performance that is as unfunny as it is repulsive.

And the Worst Script Award goes to . . . Mike Myers and Graham Gordy for writing a comedy where the funniest jokes involve Ben Kingsley crossing his eyes and a cameo appearance by Mariska Hargitay.

They Really Said It!

Guru Pitka: Intimacy is like putting your wiener on the table and having someone say, "That looks like a penis, only smaller."

Betcha Didn't Know

» Guru Pitka was conceived for, but ultimately dropped from, the 1999 Michael Myers film *Austin Powers: The Spy Who Shagged Me*.
» As the film debuted in 2008, Rajan Zed, self-important publicity hound and self-appointed spokesman of Hindus everywhere, declared the film offensive because it lampooned Hindu beliefs.

 Trivia Quiz

Mike Myers stated in an interview that before filming he tests and practices his characters and jokes in front of live audiences, just like which of the following legendary comic film performers?

A: The Marx Brothers

B: The Three Stooges

C: The Ritz Brothers

D: The Grimm Brothers

Answer: A. The Marx Brothers. The most famous routines of Groucho, Harpo, and Chico were tested and perfected—in their early films through live vaudeville performances, and in their later movies by tours organized by MGM.

ON DEADLY GROUND
Seagal-Nasso Productions/Warner Bros., 1994

PRODUCERS Jeffrey Robinov and Robert Watts (executive producers), Steven Seagal, Julius R. Nasso, and A. Kitman Ho (producers)

WRITERS Ed Horowitz and Robin U. Russin

DIRECTOR Steven Seagal

STARS Steven Seagal (*Forrest Taft*), Michael Caine (*Michael Jennings*), Joan Chen (*Masu*), and John C. McGinley (*MacGruder*)

Forrest Taft (Seagal) is an oil company employee who, after a violent near-death experience and a shamanistic spiritual reawakening, decides to kick ass and blow crap up to guard the rights of Alaskan Eskimos and the purity of Mother Nature.

Why It Sucks

There's an interesting story buried somewhere beneath the badly written dialogue, illogical plot developments, and attempt at delivering an environmental message while fighting an evil oil company through blowing stuff to pieces.

Thumbs Down Rating: 👎 👎 👎 👎

The Crappies

The Worst Director Award goes to . . . Steven Seagal for using the indigenous population of Alaska as his jumping off point, but not casting a Native American in the role of Masu, the Sexy and Wise Nature Girl.

And the Special Achievement Award for Multiculturalism goes to . . . Screenwriters Ed Horowitz and Robin U. Russin and director/coproducer Steven Seagal for their cartoonish presentation of Alaskan Native culture. Homer Simpson's "vision quests" have been more respectful of Native Americans.

They Really Said It!

Michael Jennings: Is this the slope bitch you've been banging?
Forrest Taft: No, not her.

Betcha Didn't Know

» Warner Bros. agreed to let Steven Seagal direct this film if he would star in *Under Siege 2: Dark Territory.*

» This is Steven Seagal's only directorial effort to date.

 Trivia Quiz

Which of the following facts about Steven Seagal is *not* true?

A: He owned and operated an aikido dojo in Japan.

B: He is a fully commissioned sheriff's deputy in Louisiana's Jefferson Parish and produced a reality show titled *Steven Seagal: Lawman* that followed his exploits.

C: He has been engaged in a bitter feud with Jackie Chan for nearly twenty years.

D: He won the 1995 Razzie Worst Director Award for *On Deadly Ground.*

Answer: C. By all accounts, Seagal and Chan are good friends.

THE REAPING
Dark Castle Entertainment/Village Roadshow Pictures/Warner Bros., 2007

PRODUCERS Bruce Berman, Erik Olsen, and Steve Richards (executive producers), Susan Downey, Herbert W. Gains, Joel Silver, and Robert Zemeckis (producers)

WRITERS Carey W. Hayes and Chad Hayes

DIRECTOR Stephen Hopkins

STARS Hilary Swank (*Katherine Winter*), Idris Elba (*Ben*), David Morrissey (*Doug*), and AnnaSophia Robb (*Loren McConnell*).

Katherine (Swank), a former missionary turned college professor-and-professional-debunker-of-miracles is called to an isolated Louisiana village to provide an explanation for a series of events that seem to be mirroring the Ten Plagues of Egypt. Katherine uncovers signs that something supernatural is indeed happening in the town, and it centers on a twelve-year-old girl (Robb). But is she a savior or a destroyer?

It Seemed Like a Good Idea at the Time

Why It Sucks

The Reaping comes across as a fairly standard supernatural thriller. There's only so much that can be done with a script as shallow and unemotionally involving as this one. The story turns on Katherine's loss of faith, but at no time do we get close enough to the character to care. The writers weren't up to the subject matter but were too squeamish to go for over-the-top horror. The result is a mess.

Thumbs Down Rating: 🦇🦇🦇

The Crappies

The Worst Actress Award goes to . . . Hilary Swank for playing an already underdeveloped character in such a disconnected way that the only point of interest is how she fills out her tank tops.
And the Worst Director Award goes to . . . Stephen Hopkins for an over-the-top climax when he finally realized he needed to go full-out B horror film on the audience.

They Really Said It!

Maddie: Are you here for my girl? Are you gonna kill my baby girl?
Katherine: What? No!
Maddie: Why not?

Betcha Didn't Know

» Film critic Richard Roeper named *The Reaping* as one of the ten worst movies of 2007.
» Hilary Swank has won two Best Actress Academy Awards (for *Million Dollar Baby* in 2005 and *Boys Don't Cry* in 1999).

 Trivia Quiz
What television series did Hilary Swank have a recurring role in?

A: *Buffy the Vampire Slayer*
B: *Beverly Hills 90210*
C: *Northern Exposure*
D: *The X-Files*

Answer: B. Swank appeared in *Beverly Hills 90210* as Carly Reynolds in sixteen episodes, from 1997 to 1998.

CHAPTER NINE

KINDA-SORTA BASED ON THE BOOK

Movie producers the world over have a bad habit of taking fiction and "basing" movies on it that ultimately have little to do with the source material. The movies here are not necessarily bad pieces of filmmaking, but as far as adaptations go, they miss the mark in one way or another.

THE BLACK CAT (AKA "THE HOUSE OF DOOM" AND "THE VANISHING BODY")
Universal Pictures, 1934

PRODUCER Uncredited

WRITERS Edgar G. Ulmer and Peter Ruric (script), Edgar Allan Poe (original story . . . although how they got *this* from it, I'll never know)

DIRECTOR Edgar G. Ulmer

STARS Bela Lugosi (*Dr. Vitus Werdegast*), David Manners (*Peter Alison*), Boris Karloff (*Hjalmar Poelzig*), and Jacqueline Wells (*Joan Alison*)

Honeymooners Peter and Joan Alison (Manners and Wells) are stranded in an isolated house in a Hungarian backwater. Here, they are drawn into the nets of the evil Satanist Hjalmar Poelzig (Karloff) and the revenge plans of his one-time friend Dr. Vitus Werdegast (Lugosi).

Why It Sucks

The Black Cat is a stylish and creepy movie from the Golden Age of horror at Universal Pictures. That said, it has absolutely nothing to do with Edgar Allen Poe's short story about an insane wife murderer. There aren't even traces of the Poe story. So why even bother to connect it to Poe?

Thumbs Down Rating: 👎

The Crappies

The Worst Script Award goes to . . . Edgar G. Ulmer and Peter Ruric for writing an adaptation of *The Black Cat* that has more in common with *The Fall of the House of Usher.*

And the Worst Director Award goes to . . . Edgar G. Ulmer for giving the film a cheerful denouement, ruining what could have been one of the creepiest endings in the history of film.

They Really Said It!

Poelzig: The phone is dead. Do you hear that, Vitus? Even the phone is dead.

Betcha Didn't Know

» This was Universal's biggest grossing film in 1934, with a production cost of $96,000 and a domestic box-office take of $236,000.

» This was the first screen-pairing of Boris Karloff and Bela Lugosi.

 Trivia Quiz

Which star of *The Black Cat* also appeared in Universal's second movie to bear this title?

A: Boris Karloff

B: Bela Lugosi

C: David Manners

D: Jacqueline Wells

Answer: B. Bela Lugosi has a bit-part as a creepy groundskeeper in the 1941 horror-comedy.

FROM BEYOND
Empire Pictures, 1986

PRODUCERS Charles Band (executive producer) and Brian Yunza (producer)

WRITERS Brian Yunza and David Paoli (script), H. P. Lovecraft (original short story)

DIRECTOR Stuart Gordon

STARS Jeffrey Combs (*Crawford Tillinghast*), Barbara Crampton (*Dr. Katherine McMichaels*), Ken Foree (*Buford "Bubba" Brownlee*), Ted Sorel (*Dr. Edward Pretorius*), and Carolyn Purdy-Gordon (*Dr. Bloch*)

A pair of physicists (Combs and Sorel) create a machine that causes our dimension to merge with another. They end up unleashing horrors—and sexual perversion—unlike any seen before.

Why It Sucks

The similarity between the movie *From Beyond* and the H. P. Lovecraft story it sprang from ends about ten minutes in. It's a gory, goopy movie that you do *not* want to watch while eating. Not bad in many ways, but it's got very little to do with Lovecraft's fiction.

Thumbs Down Rating: 👎

The Crappies

The Worst Special-Effects Award goes to . . . The animators who created the "mystic energy" effects. Even by 1980s low-budget sci-fi standards they were bad.

And the Worst Actress Award goes to . . . Carolyn Purdy-Gordon as Dr. Bloch for playing her part while clearly thinking "I wish I were somewhere else."

They Really Said It!

Crawford Tillinghast: It ate him! Bit his head off—like a gingerbread man!

Betcha Didn't Know

» This was one of three H. P. Lovecraft–based films that Stuart Gordon directed for companies operated by B movie mogul Charles Band.

» Jeremy Combs and Barbara Crampton also star in Gordon's two other Band-produced Lovecraft films.

 Trivia Quiz

What famous pop culture location did H. P. Lovecraft create?

A: Springfield

B: Arkham Asylum

C: The Land of Oz

D: Atlantis

Answer: B. Arkham Asylum. Several of Lovecraft's characters end up there or at least visit it. It's located in the fictional Massachusetts town of Arkham.

MODESTY BLAISE

Twentieth Century Fox, 1966

PRODUCERS Joseph Janni

WRITERS Evan Jones (script), Stanley Dubens and Peter O'Donnell (original comic strip)

DIRECTOR Joseph Losey

STARS Monica Vitti (*Modesty Blaise*), Terence Stamp (*Willie Garvin*), Clive Revill (*McWhirter/Sheik Abu Tahir*), Dirk Bogarde (*Gabriel*), Harry Andrews (*Sir Gerald Tarrant*), Michael Craig (*Paul Hagan*), and Rosella Falk (*Mrs. Fothergill*)

Adventuress Modesty Blaise (Vitti) and her sidekick Willie Garvin (Stamp) come out of semi-retirement to stop an unknown enemy from interfering with a shipment of diamonds promised to an eccentric Middle Eastern leader (Revill). Along the way Blaise clashes with her old enemy Gabriel (Bogarde).

Why It Sucks

Modesty Blaise has a timeless adventure tale. The villains manage to be creepy and funny at the same time; the film captures the relationship between Willie and Modesty perfectly. And then the filmmakers decided to go campy. Sigh. Modesty's hair color and clothes change in an instant, and she and Willie fall in love and decide to get married—something O'Donnell had specifically said would *never* happen.

Thumbs Down Rating: 👎👎👎

The Crappies

The Worst Director Award goes to . . . Joseph Losey for presiding over some of the worst fight scenes ever put on film. Not only are they badly choreographed, but he didn't seem to know how to create the illusion that blows were connecting.

And the Worst Picture Award goes to . . . Joseph Janni for a movie that was intended to be lighthearted and goofy but comes off as nonsensical. If you want to see the kind of thing Mike Myers was parodying in *Austin Powers*, rent this movie.

They Really Said It!

Gabriel: I am the villain of the piece, and I have condemned you to death.

Betcha Didn't Know

» *Modesty Blaise* creator Peter O'Donnell remarked that the only thing that remains of his original screenplay is the line "What do you know about Wilberforce?"

» Clive Revill, who plays two very different characters in the film, was a last-minute addition to the cast.

 Trivia Quiz

Which *Modesty Blaise* star voiced Emperor Palpatine in *The Empire Strikes Back*?

A: Harry Andrews

B: Dirk Bogarde

C: Clive Revill

D: Terrence Stamp

Answer: C. Clive Revill appeared as the giant holographic images that Darth Vader reports to in the original cut of *The Empire Strikes Back*. In 2004 when George Lucas recut the film, he replaced Revill with the voice and image of Ian McDiarmid.

MOONRAKER
Danjaq/Eon Productions, 1979

PRODUCERS Michael G. Wilson (executive producer) and Albert Broccoli (producer)

WRITERS Christopher Wood (script), Ian Fleming (original novel, uncredited)

DIRECTOR Lewis Gilbert

STARS Roger Moore (*James Bond*), Lois Chiles (*Dr. Holly Goodhead*), Michael Lonsdale (*Hugo Drax*), and Richard Kiel (*Jaws*)

British secret agent and one-man wrecking crew James Bond (Moore) investigates the midair theft of a space shuttle and uncovers a scheme to unleash global genocide.

Why It Sucks

None of the Bond films that share a title with a Fleming novel are as far from the original tale as this one. The film swaps the guided nuclear missiles from the book for space shuttles and orbital death satellites. London and the English countryside vanish in favor of exotic global locales and outer space, and madman Hugo Drax (in the novel a run-of-the-mill ex-Nazi bent on fulfilling the dreams of his führer) now literally wants to reshape the entire world in his image. What book did they read?

Thumbs Down Rating: 👎

The Crappies

The Al Gore Visionary Methods to Save the Earth Award goes to . . . Writer Christopher Wood for creating a villain who wants to exterminate humanity in order to improve it.

The Worst Director Award goes to . . .Lewis Gilbert for piling on one-liners and slapstick violence to the extent that the film is more comedy than anything else.

They Really Said It!

Hugo Drax: Look after Mr. Bond. See that some harm comes to him.

Betcha Didn't Know

» This eleventh James Bond movie was the most expensive in the series at the time.
» Although the script originally called for Jaws to die, director Lewis Gilbert transformed him into a good guy, because he had received fan mail from children.

 Trivia Quiz

Which British actor is a cousin to Ian Fleming, creator of James Bond?

A: Peter Cushing

B: Christopher Lee

C: James Mason

D: David Niven

Kinda-Sorta Based on the Book

Answer: B. Christopher Lee. Ian Fleming's mother was the sister of Lee's stepfather, making them cousins by marriage.

THE PUNISHER
New World Pictures, 1989

PRODUCERS Robert Gulralnick (executive producer) and Robert Mark Kamen (producer)

WRITER Boaz Yakin (script), Gerry Conway (original Punisher character)

DIRECTOR Mark Goldblatt

STARS Dolph Lundgren (*Frank Castle/the Punisher*), Louis Gossett Jr. (*Jake Berkowitz*), Jeroen Krabbé (*Gianni Franco*), and Kim Miyori (*Lady Tanaka*)

As the brutal vigilante known as the Punisher (Lundgren) struggles to avenge his family, he finds himself obligated to save the innocent children of the mobster who murdered them (Krabbé) from the clutches of the yakuza.

Why It Sucks

Frank Castle, the Punisher of the comic book, was cunning and intelligent. The movie turns him into a brutal meathead. The filmmakers, for unknown reasons, changed his profession from U.S. Marine officer to police detective, and made the murder of his family a planned hit instead of a chance encounter. These arbitrary changes turn the story from a powerful tale of obsessed vengeance into a mindless action flick.

Thumbs Down Rating: 👎👎

The Crappies

The Worst Actor Award goes to . . . Dolph Lundgren for portraying a plastic action figure with a kung fu grip rather than the Punisher. *And the Worst Director Award goes to* . . . Mark Goldblatt for first reducing the Punisher to a generic action movie character and then—much worse—making him boring.'

They Really Said It!

Frank Castle: If you're guilty, you're dead.

Betcha Didn't Know

» Production company New World Pictures was founded by B movie heavy-weight Roger Corman in 1970. He sold it to other investors in 1983.

» This was the first of three Punisher movies, each of which is disconnected from the other in its story.

 Trivia Quiz

What superhero battled the Punisher in his first appearance?

A: Captain Marvel

B: Captain America

C: Spider-Woman

D: Spider-Man

Answer: D. Spider-Man. Due to the restrictions on violence imposed by the Comics Code in the 1970s, the Punisher's automatic weapons were loaded with stun bullets during this first appearance.

THE RAVEN
Universal Pictures, 1935

PRODUCER Uncredited

WRITERS David Boehm (script), Edgar Allan Poe (poem)

DIRECTOR Louis Friedlander

STARS Bela Lugosi (*Dr. Richard Vollin*), Boris Karloff (*Edmond Bateman*), Irene Ware (*Jean Thatcher*), Samuel S. Hinds (*Judge Thatcher*), and Lester Matthews (*Dr. Jerry Halden*)

After saving a young dancer (Ware) from certain death through a miraculous feat of neurosurgery, the mentally unstable Dr. Vollin (Lugosi) becomes obsessed with her. All he has to do with the aid of a wanted murderer (Karloff) is eliminate Jean, her fiancé, and her father.

Why It Sucks

Why were Hollywood-types so afraid of making a Poe movie that's true to Poe? *The Raven*, rather than being about the haunt-

Kinda-Sorta Based on the Book

ing lament of a man for his dead love, is the tale of an evil and insane man so rich and so obsessed that he's built a house full of secret doors, secret basements, and entire rooms that serve as elevators . . . all so he can re-enact scenes from Poe's writings. That's pretty cool, I admit, but I still have to wonder.

Thumbs Down Rating: 👎👎

The Crappies

The Worst Actor Award goes to . . . Boris Karloff for playing the weakling assistant to Bela Lugosi's mad doctor. One of the great actors of B movies comes off here as dull.

And the Worst Director Award goes to . . . Louis Friedlander for tepid direction, uninspired lighting, and set design that leaves most of the potential of this film unrealized.

They Really Said It!

Judge Thatcher: Try to be sane, Vollin!

Betcha Didn't Know

» This was the first feature film directed by Louis Friedlander. He later changed his name to Lew Landers and eventually became one of the most prolific directors in Hollywood history.

» Boris Karloff's salary was larger than Bela Lugosi's on every film they appeared in together, even the ones where Lugosi had the larger part.

Trivia Quiz

What Universal Pictures comedy did Boris Karloff and Bela Lugosi both appear in?

A: *Abbott and Costello Meet Frankenstein* (1948)

B: *The Boogie Man Will Get You* (1942)

C: *A Comedy of Terrors* (1923)

D: *Gift of Gab* (1934)

Answer: D. *Gift of Gab*, where the actors had cameos in a comedy centered around an arrogant radio presenter.

113

Kinda-Sorta Based on the Book

CHAPTER TEN

MONSTROUS MONSTER MOVIES

From the moment Victor Frankenstein bellowed, "It's alive!" in James Whale's 1932 classic *Frankenstein*, monsters have been the go-to guys for horror movies. Sadly, the only horror you'll find in the movies here is that you'll never get those eighty-two minutes of your life back.

ATTACK OF THE GIANT LEECHES (AKA *"THE GIANT LEECHES"* AND *"DEMONS OF THE SWAMP"*)
American International Pictures, 1959

PRODUCERS Roger Corman (executive producer) and Gene Corman (producer)

WRITER Leo Gordon

DIRECTOR Bernard L. Kowalski

STARS Ken Clark (*Steve Benton*), Jan Shepard (*Nan Greyson*), Yvette Vickers (*Liz Walker*), Bruno VeSota (*Dave Walker*), Tyler McVey (*Doc Greyson*), and Gene Roth (*Sheriff Kovis*)

A small town located on the edge of a swamp and inhabited primarily by unpleasant hicks is menaced by giant leeches. Will the studly game warden (Clark)—one of three citizens of the county with a double-digit IQ—save the day?

Why It Sucks

Attack of the Giant Leeches is one of those movies where the characters can't get eaten by the monsters soon enough. This is partly because they're portrayed by second-rate actors delivering badly written dialogue, but also because the film screams "Cheap!!" with every frame. Bad acting, badly done monsters . . . adding up to a cinematic apocalypse.

Thumbs Down Rating: 👎👎👎👎

The Crappies

The Special Award for Lamest Creature goes to . . . The "giant leeches" are obviously large plastic bags. It takes a lot of guts to put something like that onscreen

And the Worst Script Award goes to . . . Leo Gordon for writing a story in which a law enforcement officer (in this case a game warden) brings his apparently completely untrained civilian girl-friend on potentially dangerous searches for poachers and giant blood-sucking monsters.

They Really Said It!

Nan: Where could it have come from?

Doc Greyson: I wish I knew. We'll have to do some tests. Maybe the proximity to Cape Canaveral has something to do with it.

Betcha Didn't Know

» The giant leeches were played by actors in plastic bags. (From this point of view, not all the actors in the film stink. No one's played giant leeches better. And no one is likely to play one ever again. I guess that's some sort of immortality.)

» In *On Writing*, Stephen King stated that Yvette Vickers was among the movie stars he idolized as a boy.

 Trivia Quiz

What animal has not been the monster in a Roger Corman picture?

A: Piranhas

B: Bees

C: Dogs

D: Crocodiles

Answer: C. Dogs. Every other animal has been enlarged and/or otherwise monsterfied in a Roger Corman-produced picture.

PRODUCER Anne-Marie Frigon

WRITER Jeff O'Brien

DIRECTOR Brett Kelly

STARS Mark Courneyea (*Scott*), Kerri Draper (*Gracie*), Mike Conway (*Dr. Everette*), Kevin Preece (*Sheriff Bucky*), Jody Hauke (*Walter*), Shawna McSheffrey (*Mary*), and Gary Peterson (*Grundy Miller*)

The moronic inhabitants of a small Canadian town on the edge of a marsh-bound lake start to fall victim to giant leeches. Will the wussy game warden (Courneyea) and his mildly shrewish girlfriend (Draper) save the day?

Why It Sucks

What's worse than a bad movie? One that's worse than the original. To update the story, the writers included some camping college girls who the audience keeps hoping will swim in the giant-leech infested lake. Sadly, it never happens. This film appears to have been made with a lower budget than the Corman version. "Search parties" consist of four guys paddling along the lakeshore on a cheap inflatable raft. At least Corman's production had a canoe.

Thumbs Down Rating: 🦇🦇🦇🦇🦇

The Crappies

The They Might Be Giants Memorial Award goes to . . . The leeches. Although they look more convincing in this version than in the original, they are nowhere near as much fun as guys dressed up in trash bags.

And the Worst Director Award goes to . . . Brett Kelly for failing to improve on one of Roger Corman's worst efforts.

They Really Said It!

Mary: Get out of here before I make you leave in tears.

Betcha Didn't Know

» This film saw its first wide release in July of 2008, while the original *Attack of the Giant Leeches* was released in October 1959.

» As a director, Brett Kelly makes an excellent actor, having appeared in a variety of roles in low-budget Canadian productions.

 ### Trivia Quiz
What is the greatest danger posed by leeches?

A: They can grow to giant proportions and menace towns in Canada and the United States.

B: They can potentially carry diseases.

C: They can upset the pH balance in waterways.

D: They can cause fish to grow abnormally large and threaten eco-systems.

Answer: B. Although the greatest risk to humans who are bitten by leeches is an infection to the bite area, bacteria, viruses and parasites left over from previous meals can exist in the leech for months.

ATTACK OF THE KILLER TOMATOES!
Four Squares Productions, 1978

PRODUCERS John De Bello, Steve Peace, and Mark L. Rosen

WRITERS John De Bello, Costa Dillon, Steve Peace, and Rick Rockwell

DIRECTOR John De Bello

STARS David Miller (*Mason Dixon*), George Wilson (*Jim Richardson*), Sharon Taylor (*Lois Fairchild*), Rock Peace (*Lt. Wilbur Finletter*), and Gary Smith (*Sam Smith*)

When killer tomatoes rampage through America, government beauracrats try to cover it up by putting their worst agents on the job of stopping the deadly veggies/fruits, including researcher Mason Dixon (Miller). Will the bungling agents rise above themselves to save the day, or are we all doomed?

Why It Sucks

Well, you can't say they didn't try. *Attack of the Killer Tomatoes* is a great title and the movie has an even better theme song and a hilarious concept. Where it all went to pieces was in the less-than-stellar execution. Low-budget doesn't even do justice to the movie's effects. How about no budget? To make up for this, the director padded the running time, which squashes the comedy more solidy than a stepped-on overripe tomato. (Sorry about that. But you knew there was going to be a tomato joke in this entry.)

Thumbs Down Rating: 👎👎👎

The Crappies

The Special Hope and Change Award goes to . . . John De Bello, Costa Dillon, Steve Peace, and Rick Rockwell for writing a running gag in the film about Congress being a do-nothing bunch of nitwits and the president not being any better.

And the Worst Director Award goes to . . . John De Bello for trying for sight gags that are beyond his budget and technical capabilities.

They Really Said It!

Dr. Nokitofa: Technically sir, tomatoes are fags.
Dr. Morrison: He means fruits.

Betcha Didn't Know

» The helicopter crash that marks the arrival of two of the films main characters was genuine; the helicopter was just supposed to land but the pilot clipped the stabilizer on a small rise and then lost control. The actors ad-libbed lines about the crash after they were pulled from the wreck.

» The key to defeating the tomatoes was "borrowed" in its entirety for the Tim Burton-directed sci-fi comedy *Mars Attacks* as the method for defeating the Martian invaders. In *Attack of the Killer Tomatoes*, the frightful fruits are destroyed when the song "Puberty Love" is played. In *Mars Attacks*, the Martians' heads explode when they hear Slim Whitman's "Indian Love Call."

Trivia Quiz

What is Matt Cameron, the performer of "Puberty Love," better known for?

A: Being the face of Heinz Ketchup during the 1980s

B: Being the former drummer of Soundgarden, and the current drummer of Pearl Jam

C: Being the original lead singer for pioneering grunge rock band Nirvana

D: Playing Johnny Cash in *Johnny Cash Battles the Martians*

Answer: B. Former drummer of Soundgarden, current drummer of Pearl Jam. Cameron was 16 when he recorded the song, singing in a high-pitched falsetto voice. "Puberty Love" is an awful song that kills Killer Tomatoes.

BITE ME!
E.I. Independent Cinema, 2004

PRODUCER Michael Raso

WRITER Brett Piper

DIRECTOR Brett Piper

STARS Misty Mundae (*Crystal*), Michael R. Thomas (*Ralph Vivino*), Sylvianne Chebance (*Gina*), Julian Wells (*Teresa*), Caitlin Ross (*Amber*), Rob Monkiewicz (*Terrence "Buzz" O'Reilly*), Erika Smith (*Trix*), and John Fedele (*Myles McCarthy*)

A failing strip club is invaded by monstrous spiders whose venom either brings out repressed sides of a victim's personality or turns them into hideous mutants.

Why It Sucks

The director manages to nicely spoof monster movies from the 1950s as well as soft-core porn films. But no matter how good a job the sexy actresses do—and they do better than their resumes might make you think—they can't overcome the unfocused script and its irrelevant subplots.

Monstrous Monster Movies

Thumbs Down Rating: 🎬🎬🎬

The Crappies

The Worst Director Award goes to . . . Brett Piper for failing to recognize that when someone picks up a DVD starring Misty Mundae, Julian Wells, and Caitlin Ross he expects to see a *whole* lot more nakedness and sex than *Bite Me!* contains.

And the Worst Writer Award goes to . . . Brett Piper for failing to recognize that the heart and soul of his story was the strip club and its denizens. Not to mention the idea that the bugs mutate as a result of ingesting tainted marijuana.

They Really Said It!

Ralph: Somebody better get that God dame off the stage, right now!

Betcha Didn't Know

» Misty Mundae has been working toward a film studies degree in recent years, and she has released one of her student films (*Voodoun Blues* in 2004) on DVD.

» In an age of cheap CGI, Brett Piper continued to use stop-motion miniatures in his films.

 Trivia Quiz

Why did actress Misty Mundae change her name to Erin Brown?

A: She wanted to disassociate herself from the soft-core porn of her early career

B: She was tired of having a name that invoked a New Order song

C: She entered the Federal Witness Protection program

D: She parted ways with the production company for which she had made virtually all of her early films, but she did not own the rights to the Misty Mundae stage name.

Answer: D. Mundae from 1999–2004 starred in over thirty-five soft-core horror- and/or comedy tinged soft-core porn films produced by E.I. Independent for its various labels. By 2004 she had tired of erotic filmmaking and wanted to branch out into other things. E.I., which had invested much in making Misty Mundae a symbol of their brand of entertainment, did not let her take the name with her, so she started making movies as Erin Brown.

BOOGEYMAN

Screen Gems, 2005

PRODUCERS Gary Bryman, Joe Drake, Steve Hein, and Nathan Kahane (executive producers), Sam Raimi and Rob Tapert (producers)

WRITERS Eric Kripke, Juliet Snowden, and Stiles White

DIRECTOR Stephen Kaye

STARS Barry Watson (*Tim*), Emily Deschanel (*Kate Houghton*), and Skye McCole Bartusiak (*Franny Roberts*)

A young magazine editor finds himself and his loved ones endangered when a childhood closet-monster comes back to haunt him in adulthood.

Why It Sucks

This attempt at a horror movie might have worked if someone had bothered writing a coherent script. If, for instance, we had an explanation of why the monster attacks . . . other than "just because." It's astonishing that Sam Raimi and Rob Tapert could miss the mark by so much, since they were involved in such great horror fests as *Evil Dead II* and *Drag Me to Hell*.

Thumbs Down Rating: 👎👎👎👎

The Crappies

The Worst Script Award goes to . . . Erik Kripke, Juliet Snowden, and Stiles White, because between the three of them they couldn't come up with a sensible story.

And the Worst Director Award goes to . . . Stephen Kaye for failing to recognize that repeatedly building an atmosphere of dread and then dispelling it without a payoff doesn't make a move scary, it just makes it annoying.

They Really Said It!

Franny: I wanted to tell you something. Is it true, the boogeyman took your Dad? Are you scared?

Betcha Didn't Know

» To date, two direct-to-video "sequels" have been made to this movie. They aren't any better that the original, despite the fact that neither has anything to do with the other or the movie they follow.

» Troma Entertainment produced a boogyman-centric horror spoof in 1986 titled *Monster in the Closet*. It is scarier than this.

 Trivia Quiz

What series of superhero movies did *Boogeyman* producer Sam Raimi direct three of?

A: *Superman*

B: *Darkman*

C: *Batman*

D: *Spider-Man*

Answer: D. Raimi directed the first three Spider-Man movies.

CRY OF THE BANSHEE
American International Pictures, 1970

PRODUCERS Louis M. Heyward (executive producer), Samuel Z. Arkoff and Gordon Hessler (producers)

WRITERS Tim Kelly (story), Christopher Wicking (script)

DIRECTOR Gordon Hessler

STARS Vincent Price (*Lord Edward Whitman*), Hilary Dwyer (*Maureen Whitman*), Patrick Mower (*Roderick*), and Elisabeth Bergner (*Oona*)

When the ruthless, psychopathic Lord Edward Whitman (Price) orders a coven of witches massacred, the leader (Bergner) escapes and calls forth a banshee that will visit death and destruction upon the entire Whitman line until it exists no more.

Why It Sucks

Cry of the Banshee is so badly written and the characters so badly drawn that we're rooting for the banshee from the start. Vincent

Price is a bloodthirsty upper-class twit in Elizabethan England who gets off on killing buxom peasant wenches suspected of performing pagan rituals in the woods. As his nemesis, Oona (Really? *Oona*? Where do they get these names?), Bergner confuses chewing scenery with acting.

Thumbs Down Rating: 🖓 🖓 🖓

The Crappies

The Special Award for Exceptionalism in the Area of Ignorance goes to . . . Everyone involved with the writing, producing, and marketing of this film. If someone had bothered finding out what a banshee is, the film would have been significantly less dumb. (Spoiler: There is no banshee, in the general definition of the word, in this movie.)

And the Worst Director Award goes to . . . Gordon Hessler for not noticing that his movie has *no* likeable characters in it. Or banshees.

They Really Said It!

Lady Patricia: Don't you know this house is cursed? You are cursed, and Edward's cursed, and everybody's cursed.

Betcha Didn't Know

» The opening title sequence was created by Terry Gilliam of *Monty Python's Flying Circus* and *Time Bandits* fame. It's better than *Cry of the Banshee* deserves.
» It wasn't until the 1950s that Vincent Price became firmly associated with horror films. Although he had starred in *The Invisible Man Returns* in 1940, he was still thought of primarily as a serious dramatic actor.

 Trivia Quiz

In what other movie did Vincent Price play a bloodthirsty witch hunter?

A: *The Conqueror Worm* (1968)

B: *Masque of the Red Death* (1964)

C: *War-Gods of the Deep* (1965)

D: *The Bat* (1959)

Answer: A. *The Conqueror Worm.* In this 1968 horror movie (also known as *Witchfinder General*), Price plays Matthew Hopkins, a real-world witch hunter who brutally killed as many as 400 "witches."

DIE HARD DRACULA
Peter Horak Productions, 1998

PRODUCER Peter Horak

WRITER Peter Horak

DIRECTOR Peter Horak

STARS Denny Sachen (*Steven Hillman*), Bruce Glover (*Dr. Van Helsing*), Kerry Dustin (*Carla/Julia*), and Ernest M. Garcia and Tom McGowan (*Dracula*)

After his fiancée (Dustin) drowns, Steven (Sachen) goes on a European vacation to get over his loss. Naturally, being in mourning, he heads for Transylvania, where he encounters a woman who is the exact double of his dead love (also played by Dustin)—who actually is his dead love, having been brought magically back to life by a shooting star. Steven also ends up fighting Dracula.

Why It Sucks

If you're thinking John McClane going up against vampires, you're not that far off. In fact, if they'd stuck with that, the filmmakers would have been better off. Unfortunately, they had a minuscule budget, not to mention writer/director Peter Horak, and a rancid collection of actors and crew. That said, the script is the best thing here. Maybe someone should think about a remake.

The Crappies

The Worst Autuer Award goes to . . . Peter Horak for taking a fun idea and turning it into a film that displays just about every kind of bad filmmaking there is.

And the Worst Acting Award goes to . . . Denny Sachen for playing an Everyday Joe who is as boring as a real-life Everyday Joe.

They Really Said It!

Steven: I'm an American. We're tough.

Betcha Didn't Know

» Peter Horak worked as stuntman in a number of movies and television shows throughout the 1980s and 1990s, including such high-profile productions as the 1988 Steven Seagal film *Above the Law* and 1998's superhero comedy *Mystery Men*.
» Bruce Glover is a prolific character who has played villains in A-list movies such as *Diamonds Are Forever*, *China Town*, and countless television series. Somewhere along the way, he slipped into Z-grade horror movies, including this one and *Warlock: The Armagedon*.

Trivia Quiz

Which of the following actors has not played Dracula onscreen?

A: Gary Oldman

B: Jack Palance

C: George Hamilton

D: George Clooney

Answer: D.George Clooney. Gary Oldman played Dracula in the oh-so-inaccurately named *Bram Stoker's Dracula* in 1992; George Hamilton took a crack at the character's comedic side in 1979's *Love at First Bite*; and Jack Palance amped up the tragically romantic qualities of the character, in 1973's *Dracula*.

EVIL BONG
Talos Entertainment/Forbidden Worlds/Shoot Productions, 2006

PRODUCERS Thomas Smead (executive producer) and Joe Dain (producer)

WRITER August White

DIRECTOR Charles Band

STARS David Weidoff (*Alistair*), Brian Lloyd (*Brett*), John Patrick Jordan (*Larnell*), Kristyn Green (*Janet*), Robin Snyder (*Luann*), Mitch Eakins (*Bachman*), Michele Mais (*Voice of the Evil Bong*), and Tommy Chong (*Jimbo Leary*)

When his pot-smoking roommates and the lovely Janet (Green) fall victim to the mysterious powers of the Voodoo-cursed Evil Bong, it's up to the nerdy, straight-laced Alistair (Weidoff) to save them all.

Why It Sucks

Evil Bong is part stoner comedy, part horror movie spoof. It's also a far more effective antidrug movie than say, *Reefer Madness* or a lot of the antidrug after-school specials. Unfortunately, this is a sad, under-budgeted movie that falls short of its potential. It feels as if the filmmaker put together the footage and said, ''That's the outline of the movie I want to make.''

Thumbs Down Rating: 🍗🍗🍗

The Crappies

The Worst Picture Award goes to . . . Producer Joe Dain for failing to get this film the resources it needed to make a good movie.

And the Worst Director Award goes to . . . Charles Band for his inability to make the picture work within the tiny budget. I mean, it's been done before, but he couldn't do it. What we get is a talking bong with a badly animated face and a "Bongworld" that feels like a hangover in a skid row strip club at 10 A.M.

They Really Said It!

Larnell: If there's one thing this pad is lacking, it's a killer fucking bong.

Betcha Didn't Know

» Tommy Chong, true to his comedy stoner image, ran an Internet business that sold bongs and marijuana pipes. He was among fifty-five people arrested in 2003 on federal drug paraphernalia charges and was sentenced to nine months in prison and $120,000 in fines.

» The 2009 sequel, *Evil Bong 2: King Bong*, unites the cast of the first film to battle a lingering curse cast upon them.

 Trivia Quiz

What movie made to warn about the dangers of marijuana use became a cult comedy hit among stoners?

A: *Harold and Kumar Go to White Castle* (2004)

B: *Reefer Madness* (1936)

C: *Jailbait* (2004)

D: *Up In Smoke* (1978)

Answer: B. *Reefer Madness*. Originally titled *Tell Your Children*, this 1938 film is an over-the-top cautionary tale about the evils of drugs.

THE FURY OF THE WOLFMAN
(AKA *"THE WOLFMAN NEVER SLEEPS"*)
Maxper Producciones, 1972

PRODUCER Maximiliano Pérez Floréz

WRITER Jacinto Molina Álvarez

DIRECTOR José María Zabalza

STARS Paul Naschy (*Waldemar Daninsky*), Perla Cristal (*Dr. Ilona Elmann*), and Veronica Lujan (*Karen*)

When a globe-trotting scientist (Naschy) contracts lycanthropy, he becomes the latest subject of the twisted experiments of a mad scientist (Cristal) and her all-woman team of graduate student assistants.

Why It Sucks

The Fury of the Wolfman should have been titled *Moonlight Strolls of the Wolfman*. Or possibly *The Tasmanian Devil's Really, Really Bad Day*. Rather than dismembering hapless peasants, the wolfman spends much of his time wandering about. And when he's snarling, he sounds exactly like the Tasmanian Devil from old Bugs Bunny cartoons. All in all, this is an unintentionally hilarious rather than horrifying film.

Thumbs Down Rating: 👎 👎 👎

The Crappies

The Worst Script Award goes to . . . Jacinto Molina Álvarez for a script that tries to cram every single werewolf legend into a single story.

And the Worst Actor Award goes to . . . Paul Naschy for portraying the most laid-back werewolf to ever saunter through the moonlit countryside.

They Really Said It!

Sexy Grad Student (as she becomes the subject of an evil experiment): This can't be scientific! This can't be scientific!

Betcha Didn't Know

» Jacinto Molina Álvarez is the true name of Paul Naschy.

» Although it was the fifth movie in which Paul Naschy portrayed werewolf Waldemar Daninsky, it is actually a prequel to the other films, explaining how Waldemar develops his condition.

Trivia Quiz

Which if these actors portrayed a werewolf in the most movies?

A: Lon Chaney Jr.

B: Peter Cushing

C: Paul Naschy

D: Bela Lugosi

Answer: C. Paul Naschy has thirteen werewolf credits to his name. Peter Cushing, on the other hand, never played a werewolf onscreen.

THE GIANT CLAW
Clover Production, 1957

PRODUCER Sam Katzman

WRITERS Paul Gangelin and Samuel Newman

DIRECTOR Fred F. Sears

STARS Jeff Morrow (*Mitch MacAffee*), Mara Corday (*Sally Caldwell*), Robert Shayne (*General Van Buskirk*), and the goofiest bird puppet you'll ever see.

An electrical engineer who happens to dabble in molecular physics on the side (Morrow) and his mathematician Girl Friday (Corday) work with the United States military to defeat a giant antimatter bird from outer space.

Why It Sucks

The pacing, tone, and quality of acting and the special effects in *The Giant Claw* compare favorably to the present-day cheesy monster movies that appear regularly under the banner of "A Sci-Fi Channel Original" on cable television's "most dangerous night of television." This movie has the added "benefit" of a giant bird that has come to Earth to nest (!) and, in the process, eat planes, trains, the UN building in New York City, and the odd pair of joyriding teenagers.

Thumbs Down Rating: 🦅🦅🦅

The Crappies

The Worst Writing Award goes to . . . Paul Gangelin and Samuel Newman for writing sexual harassment with a style that only a scientist in a 1950s sci-fi movie can deliver.
And the Goofiest Monster Award goes to . . . The giant, antimatter, indistructable space buzzard that causes a global panic.

They Really Said It!

Mitch: Keep your shirt on, and I'll go put my pants on.

Betcha Didn't Know

» Between 1933 and 1972 Sam Katzman produced and/or directed some 250 features and serials.

» Mara Corday started her show-biz career as a chorus girl and model at the age of seventeen. She later turned to acting and has appeared in just about every type of picture genre.

 Trivia Quiz

What movie about aliens invading Earth was produced by Sam Katzman?

A: *Invaders from Mars* (1953)

B: *Devil Girl From Mars* (1954)

C: *Earth vs. the Flying Saucers* (1956)

D: *The Last Blitzkrieg* (1959)

Answer: C. *Earth vs. the Flying Saucers*. Katzman also produced *The Last Blitzkrieg*, an over-the-top spy thriller set during World War II.

HUMANOIDS FROM THE DEEP
New World Pictures, 1980

PRODUCERS Roger Corman and Martin B. Cohen

WRITERS Frank Arnold and Martin B. Cohen (story), William Martin (script)

DIRECTOR Barbara Peeters

STARS Doug McClure (*Jim Hill*), Ann Turkel (*Dr. Drake*), Vic Morrow (*Hank Slattery*), Cindy Weintraub (*Carol Hill*), and Lynn Theel (*Peggy Larson*).

Humanoids evolved from mutant salmon emerge from the ocean to terrorize a small coastal town, killing the men and raping the women. Will they ruin the annual carnival with their urge to head up the road and spawn?

Why It Sucks

One never expects much of an explanation for the "how" and "why" of the green, slimy fishmen who attack the town in a Z-grade monster movie like this, but a little background about how salmon mutated into green, amphibious rapists would have been nice. And then there's the weird scene where a ventriliquist dummy is a bigger turn-on for a hot chick than a big bank account.

Thumbs Down Rating: 👎👎

The Crappies

The Worst Producer Award goes to . . . Roger Corman and Martin B. Cohen for "sexing up" what they felt was a weak movie with boobs and fish-man rape-scenes instead of starting with a script that actually had a little more content and logic to it. Most of the credit belongs to Corman, though.

And the Special Award for the Creepiest Fetish goes to . . . The chick who is so turned on by a ventriloquist dummy she strips naked.

They Really Said It!

Dr. Drake: Look at the size of that cranium. That means they have tremendous brain capacity. Doesn't mean, though, they have the ability to use it.

Betcha Didn't Know

» Director Barbara Peeters was fired from the picture after she refused to film certain scenes requested by producer Roger Corman.

» The music for the soundtrack was composed by James Horner and it's better than the film itself.

Trivia Quiz
For what movie did Roger Corman win an Academy Award?

A: *The Haunting of Hell House* (1999)

B: *Black Rose of Harlem* (1996)

C: *Revenge of the Red Baron* (1994)

D: None of the Above

Monstrous Monster Movies

JACK FROST
Frost Bite Films, 1997

PRODUCERS Barry L. Collier and Barbara Javitz (executive producers), Jeremy Paige and Vicki Slotnick (producers)

WRITERS Michael Cooney and Jeremy Paige

DIRECTOR Michael Cooney

STARS Christopher Allport (*Sam*), Scott MacDonald (*Jack Frost*), Stephen Mendel (*Agent Manners*), and Eileen Seeley (*Anne*)

A homicidal maniac named Jack is killed in a freak accident as he is being transported from one prison to another and resurrected as a snowman—a mass-murdering homicidal maniac snowman. Naturally, he sets about getting revenge on the small-town sheriff who captured him (Allport), but happily kills anyone else who crosses his path.

Why It Sucks

It's a movie about a killer snowman who, among other things, rapes a girl to death with his carrot nose. And there's the amazingly lame special effects, the godawful acting, and the fact that Jack is "killed" at the end of the movie by antifreeze. Oh, yeah—and just to hit you over the head with it, the town where all this takes place is named Snowmaton.

Thumbs Down Rating: 🖓🖓🖓

The Crappies

The Worst Director Award goes to . . . Michael Cooney for not coaxing even minimally competent performances from his actors.
And the Worst Writing Award goes to . . . Michael Cooney and Jeremy Paige for a horror movie in which one of the key scenes is of a girl being raped to death with a carrot.

They Really Said It!

Jack Frost: Is it cold in here, or is it just me?

Betcha Didn't Know

» This was the first screen appearance of Shannon Elizabeth, who would go on to star in *American Pie*.

» In 1998 Michael Keaton starred in a completely different film about a man reincarnated as a snowman, also titled *Jack Frost*. The Keaton film is a children's movie.

 Trivia Quiz

Which star of Jack Frost was killed by an avalanche in 2008?

A: Eileen Seeley

B: Christopher Allport

C: Scott MacDonald

D: Stephen Mendel

Answer: B. Christopher Allport. In January 2008, Allport was killed while skiing in an off-trail canyon near the Mountain High ski resort in the San Gabriel mountains.

JEEPERS CREEPERS
United Artists/American Zoetrope, 2001

PRODUCERS Francis Ford Coppola, Willi Baer, Eberhard Kayser, Mario Ohoven, and Linda Reisman (executive producers), Tom Luse and Barry Opper (producers)

WRITER Victor Salva

DIRECTOR Victor Salva

STARS Gina Philips (*Trish Jenner*), Justin Long (*Derry Jenner*), Patricia Belcher (*Jezelle Gay Hartman*), and Jonathan Breck (*the Creeper*)

A brother and sister on their way home from college (Long and Phillips) are stalked by a flesh-eating monster on an isolated stretch of highway.

Why It Sucks

About forty minutes into the film you're looking at your watch, tapping your feet, going to the fridge for another beer. Finally some tension and atmosphere start manifesting themselves. Of course, by that time most viewers have passed out on the couch. The story keeps going, sadly, but only because the characters are stupid beyond words.

Thumbs Down Rating: 👎 👎 👎 👎

The Crappies

The Worst Writer Award goes to . . . Victor Salva for populating his story with the dumbest horror movie characters ever. How many times do we have to tell characters not to go into the dark basement if they think the insane killer is hiding there?

And the Worst Director Award goes to . . . Victor Salva for a movie that starts boring and ends in a cavalcade of stupidity.

They Really Said It!

Trish: You know that part in scary movies where somebody does something really stupid and everyone hates them for it? This is it.

Betcha Didn't Know

» A financial success, *Jeepers Creepers* cost around $10 million to make, but earned over $37 million during its U.S. theatrical run alone.

» Gina Philips declined to return for *Jeepers Creepers II*, but Victor Salva announced in September of 2009 that she would be reprising her role as Trish in *Jeepers Creepers III*.

 Trivia Quiz

What is Justin Long best known for?

A: Marrying Demi Moore, a woman more than twice his age.

B: Playing "Mac" on television commercials that pit Macintosh computers against computers using Microsoft Windows software.

C: Being a regular on the SyFy Channel's *Ghosthunters* series.

D: Moving to Malaysia in protest over Barack Obama's election as president of the United States.

Answer: B. From 2006 to the present, Long has portrayed "Mac" opposite John Hodgeman's "PC."

KUNG FU ZOMBIE

The Eternal Film Company/Transmedia, 1982

PRODUCER Ming Pal

WRITER Yi-Jung Hua

DIRECTOR Yi-Jung Hua

STARS Billy Chong (*Pang*) and Lau Chan (*the Magician*)

When the ghost of a small-town thug bullies a third-rate priest/magician (Lau) into binding him to a recently dead corpse so he can take revenge on the young martial artist who accidentally caused his demise (Chong), everything that can go wrong, does go wrong.

Why It Sucks

Kung Fu Zombie has moments of inspired and hilarious weirdness that defy description. Unfortunately, the fight scenes are mediocre, and the film is cluttered up with un-scary hopping vampires. (Yes, I said hopping!) It's sad, really, because this could have been a fun flick if just a little more effort had gone into staging and choreography.

Thumbs Down Rating: 🦇 🦇 🦇

The Crappies

The Worst Acting Award goes to . . . The entire cast of voice actors who dubbed the American version. They sound as if they swallowed hot potatoes.

And the Worst Writing Award goes to . . . Yi-Jung Hua for writing a "hero" who we hope throughout the movie will die horribly at the hands of the villains.

They Really Said It!

Pang: Go to hell, old man.

Betcha Didn't Know

» The zombies in this film are what are commonly referred to as "Chinese Hopping Vampires," the most commonly used undead in Chinese popular fiction and culture.

» Billy Chong's real name is Willy Dozan, and he hails from Indonesia.

 Trivia Quiz

According to folklore, what's the most effective way to make your home hopping-vampire proof?

A: Have it blessed by Taoist priests

B: Have hinged doors that open outward and from right to left, as it will confuse the undead

C: Put a threshold in external doorways that's at least six inches tall

D: Use paint containing the ashes of a cremated Taoist priest on the door frames

Answer: C. Put a threshold in external doorways that's at least six inches tall, as the hopping vampires can't jump higher than that. Most traditional Taoist temples are equipped with such thresholds.

THE MANSTER (AKA *"THE SPLIT"*)
United Artists/Lopert Pictures, 1959

PRODUCERS William Shelton (executive producer) and George Breakston (producer)

WRITERS Walt Sheldon (story), George Breakston (script)

DIRECTORS George Breakston and Kenneth Crane

STARS Peter Dyneley (*Larry Stanford*), Satoshi Nakamura (*Dr. Robert Suzuki*), Terri Zimmern (*Tara*), Norman Van Hawley (*Ian Matthews*), Jane Hylton (*Linda Stanford*), and Jerry Ito (*Police Superintendant Aida*)

Larry (Dyneley), an American journalist working in Japan, travels to interview a reclusive scientist (Nakamura) about his strange experiments. But soon, the usually mild-mannered reporter is partying all night with Japanese hookers, going on killing sprees, and growing a second head.

Why It Sucks
It starts with a classic theme: Jekyll and Hyde—a man's hidden desires and passions coming to the surface. And then . . . he starts to grow a second head. And ultimately splits into two separate beings, who, through the wonders of mad science, are both fully clothed immediately after the transformation! The *Manster* is a monster movie that's so jaw-droppingly stupid that it transcends its own badness. It all culminates in a fiery climax atop a volcano . . . .

Thumbs Down Rating: 🙌 🙌 🙌

The Crappies
The Worst Acting Award goes to . . . The entire cast. You can actually see them looking off camera for their cue cards.
And the Worst Picture Award goes to . . . George Breakston. Even by low-budget standards of the 1950s, this two-headed man looks cheesy.

They Really Said It!
Ian: Do you realize that your behavior lately has had every aspect of a man flipping his lid?
Larry: What are you trying to say, Ian?!

Betcha Didn't Know
» Star Peter Dyneley was a British actor who was best known for his stage work, but he appeared in a number of crime dramas and sci-fi films over the course of his career.
» Kenneth Crane is sometimes mistakenly credited with directing one of Edward D. Wood's final science fiction films—*The Double Garden* (aka *Venus Flytrap*) in 1970. He did, however, not direct such a movie. Crane spent most of his career as an editor, and directed only four low-budget horror films during 1958–1959, the most notable being this one and *The Monster from Green Hell*.

Trivia Quiz

What famous horror comedy has a sequence that was clearly inspired by this film?

A: *The Evil Dead* (1981)

B: *The Grudge* (2004)

C: *The Boogey Man* (1980)

D: *Army of Darkness* (1992)

Answer: D. The scene in *Army of Darkness* in which Ash is split in two—Good Ash and Evil Ash—is a clear and obvious echo of the transformation and eventual doubling of Larry.

MONSTURD

4321 Productions, 2003

PRODUCER Rick Popko

WRITERS Rick Popko and Dan West

DIRECTORS Rick Popko and Dan West

STARS Paul Weiner (*Sheriff Duncan*), Beth West (*Agent Hannigan*), Dan Burr (*Dr. Stern*), Dan West (*Deputy Dan*), Rick Popko (*Deputy Rick*), and Brad Dosland (*Jack Schmidt*)

Serial killer Jack Schmidt (Dosland) is reborn as a living turd, after mad scientist Dr. Stern (Burr) dumps bioengineered bacteria in the sewers. Now, Schmitt is killing the residents of the town as they Do Their Business, and growing bigger and bigger.

Why It Sucks

Well . . . hmmm . . . I'm at a loss for words. It does more with "Number Two" than any other movie has ever done before—and hopefully ever will again. Of course, if you enjoy scatological humor, you'll have a great time. (Confession: I enjoyed this film very much.) That said, it was a first-time effort and it shows in the uneven editing and choppy camera work.

Thumbs Down Rating: 👎👎

The Crappies
The Worst Actress Award goes to . . . Beth West for her flat (we might almost say, flatulent) and uninspired performance as Agent Hannigan.
And the Worst Director Award goes to . . . Rick Popko and Dan West for using jump cuts and the "shakey-cam technique" to excess.

They Really Said It!
Agent Hannigan: You've been watching too many crappy horror movies, Sheriff.

Betcha Didn't Know
» *Monsturd* was the first film effort from Popko and West. They were inspired to make it by the crappiness of *Jack Frost*.
» The movie was successful enough to spawn a sequel in 2008, *RetarDEAD*, that saw Dr. Stern attempt to turn a bunch of "special" children into geniuses, unleashing a zombie plague instead.

 Trivia Quiz

What horror movie has monsters bursting from the backside of victims?

A: *Dreamcatcher* (2003)
B: *Ghoulies* (1985)
C: *It* (1990)
D: *The Stuff* (1985)

Answer: A. *Dreamcatcher.* From a novel by Stephen King, this 2003 horror movie has as one of its highlights a man being killed by monsters while sitting on the crapper.

THE MUMMY'S SHROUD
Hammer Film Productions, 1967

PRODUCER Anthony Nelson Keys

WRITERS John Elder (story) and John Gilling (script)

DIRECTOR John Gilling

STARS André Morrell (*Sir Basil Walden*), Maggie Kimberly (*Claire de Sangre*), David Buck (*Paul Preston*), John Phillips (*Stanley Preston*), Elizabeth Sellars (*Barbara Preston*), Roger Delgado (*Hasmid*), Michael Ripper (*Longbarrow*), and Catherine Lacey (*Haiti*)

When British archaeologist Sir Basil (Morrell) and his obnoxious American financier (Phillips) ignore the warning of a crazed tomb guardian (Delgado) and move the mummified body of an ancient child-king to a museum, they unleash a deadly curse . . . and, of course, a revived mummy bodyguard hell-bent on revenge.

Why It Sucks

Mummies are great, but here we have to have one that looks like a guy in a rubber Halloween mask, wearing tan coveralls with some bandages glued on? This costume ties with 2002's *Mummy Raider* for Worst Mummy Costume to Ever Appear on Screen (and if there's not an award for that, there ought to be!).

Thumbs Down Rating: 👎👎👎

The Crappies

The Worst Actor Award goes to . . . Roger Delgado for his lackluster performance. Mummy guardians are supposed to be sinister and evil—not *booooring*.

And the Worst Director Award goes to . . . John Gilling for making a horror movie with only one (one!!) scary scene, the one in which a delirious Sir Basil stumbles upon the lair of a creepy gypsy woman. As a matter of fact, the scene may be scary, but it's also completely illogical.

Monstrous Monster Movies

They Really Said It!

Haiti: You will soon be dead. Then you can rest. Ah death, death can be sweet. Sweet death, I pray for it because I am old and tired, you pray for it because you are sick. There is nothing left for you but death.

Betcha Didn't Know

» John Elder was the pen name used by Hammer Films executive and co-owner Anthony Hinds.

» This was the last Hammer production to be shot at Britain's legendary Bray Studios, ending a fifteen-year association.

Trivia Quiz

What cast member was a regular on the long-running BBC science fiction series *Dr. Who?*

A: Michael Ripper

B: Roger Delgado

C: Andre Morrell

D: Elizabeth Sellars

RETURN OF THE LIVING DEAD: RAVE TO THE GRAVE
Aurora Entertainment/Castel Film Romania, 2005

PRODUCERS Vladimir Dostal, Tom Fox, and Nikolai Makarov (executive producers), Anatoly Fradis and Steve Scarduzio (producers)

WRITERS William Butler and Aaron Strongoni

DIRECTOR Ellroy Elkayem

STARS John Keefe (*Julian*), Jenny Mollen (*Jenny*), Cory Hardrict (*Cody*), Cain Mihnea Manoliu (*Jeremy*), Claudiu Bleont (*Aldo*), Sorin Cocis (*Gino*), Catalin Paraschiv (*Skeet*), and Peter Coyote (*Uncle Charles*)

Dimwitted college kids unleash a zombie plague after making a designer drug with chemicals used to reanimate dead tissue.

Why It Sucks

The cheapness of the film wafts from it like the smell of urine from a drunk bum passed out in a doorway. It's inconsistent with the zombie lore established in the first two *Return of the Living Dead* movies and, to make matters even worse, very little in the film is funny. There is even less that is scary. The key to the movie is to realize if there's an idiotic and illogical thing to do, one of the characters will do it.

Thumbs Down Rating: 👎👎👎👎

The Crappies

The Worst Writing Award goes to . . . William Butler and Aaron Strongoni for a script so lazily written that it gets the name of the zombie-creating drug wrong and is inconsistent with *Return of the Living Dead 4*, the film it's a direct sequel to.

And the Worst Actress Award goes to . . . Jenny Mollen for her role as Jenny. Sigh. So cute. And so, so untalented.

They Really Said It!

Skeet: Listen, if you can't trust your drug dealer, who can you trust?

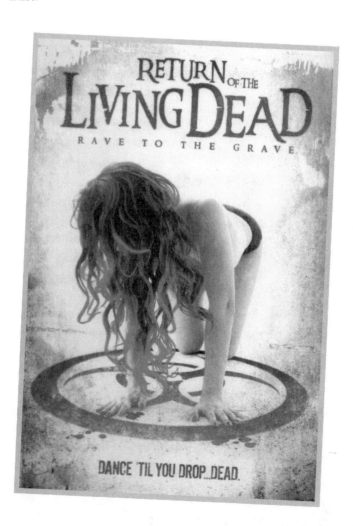

Betcha Didn't Know

» Executive producer Tom Fox produced the original *Return of the Living Dead* film. He has been involved with the production of all films in the series so far except the third one.

» This movie was released twenty years after the first film in the series debuted in movie theaters.

 Trivia Quiz

What is the main difference between the zombies in this film and most other installments in the series?

A: The zombies are animated by Trioxin.

B: The zombies create other zombies through their bites.

C: They aren't unstoppable killing machines, but can be brought down with a single gunshot.

D: The zombies are obsessed with eating brains.

Answer: C. They can be killed with one gunshot. In the first three movies, the zombies are virtually indestructible.

SNOWBEAST
Douglas Cramer Productions, 1977

PRODUCERS Douglas S. Cramer (executive producer) and Wilford Lloyd Baumes (producer)

WRITER Joseph Stefano

DIRECTOR Herb Wallerstein

STARS Robert Logan (*Tony Rill*), Syliva Sidney (*Carrie Rill*), Bo Svenson (*Gar Seberg*), Yvette Mimieux (*Ellen Seberg*), and Clint Walker (*Sheriff Paraday*)

As a small ski resort prepares to celebrate its fiftieth winter carnival, a violent Sasquatch-like creature descends from the mountaintop to snack on the skiers.

Why It Sucks

It's a cross between *Jaws* and a disaster movie that suffers from an excess of padding (and no, I'm not talking about the costume the Sasquatch wears). There are *waaaay* too many montage shots of

Monstrous Monster Movies

characters zooming downhill on skis or trudging through the frozen winter forest in search of Bigfoot tracks. We want to scream at the screen, "Just *kill someone*, dammit!"

Thumbs Down Rating: 🖒🖒🖒

The Crappies

The Worst Writer Award goes to . . . Joseph Stefano for lack of basic writing skills. Dude, if you write a movie about people getting killed by a monster, we have to care about the characters a little. *And the Worst Director Award goes to* . . . Herb Wallerstein for filling his movie with obvious and dull scenes merely in order to meet the format-dictated made-for-television running time.

They Really Said It!

Tony Rill: I must have seen her somewhere. Maybe I'll recognize her when I see her face.
Sheriff Paraday: She doesn't have one.

Betcha Didn't Know

» Joseph Stefano wrote the screenplay for Alfred Hitchcock's masterful thriller *Psycho*. Stefano later felt that the success of that film made it difficult for him to find work on any films other than horror and thrillers.
» In 2009, sixty-eight-year-old Bo Svenson took the silver medal in the USA Judo National Championships. Svenson took the prize despite three broken ribs received during an accident while filming *ICARUS* two weeks earlier.

 Trivia Quiz

Whose allegedly real Bigfoot encounter did Joseph Stafano use as inspiration for his *Snow Beast* script?

A: Film critic and talk show host Michael Medved

B: Author and Bigfoot-tracker Roger Patterson

C: Writer and director Roger Corman

D: Former United States president Jimmy Carter

Answer: B. In 1967, Roger Patterson shot a minute-long film of an alleged Bigfoot crossing a stream deep within a California wilderness.

THE SOUND OF HORROR
Zurbano Films, 1964

PRODUCER Gregorio Sacristán

WRITERS Sam X. Abarbanel, José Antonio Nieves Conde, G. Sacristán, and Gregg C. Tallas

DIRECTOR José Antonio Nieves Conde

STARS Arturo Fernández (*Professor Andre*), James Philbrook (*Dr. Pete Asilov*), Soledad Miranda (*Maria*), Lola Gaos (*Calliope*), José Bódalo (*Mr. Dorman*), and Ingrid Pitt (*Sofia Minelli*)

A group of treasure hunters blast openings in a series of caves and unleash invisible, flesh-eating dinosaurs that have been dormant for thousands of years.

Why It Sucks

It's a movie about invisible dinosaurs. Of course, it's a clever idea if you want to make a monster movie without any budget for special effects. But the filmmakers "show" the dinosaurs by filming long scenes of empty cave sets. I'm not kidding. Almost as bad a choice are dance routines by Soledad Miranda and Ingrid Pitt.

Thumbs Down Rating: 👎👎👎

The Crappies

The Don't Quit Your Day Job Award goes to . . . Soledad Miranda and Ingrid Pitt for proving they would have been finished as of the first episode of *Dancing with the Stars*.

And the Worst Director Award goes to . . . José Antonio Nieves Conde for turning invisible dinosaurs into show-killing pictures of empty caves.

They Really Said It!

Maria: And just how was he killed? This something, do you know what it was, Uncle Andre?

Professor Andre: Maybe a heart attack.

Dorman: Oh . . . and did he slash himself when he was dying?

Betcha Didn't Know

» This was Ingrid Pitt's first screen appearance. She later appeared in *Where Eagles Dare*, alongside Clint Eastwood and Richard Burton, and many other films.

» Soledad Miranda had just signed a contract with a German film-maker for a role that promised to be her big break when she was killed in a car accident in 1970. She was twenty-seven years old.

Trivia Quiz
Which of the following movies does *not* feature dinosaurs snacking on humans?

A: *Jurassic Park* (1993)

B: *One Million Years B.C.* (1966)

C: *Galaxy of Dinosaurs* (1992)

D: *Year One* (2009)

Answer: D. It may have mangled history, but at least *Year One* was dinosaur-free.

TSUI HARK'S VAMPIRE HUNTERS (AKA *"THE ERA OF VAMPIRES"*)
Film Workshop, 2002

PRODUCERS Wouter Barendrecht, Satoru Iseki, Nansun Shi, and Michael J. Werner (executive producers), Tsui Hark (producer)

WRITER Tsui Hark

DIRECTOR Wellson Chin

STARS Ji Chun Hua (*Master Mao Shan*), Kwok-Kwan Chan (*Choi*), Ken Chang (*Hei*), Suet Lam (*Kung*), Michael Chow Man-Kin (*Fat*), Rongguang Yu (*Master Jiang*), and Anya (*Sasa*)

When master vampire hunter (Hua) and his four apprentices (Chan, Chang, Lam, and Chow Man-Kin) are separated after a disastrous confrontation with a Vampire King, the four young men take up jobs as servants in the house of a mysterious embalmer. Meanwhile, the vampire continues to kill . . . .

Why It Sucks

Vampire Hunters is full of subplots, sub-subplots, and characters who jam up the screen like an LA freeway at rush hour. Nothing gets resolved or explained because the various elements are tripping over each other. Of four vampire-busting heroes only one plays a major role. The rest disappear for most of the film.

Thumbs Down Rating: 🦃🦃🦃

The Crappies

The Fool Me Once Award goes to . . . Wellson Chin for making a movie with an exciting first ten minutes that sink into confusion. *And the Worst Writer Award goes to* . . . Tsui Hark for giving us four vampire hunters, each with a form of elemental magic . . . but not ever letting us see them use it.

They Really Said It!

Master Jiang: What kind of dumb names are those? From now on, you're Kung, you're Hei, you're Fat, and you're Choi. Good Chinese names!

Betcha Didn't Know

» The film is set in the seventeenth century, yet the American DVD release states it takes place in the nineteenth century.
» *The Legend of the Seven Golden Vampires*, a co-production between British Hammer Films and the Hong Kong-based Shaw Brothers and the first film to cross martial arts with the horror genre, was released in 1974. It was released in the U.S. in a highly re-edited version under title *The Seven Brothers Meet Dracula*.

 Trivia Quiz

Which of the creatives involved with this movie studied filmmaking at the University of Texas, Austin?

A: Wellson Chin

B: Ken Chang

C: Tsui Hark

D: Anya

Answer: C. Tsui Hark graduated in 1974.

UNDEAD OR ALIVE

Odd Lot Entertainment, 2007

PRODUCERS Deborah Del Prete, David S. Greathouse, and Gigi Pritzker

WRITERS Scott Pourry and Glasgow Phillips (story), Glasgow Phillips (script)

DIRECTOR Glasgow Phillips

STARS James Denton (*Elmer*), Chris Kattan (*Luke*), Navi Rawat (*Sue*), Matt Besser (*Claypool*), Chris Coppala (*Cletus*), and Leslie Jordan (*Padre*)

Two hapless outlaws (Denton and Kattan) team up with Geronimo's niece (Rawat) to escape an Indian curse that's rapidly turning southwest America into a land of flesh-eating zombies. All the while, an undead corrupt sheriff (Besser) and his zombie posse is hot on their trail.

Why It Sucks

Undead or Alive is a fun zombie-Western comedy (yes, you read that right!) if—and it's a big *if*—you can tolerate the notion of a zombie Western and you have a high tolerance for anachronisms and films driven by plot conveniences. If, on the other hand, you're not turned on by these things, this is just a big mess.

Thumbs Down Rating: 🖓🖓

The Crappies

The Special "Isn't That the Other Way Around?" award goes to . . . The casting director for casting Indian-American Navi Rawat as American-Indian Sue, Geronimo's granddaughter.

And the Worst Director Award goes to . . . Glasgow Phillips for telegraphing the film's twist ending so heavily that we see it twenty minutes away.

They Really Said It!

Claypool: You say another word and I'm gonna shoot your jaw clear off your face. Then I'm gonna take a shit in your chin hole.

Betcha Didn't Know

» According to Glasgow Phillips, the roles played by Chris Kattan and James Denton were originally reversed. When it turned out that Denton was an expert horseman, he and Kattan changed parts.

» Navi Rawat is a native-born American from Malibu, California. Her father is of Indian descent while her mother's heritage is German.

 Trivia Quiz

What long-running animated television series was Glasgow Phillips a writer for?

A: *South Park*

B: *The Simpsons*

C: *Family Guy*

D: *King of the Hill*

Answer: A. *South Park*. He worked on the long-running Comedy Central series for the 2002 season, making contributions to eleven episodes.

THE WASP WOMAN
Film Group Feature, 1959

PRODUCER Roger Corman

WRITERS Leo Gordon (script), Kinta Zertuche (story)

DIRECTOR Roger Corman

STARS Susan Cabot (*Janice Starlin*), Michael Mark (*Eric Zinthrop*), Fred Eisley (*Bill Lane*), Barboura Morris (*Mary Dennison*), and William Roerick (*Arthur Cooper*)

Cosmetics industry queen and aging "glamor girl" Janice Starlin (Cabot) undergoes an experimental treatment developed from the jelly of queen wasps. She regains her youth, but transforms into a giant flesh-eating wasp woman when the sun goes down.

Why It Sucks

If you look up the word "tedious" in the dictionary, you'll find a poster for *The Wasp Woman*. There isn't a scene that doesn't drag on and on. Although the pace is picked up a little in the film's final

Monstrous Monster Movies

twenty minutes, getting there is an experience that makes you wonder if watching wasps build a nest might be more interesting.

Thumbs Down Rating:

The Crappies
The Worst Actor Award goes to . . . Fred Eisley for playing hero Bill Lane as if he were nothing but a pretty face on an empty head. *And the Worst Director Award goes to* . . . C'mon, Roger. The most frightening thing about the movie is that you'll die of old age before anything interesting happens.

They Really Said It!
Bill Lane: You can call it male intuition if you like, except there's something about this whole business that doesn't smell right. A private laboratory. A secret experiment. Zinthrop himself. The only thing that's missing is a genie with a lamp.

Betcha Didn't Know
» Susan Cabot had a well-publicized romance with King Hussein of Jordan. The relationship ended in 1959 when he discovered she was Jewish.
» Susan Cabot retired from acting after making this film.

Trivia Quiz

What cast member was bludgeoned to death by his or her own child?

A: William Roerick

B: Micheal Mark

C: Barboura Morris

D: Susan Cabot

WEREWOLF IN A GIRLS' DORMITORY (AKA *"LYCANTHROPUS"* AND *"MONSTER AMONG THE GIRLS"*)
Royal Film, 1961

PRODUCER Jack Forrest

WRITER Ernesto Gastaldi

DIRECTOR Richard Benson

STARS Barbara Lass (*Priscilla*), Carl Schell (*Dr. Julian Olcott*), Curt Lowens (*Director Swift*), Maurice Marsac (*Sir Alfred Whiteman*), Maureen O'Connor (*Leonor MacDonald*), Mary MacNeeren (*Mary Smith*), Grace Neame (*Sandy*), and Annie Steinert (*Sheena Whiteman*)

Dr. Julian Olcott (Schell), a disgraced research physician, is hired as a science professor at an isolated reform school for girls. Olcott arrives just in time for a series of brutal murders. Together with a spunky "good girl," he seeks the identity of the killer—possibly the marauding werebeast that appeared on the scene when Olcott arrived.

Why It Sucks

Great title, but a sucky film—it's too bad. But the movie's too talky (and *how* is this possible in a film about werewolves and girls' dormitories?) and one exciting moment turns Monte Python–skit when the victim of the werewolf, after being mauled to death, keeps getting back up. Not to mention that the skimpy nightie quotient is entirely too low.

Thumbs Down Rating: 👎👎👎

The Crappies
The Special PT Barnum Memorial Award goes to . . . Producer Jack Forrest for making a movie titled *Werewolf in a Girls' Dormitory* where the werewolf never makes it into the girls' dormitory.
And the Worst Director Award goes to . . . Richard Benson for failing to recognize that his film needed girl-on-werewolf action.

They Really Said It!
Julian Olcott: I was successful with the extract from the brain of a wolf, while I was experimenting on [a patient]. One night, she gave herself an overdose. Perhaps I made it too strong. And the police then accused me of killing her.

Betcha Didn't Know
» German actor Curt Lowens made a steady career of appearing in cheap horror and sci-fi films starting in the 1950s and continuing through the late 1990s, including a number of productions from B movie mogul Charles Band.
» Polish-born actress Barbara Lass was married to disgraced director and convicted child rapist Roman Polanski from 1959 to 1963.

 Trivia Quiz
Maurice Marsac is best known for playing what character, again and again?

A: A French waiter or maitre d'
B: A British nobleman with a fondness for fondling wayward girls
C: A NASA scientist or administrator
D: A pirate

Answer: A. Marsac played these roles well over twenty times. His first time was in the 1944 comedy *Our Hearts Were Young and Gay*.

ZOMBIES OF MORA TAU
(AKA *"THE DEAD THAT WALK"*)
Clover Productions, 1957

PRODUCER Sam Katzman

WRITERS Raymond T. Marcus (script), George Plympton (story)

DIRECTOR Edward L. Cahn

STARS Gregg Palmer (*Jeff Clark*), Autumn Russell (*Jan Peters*), Allison Hayes (*Mona Harrison*), Joel Ashley (*George Harrison*), Marjorie Eaton (*Grandma Peters*), and Morris Ankrum (*Dr. Jonathan Eggert*)

A group of callous treasure hunters and the residents of an isolated African farm are beset by swimming zombies protecting a treasure trove of cursed diamonds.

Why It Sucks

Even with swimming zombies, it's a shaky script being performed by a cast who are devoid of any actual talent. The idea of underwater zombie attacks is cool, but it would have been cooler if they'd look believable. Or maybe underwater zombies dry immediately upon exiting the water?

Thumbs Down Rating: 🔻🔻🔻

The Crappies

The Worst Actress Award goes to . . . Allison Hayes for giving such a wooden performance that when she's zombified, you can't tell the difference.

And the Worst Director Award goes to . . . Edward L. Cahn for not even sprinkling water on the supposedly water-born zombies when they're on dry land. Not to mention having them sleeping in coffins on dry land during the day.

They Really Said It!

Mona: Do you believe in the walking dead, Dr. Eggert?
Dr. Eggert: All I know is what I've read.

Jeff: What does it say in the books, Doc? Are they supposed to be good swimmers?

Betcha Didn't Know

» Before George Romero made *Night of the Living Dead*, the zombies featured in this film were the standard pop culture version, as established in the 1932 film *White Zombie*. Well, aside from the whole swimming thing.

» Unlike many early (and even some contemporary) zombie films, the living dead are there from the beginning. One is run over by a car in the first ten minutes of the film.

 Trivia Quiz

Bela Lugosi appeared both in Universal's classic *Dracula* and in the first-ever zombie movie *White Zombie*. What else do those two classic films have in common?

A: Both take place in England

B: Both take place in Haiti

C: Both were directed by Tod Browning

D: Many of the same set pieces appear in both films.

Answer: D. Low-budget director Victor Halperin shot *White Zombie* on many of the same sets that had been used for *Dracula*.

CHAPTER ELEVEN

MYSTERIES OF THE ORIENT

Popular culture is often specific to the society that creates it. That is very plain in many films from China, Japan, and Korea that have been showing up in video stores and on late-night television since the 1980s. Even if you carefully follow the subtitles, you often find yourself baffled and doubting if you really read what you think you read, or saw what you think you saw. This is often even more true if a film is dubbed. In the pages that follow are a dozen or so films that illustrate there are many things that come from Asian culture that make even less sense than feng shui.

ATTACK OF THE MONSTERS
(AKA "GAMERA VS. GUIRON")
Daiei Motion Picture Company, 1969

PRODUCERS Masaichi Nagata (executive producer), Hidemasa Nagata and Sandy Frank (producers)

WRITER Fumi Takahashi

DIRECTOR Noriaki Yuasa

STARS Christopher Murphy (*Tom*), Yuko Hamada (*Kuniko*), Nobuhiro Kajima (*Aiko*), Miyuki Akiyama (*Tomoko*), Reiko Kasahara (*Flobella*), Hiroko Kei (*Barbella*), and Kon Omura (*Officer Kondo*)

When two boys (Hamada and Murphy) are abducted by aliens, it's Gamera to the rescue! But will even the mighty Gamera be able to defeat the evil space babes (Kasahara and Akiyama) and the horrible Guiron?!

Why It Sucks

It's a movie about monster turtle that is propelled through space by rockets up its butt. That's for a start. And then we have the pair of plucky youngsters. And a couple of evil vixens in tight clothes . . . who want to eat the kids' brains for lunch. Actually, there's something here for everyone: the kids can watch the kids, Mom can watch the giant flying turtle do Olympic gymnastics, and Dad can watch the vixens. You can't say that's not family entertainment!

Thumbs Down Rating: 🦃🦃🦃

The Crappies

The Worst Acting Award goes to . . . The anonymous voice actor who dubbed Officer Kondo in the American version. "Effeminate" is almost too mild a word.

And the Special Award for Explaining the Facts of Life goes to . . . Screenwriter Fumi Takahashi for telling a story spotlighting what all adolescent boys suspect about girls: sexy chicks might as well eat our brains because they make us stupid.

They Really Said It!

Akio: Let's make the Earth a great place to live, without war and traffic accidents.

Betcha Didn't Know

» Although created by a rival studio to capitalize on the success and popularity of Godzilla, Gamera survived the bankruptcy of his original owners and is nearly Godzilla's equal on the pop culture scene.

» The original actor who played Gamera remains anonymous to this day.

Trivia Quiz

What does the Japanese word *kaiju* decribe?

A: "Strange beast," it refers to films featuring creatures like Gamera.

B: "Strange men," it refers to adults who like movies made for kids.

C: "Strange turtle," it is a nickname for Gamera.

D: *Kaiju* is the name of the Japanese alphabet.

Answer: A. The phrase can also be translated as "strange monster."

BLACK MAGIC WARS
(AKA *"DEATH OF A NINJA," "NINJA WARS,"*
"IGA MAGIC STORY," AND *"BLACK MAGIC STORY"*)
Toei Pictures/Kadokawa Productions, 1982

PRODUCERS Haruki Kadokawa (executive producer), Izumi Toyoshima, and Masao Sato (producers)

WRITER Ei Ogawa (script), Kazetaro Yamada (original novel)

DIRECTOR Mitsumasa Saito

STARS Hiroyuki Sanada (*Jotaro*), Noriko Watanabe (*Kagaribi/Lady Ukyo*), Akira Nakao (*Matsunaga Danjo*), Jun Miho (*Isaribi*), Mikio Narita (*Kashin*), Noboru Matsuhashi (*Miyoshi*), Hiroshi Tanaka (*Hanzo Hattori*), and Sonny Chiba (*Shinzaemon Yagyu*)

A Japanese feudal warlord (Nakao) allies with a demon (Narita) and the five monks in his service after it is prophesized that if he wins the heart of a beautiful princess (Watanabe), he will some-day rule the world. To ensure their success, the demon monks kidnap the princess's virginal twin sister (also Watanabe). But they didn't take her fellow ninja and sweetheart Jotaro (Sanada) into account.

Why It Sucks

Actually the plot's got a lot more wild twists and turns than the summary above would imply. It's got all the elements of high fantasy with romance, spectacular battles, evil magic applied in bizarre ways. It's got pure-hearted virgins, brave ninjas, honor-less nobles, and samurai who are more than what they seem. And it's got countless extreme and over-the-top moments when you'll say, "No . . . they didn't just do *that*, did they?!"

Thumbs Down Rating: 👎

The Crappies

The Special Achievement Award in Unexpected Plot Twists Award goes to . . . Ei Ogawa and Kazetaro Yamada for suddenly behead-ing a main character halfway through the film.
And the Worst Director Award goes to . . . Mitsumasa Saito, who feels we can't remember something we sat through ten minutes ago without a flashback to remind us.

They Really Said It!

Devil Monk: Oh yes. We must have the most famous spider tea kettle.

Betcha Didn't Know

» Many of the heroes and villains featured in this film are loosely (one assumes loosely, unless seventeenth-century Japan was a very, very strange place) based on historical figures and events.

» Hanzo Hattori is a well-known hero in Japan. Train stations and other landmarks bear his name.

Trivia Quiz

How did the historical figure Matsunaga Danjo meet his end?

A: He drowned while bathing drunk on sake.

B: He committed seppuku while enemy troops stormed his castle, and his severed head was tied to a tea kettle and blown up so that it could not be displayed as a trophy.

C: He choked on his own vomit (or possibly suffocated on vomit spewed by demon monks).

D: He slipped on icy stairs while chasing his mistress in a fit of passion.

Answer: B. Really! After his head was tied to the tea kettle, his enemies filled it (the tea kettle, that is) with gun powder and blew it up. This tea kettle features prominently in *Ninja Wars*.

CITY HUNTER
Golden Harvest, 1993

PRODUCERS Raymond Chow and Leonard Ho (executive producers), Lam Chua (producer)

WRITERS Jing Wong (script), Tsukasa Hōjō (original characters and comic book)

DIRECTOR Jing Wong

STARS Jackie Chan (*Ryu Saeba*), Chingmy Yau (*Saeko Nogami/Anna*), Joey Wang (*Kaori Makimura/Carrie*), Richard Norton (*Col. MacDonald*), Kumiko Goto (*Shizuko Imamura/Kyoko*), Michael Wong (*Hideyuki Makimura*), and Gary Daniels (*MacDonald's henchman*)

Private detective Ryu Saeba (Chan), hired to track down a runaway heiress, ends up on a luxury liner, trapped between his jealous secretary/partner (Wang), the attractive heiress, a sexy gun-happy female cop (Yau), and a group of terrorists bent on capturing the ship and holding the passengers for ransom. And all the poor guy wants is a bite to eat, because he skipped breakfast!

Why It Sucks

City Hunter was adapted from a Japanese comic book and animated series of the same name . . . and it shows. The actors do the kind of double-takes, gestures, and poses that you'd expect from, well, a comic book. Not to mention the fact that this "action" film has a musical production number halfway through. Be forewarned: If you don't know the comic book, the chaotic story is going to be mindblowingly confusing.

Thumbs Down Rating: 👎👎

The Crappies

The Worst Picture Award goes to . . . Producers Raymond Chow, Leonard Ho, and Lam Chua for making a movie with Jackie Chan where he doesn't do any of his signature physical comedy.

And the Worst Writing Award goes to . . . Writer/director Jing Wong for not taking just a couple of minutes (that's *all* it would take!) to set up the characters for the uninitiated.

They Really Said It!

Ryo Saeba: How do I get to the casino from here?

Hideyuki Makimura: Take the elevator.

Ryo Saeba: I mean by stealth.

Hideyuki Makimura: Take the elevator and don't tell anyone.

Betcha Didn't Know

» Jackie Chan has often named this film as one of his least favorites.

» One of the characters from the Street Fighter II game was renamed E. Honde instead of E. Honda, because Jackie Chan was a spokesman for Mitsubishi Motors and any mention of competitor Honda had to be avoided.

 Trivia Quiz

What star of this film is nicknamed "Dangerman"?

A: Jackie Chan

B: Richard Norton

C: Gary Daniels

D: Joey Wang

Answer: C. Gary Daniels is a world champion kickboxer who retired from the sport and turned to acting. He's appeared in more than forty-five films and TV series.

FANTASY MISSION FORCE

Original Production Company Unidentified, 1982

PRODUCER Hsiao Yin Shen

WRITER Hsin Wei

DIRECTOR Yen-Ping Chu

STARS Jimmy Wang Yu (*Lt. Don*), Brigitte Lin (*Lily*), Jackie Chan (*Sammy*), Gou Ling Feng (*Greased Lightning*), Sun Yueh (*Old Sun*), Ling Chang (*Emily*), and Adam Cheng (*Amazon Leader*)

When the Japanse capture the top Allied generals, including Abraham Lincoln, during the invasion of Arctic Canada at the height of World War II, it's up to a group of super-weird commandos to rescue them and defeat the Imperial Japanese Army, cannibal Amazons, and hopping vampires. In Luxembourg.

Why It Sucks

If you've ever wanted to find out what an acid trip might be like without actually dropping LSD, then you might want to watch this movie. To really get the effect, have a couple of drinks first. The plot makes no sense (I mean, Abraham Lincoln in World War II?), there's no story or character development, and even the action scenes are so far out you can't take any of them seriously. But it does have cannibal Amazons.

Thumbs Down Rating: 👎👎👎👎

The Crappies

The Worst Continuity Award goes to . . . Everyone invovled with the production of *Fantasy Mission Force*. The stunt doubles are matched so badly with the actors, and the filming is so inept, that they barely bothered to dress them in similar costumes.

And the Worst Self-Referential Supporting Role goes to . . . Adam Cheng, who appears as a tuxedo-clad King of the Amazons. At the time this movie was made, he was winding down a successful singing career and transitioning into acting.

They Really Said It!

Lily: The nice people always die first. Do I look like a nice person?

Betcha Didn't Know

» Many VHS and DVD versions of this film give Jackie Chan top billing. He is, in fact, in the film for less than fifteen minutes and plays a small supporting role.

» Jackie Chan wrote in his autobiography *I Am Jackie* that he did this movie as a favor to Jimmy Wang Yu. He didn't have anything good to say about it.

 Trivia Quiz

What movie star is usually credited with jump-starting the kung fu movie craze that turned Hong Kong into an international film center?

A: Jackie Chan

B: Adam Cheng

C: Brigitte Lin

D: Jimmy Wang Yu

Answer: D. Jimmy Wang Yu starred in *The Chinese Boxer*, a hit for the Shaw Bros. and usually credited with starting the kung fu craze.

FOR YOUR HEIGHT ONLY
(AKA *"FOR Y'UR HEIGHT ONLY"*)
Liliw Productions, 1981

PRODUCERS Peter M. Caballes and Dick Randall

WRITER Cora Ridon Caballes

DIRECTOR Eddie Nicart

STARS Weng Weng (*Agent 00*) and Beth Sandoval (*Irma*)

When the odds of success appear insurmountable, the Phillipine Secret Agency (PSA) calls upon its smallest operative—Weng Weng, a dwarf code-named Agent 00 (Weng). But can even he rescue a kid-napped American scientist before the mysterious criminal mastermind Mister Giant forces the scientist to build him a deadly N-bomb? And, more importantly, will the swingin' Weng Weng nail his beautiful collegue, Irma (Sandoval).

Why It Sucks

It's a James Bond spoof about a dwarf who cock-punches opponents while giggling maniacally. The joke's funny once, but that's about it. The film is so low budget that the villain's minions cruise around in a VW Bug, and Weng Weng's spy gadgets look like they were made in someone's garage—which they probably were.

Thumbs Down Rating:

The Crappies

The Special Achievement in Unsportsmanlike Behavior Award goes to . . . Weng Weng for almost always leading with a punch or a kick to the groin. Sometimes, for good measure, he stomps on the balls of an already defeated bad guy. All this while giggling.
And the Worst Script Award goes to . . . Cora Ridon Caballes or whoever wrote the English-language dialogue. It features some of the strangest non sequiturs you'll ever hear.

They Really Said It!

Irma: You're such a little guy, though. Very petite like a potato.

Betcha Didn't Know

» *For Your Height Only* was successful enough to spawn a sequel, *The Imposssible Kid.*
» Weng Weng reportedly died of progeria at the age of thirty-five.

Trivia Quiz
What degree of martial arts did actor Weng Weng achieve?

A: Green Belt

B: Red Belt

C: Black Belt

D: Weng Weng did not practice martial arts in real life.

Answer: B. According to Weng Weng scholar Andrew Leavold (who created a documentary, *The Search for Weng Weng*), the actor's first movie listed his vital statistics as: Weight, 30 pounds; Red Belt; Blood pressure 120/80.

GAMMERA THE INVINCIBLE

Harris Associates, 1966

PRODUCERS Ken Barnett (executive producer) and Masaichi Nagata (producer)

WRITERS Nizo Takahashi and Richard Kraft

DIRECTORS Noriaki Yuasa and Sandy Howard

STARS Eiji Funakoshi (*Dr. Hidaka*), Michiko Sugata (*Nobuyo*), Brian Donlevy (*Gen. Terry Arnold*), Diane Findlay (*Sgt. Susan Embers*), and Dick O'Neill (*Gen. O'Neill*)

The prehistoric (yet radioactive) monster Gammera is awakened by a nuclear explosion in the Arctic. Like any self-respecting giant monster, he heads straight for Tokyo, leaving chaos in his wake. Along the way, however, he befriends a little boy and saves him from certain death. Will evil warmongers see the kindness in Gammera's heart and leave him to level Tokyo in peace?

Why It Sucks

To remind you, Gammera is a giant turtle with two rocket engines in his ass. He also breathes fire . . . or radioactivity . . . or gas (understandable, given where the two rocket engines are). That alone files this movie in the cinematic disasters folder. Gammera's name also changes in spelling, between this film and those that follow, as one of the "m"s vanishes. (Now *that* is some serious budget cutting.)

Thumbs Down Rating: 🐾🐾🐾

The Crappies

The Worst Soundtrack Award goes to . . . Artie Butler for "The Gammera Theme." And it lodges itself in your head and stays there for *weeks.*

And the Cynical Ripoff Award goes to . . . Masaichi Nagata, who created Gammera to cash in on Godzilla's popularity. As it happens, Gammera trancended his roots, partly due to the inexplicable scene where he chooses to not kill an obnoxious brat.

They Really Said It!

Dr. Hidaka: Evacuate the area, or at least the civilians. And call me a car.

Betcha Didn't Know

» Gammera is an enduring Japanese pop culture icon (at least when his name is spelled with one *m*). The 1966 film has spawned thirteen sequels to date.

» Much like Godzilla was Americanized for release in this country, so was Gammera. With an extra *m* added to his name, new scenes featuring B movie mainstay Brian Donlevy, and recutting of the existing footage, Gammera hit the American shores in 1966 and captured the imagination of kids and geeks everywhere.

 Trivia Quiz

Who was the first giant monster to trash cinematic Tokyo?

A: King Kong (in 1933)

B: Gigan (in 1953)

C: Godzilla (in 1954)

D: Gadzooke (in 1956)

Answer: C. Godzilla, the original stomper of Tokyo landmarks, breathed his first gout of flame in 1954.

KUNG FU HUSTLE
Columbia Pictures/Sony Pictures Classics, 2004

PRODUCERS Bill Borden, David Hung, Zhonglei Wang, and Hai Cheng Zhao (executive producers), Stephen Chow, Po Chu Chui, and Jeffrey Lau (producers)

WRITERS Stephen Chow, Xin Huo, Chan Man Keung, and Kan-Cheung Tsang

DIRECTOR Stephen Chow

STARS Stephen Chow (*Sing*), Danny Chan (*Brother Sum*), Wah Yuen (*Landlord*), Qiu Yuen (*Landlady*), Suet Lam (*Axe Gang Vice General*), and Siu-Lung Leung (*the Beast*)

In 1920s Shanghai, an underachieving con man and could-be martial artist (Chow) finds himself in the middle of a gaggle of kung fu masters and a final showdown with the brutal Axe Gang.

Why It Sucks

It has the feel of an old Shaw Bros. martial arts flick crossed with a Warner Bros. cartoon. Like all of writer/director/actor Stephen Chow's pictures, it leans heavily on Chinese pop cultural references for much of its humor. The silliness translates to an international audience, but many of the actual jokes do not. Still, if you enjoy over-the-top action scenes, this might be for you.

Thumbs Down Rating: 👎

The Crappies

The Worst Writing Award goes to . . . Stephen Chow, Xin Huo, Chan Man Keung, and Kan-Cheung Tsang for writing a story as unfocused and aimless as those featured in the 1970s kung fu films it echoes.

And the Strangest Use of a Musical Number Award goes to . . .
Director Stephen Chow for including a large-scale dance production number performed by the psychotic leader of the Axe Gang and his minions.

They Really Said It!
Landlady: You may know kung fu, but you're still a fairy.

Betcha Didn't Know
» Many of the films characters and martial arts styles are based on or inspired by elements and characters from novels by popular Chinese pulp fiction writer Louis Cha.
» Stephen Chow draws on his own impoverished childhood and youth for many of the characters and story elements featured in his films.

 Trivia Quiz
What leisure activity/sport has not yet been used as a backdrop for a Stephen Chow film?

A: Soccer

B: Cooking

C: Fly-fishing

D: Judo

Answer: C. Fly-fishing. Soccer was the center of *Shaolin Soccer* (2001), cooking was the focus of *God of Cookery* (1996), and Judo featured prominently in *Love on Delivery* (1994).

NINJA CHAMPION
IDF Film and Arts, 1985

PRODUCERS Betty Chan and Joseph Lai

WRITER Godfrey Ho

DIRECTOR Godfrey Ho

STARS Nancy Chang (*Rose*), Bruce Baron (*Donald, the Good Ninja*), Jack Lam (*George*), Richard Harrison (*Richard*), and Pierre Tremblay (*Maurice, the Evil Ninja*)

A rape victim, Rose (Chang), infiltrates a diamond-smuggling ring so she can more effectively stalk and kill the three men who raped her (as well as uncover who ordered them to do it). Meanwhile, the Good Ninja (Baron), an Interpol agent, is attacking and killing the followers of the Evil Ninja (Tremblay) because . . . um . . . well, just because.

Why It Sucks

The movie was cobbled together using bits of unfinished films and footage of actors running around, being goofy in ninja costumes. The resulting "storyline" makes little sense, but the ninja stuff is so stupid that it doesn't make any sense at all. And that's even after the Evil Ninja (who is named Maurice; that alone might have made him turn to wickedness) explains his plot to the Good Ninja.

Thumbs Down Rating: 👎👎👎👎👎

The Crappies

The My Body is a Weapon Award goes to . . . Nancy Chang as Rose for performing an assassination with her poisoned nipples.
And the Worst Auteur Award goes to . . . Godfrey Ho for making an ill-assembled patchwork picture featuring ninjas named Maurice and Donald.

They Really Said It!

Donald: What's the use of those photos you sent me? It's only Maurice and his three assholes.

Betcha Didn't Know

» According to both Richard Harrison and Godfrey Ho, the footage of Harrison in this film was actually shot for other pictures, most likely *Diamond Ninja Force*, one of Ho's nonpatchwork projects.
» One of Richard Harrison's final film appearances before retiring from the movie business was as a zombie in *Nudist Colony of the Dead* (discussed in Chapter 12).

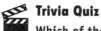

Trivia Quiz

Which of these actors has played a ninja onscreen?

A: Peter Cushing

B: John Candy

C: George Zucco

D: Chris Farley

Answer: D. Chris Farley. He portrayed a most unconventional ninja in the comedy *Beverly Hills Ninja*.

NINJA THE PROTECTOR
(AKA *"PROJECT NINJA DAREDEVILS,"* *"MOTOR DEVILS,"* AND *"NINJA'S TERROR"*)
IFD Films and Arts, 1986

PRODUCERS Betty Chan and Joseph Lai

WRITER Godfrey Ho

DIRECTOR Godfrey Ho

STARS Richard Harrison (*Jason Hart*), Warren Chan (*Warren*), and David Bowles (*Bruce, Master of Evil Ninjas*)

Interpol officer Jason Hart (Harrison), who is secretly a Ninja Master, brings all his wits, Ninja Magic, and dimwitted fellow Interpol officers to bear against a counterfeiting ring and modeling school that is being operated by a cult of Evil Ninjas and their leader, Bruce (Bowles)!

Why It Sucks

Bruce the Evil Ninja Master uses a modeling school as a front for his counterfeiting ring, which is in turn a front for his Evil Ninja Cult. The film is so full of nonsensical ninja high jinks (such as ninjas jousting on motorcycles) that it plays more like a spoof than a serious movie. Finally, it's another Godfrey Ho patchwork cinematic disaster in which the pieces and plot threads don't fit together because they were taken from other movies.

Mysteries of the Orient

173

Thumbs Down Rating: 🦇🦇🦇🦇

The Crappies

The Worst Stunt Award goes to . . . The Good Ninja and Bruce, the Evil Ninja, jousting while riding motorcycles.

And the Al Gore Special Recognition Award for Exceptional Acheivement in Recycling goes to . . . Godfrey Ho for showing that any unfinished film can be turned into a ninja epic.

They Really Said It!

Agent: I like people who are honest, and you lied to me earlier, but now you're telling me the truth, so I'll hire you.

Betcha Didn't Know

» There are two different *Ninja the Protector* films, both written and directed by Godfrey Ho and both featuring Richard Harrison. The other film is actually a geniune Godfrey Ho picture—original from beginning to end—and its plot revolves around an Evil Ninja Cult that's gotten its hands on a deadly bio-weapon. It's sometimes known as *Ninja Thunderbolt*, *To Catch a Ninja*, and *Ninja Hunt*.

» When action film star David Carradine was found dead in a hotel room in 2009, some conspiracy theorists—including supposed representatives of the Carradine family—suggested that he had been killed by ninjas or some other secretive martial arts cult to preserve its secrets and/or to avenge an insult. (Of course, if ninjas really were running around killing actors and filmmakers, Godfrey Ho would be dead many times over.)

 Trivia Quiz
How many films has Godfrey Ho directed?

A: 45

B: 75

C: 115

D: No one, not even Godfrey Ho, knows for sure.

Answer: D. While Internet Movie Database lists 115 films directed by Ho, it admits that the actual number hasn't been confirmed. Ho has commented that some movies that list him as director were actually directed by others, but that his name was used to secure distribution.

REINCARNATION

Geneon Entertainment/Nikkatsu/Oz Company/Toho Company/TBS, 2005

PRODUCERS Kazuya Hamana, Yashushi Kotani (executive producers), Takashige Ichise (producer)

WRITERS Takashi Shimizu and Misaki Adachi

DIRECTOR Takashi Shimizu

STARS Yuka (*Nagisa Sugiura*), Karina (*Yayoi Kinoshita*), Marika Matsumoto (*Yuka Morita*), Kippei Shiina (*Ikuo Matsumura*), and Tetta Sugimoto (*Tadashi Murakawa*)

After landing a part in a horror movie based on a true-life mass-murder at a vacation resort over thirty years ago, Nagisa (Yuka) starts having strange visions . . . as if the past is somehow trying to reach out to her. Meanwhile, mysterious phantoms are causing men and women from all walks of life to vanish all across Japan. Can there be a connection?

Why It Sucks

It's a ghost story and a tale of revenge that crosses time, space, and the boundary of life and death. That would be cool, but the director/cowriter Takashi Shimizu never bothers to explain or give the viewer insight into what's going on in the film. It's full of creepy imagery but the underdeveloped story never adds up to anything more than nonsense.

Thumbs Down Rating: 🖓🖓🖓

The Crappies

The Worst Actress Award goes to . . . Yuka for continuing to prove that performers who go by one name (*Cough! Madonna! Cough!*) shouldn't take roles that require them to act.

And the Worst Director Award goes to . . . Takashi Shimizu for failing to realize a good horror movie needs more than pretty girls and random spooky stuff.

Mysteries of the Orient

They Really Said It!

Yuka: That's not me!

Betcha Didn't Know

» This was one of the films the term "J-Horror" was originally coined to market.

» Was originally brought to North America by distributor After Dark for one of the annual Eight Films to Die For horror film series.

Trivia Quiz

What do some researchers like to hold up as proof of reincarnation?

A: Nothing. There can be no physical proof.

B: Similarities in eating habits

C: Similarities in dexterity

D: Similarities in facial bone structure

Answer: D. Who knew? Apparently the spirits of the dead play a bigger role in determining facial structure than parentage, DNA, or silly stuff like that.

SISTER STREET FIGHTER
Toei Tokyo, 1974

PRODUCERS Kenji Takamura and Kineo Yoshimine

WRITERS Masahiro Kakefuda and Norifuma Suziki

DIRECTOR Kazuhiko Yamaguchi

STARS Etsuko "Sue" Shihomi (*Tina Long*), Masashi Ishibashi (Hammerhead), Emi Hayakawa (*Amy*), and Sonny Chiba (*Sonny Kawasaka*)

Martial arts prodigy Tina Long (Shihomi) travels to Japan to locate her brother after he vanishes while investigating a drug-smuggling ring. Her search brings her into conflict with dozens of martial artists, including the deadly Hammerhead (Ishibashi). Long is joined by two Japanese martial artists (Chiba and Hayakawa) who, although belonging to a karate school that espouses pacifism, kicks ass every bit as efficiently as Tina.

Why It Sucks

Sister Street Fighter plays more like a video game than most movies that proport to adapt video games to the screen. The illogical plot is almost nonexistent for most of the movie. When it surfaces, it's just an excuse to move from one fight scene to the next. The English-language version is made even more disjointed due to careless editing, done to avoid an X rating for violence.

Thumbs Down Rating: 👎👎

The Crappies

The Worst Editing Award goes to . . . The drunken louts who, presumably in an effort to please the MPAA ratings board, ruined the film's otherwise well-staged fight scenes. This includes screwing up Tina's first confrontation with Hammerhead, which raises the question of how Tina survives a fall from a bridge.

And the Worst Actress Award goes to . . . Etsuko "Sue" Shihomi has the martial arts moves, but she's no actress.

They Really Said It!

Hammerhead: There is only room for one champion.

Betcha Didn't Know

» This film is occasionally misidentified as a sequel to *The Street Fighter.* While the films share similar titles and several of the same actors, none play the same roles and the tone of this film is different from anything found in the two actual sequels to *The Street Fighter,* let alone the original.

» Etsuko Shihomi retired from acting in 1987 after marrying Japanese singer and actor Tsuyoshi Nagabushi.

Trivia Quiz

How did Sue Shihomi become a cinematic martial artist?

A: She joined Sonny Chiba's Japan Action Club.

B: She dated Sonny Chiba and he gave her jobs.

C: She became an impromptu replacement for a stunt-woman killed on a set she was passing by.

D: She funded *Sister Street Fighter* with money made from shrewd stock investments.

Answer: A. Chiba's Japan Action Club was created to improve the physical fitness of actors so they could perform better in action and martial arts films. Shihomi quickly rose to its top ranks.

CHAPTER TWELVE

INDEPENDENT ODDITIES

If you love movies, you've undoubtedly got friends who love movies. Among them, there may be someone who minored in film studies and who likes to pontificate on the superior nature of independent films. If you want to shut him up, mention one of the movies in this chapter.

THE APE MAN (AKA *"LOCK YOUR DOORS"*)
Banner Productions, 1943

PRODUCERS Jack Dietz and Sam Katzman

WRITERS Barney A. Sarecky (script) and Karl Brown (original short story, "They Creep in the Dark")

DIRECTOR William Beaudine

STARS Bela Lugosi (*Dr. James Brewster*), Wallace Ford (*Jeff Carter*), Minerva Urecal (*Agatha Brewster*), Louise Currie (*Billie Mason*), Henry Hall (*Dr. George Randall*), and Emil Van Horn (*the Ape*)

Dr. Brewster (Lugosi) decides to prove his evolutionary theory by using a serum to turn himself into a "missing link." He soon regrets this and sets out to create a cure. Unfortunately, his cure requires lots of fresh spinal fluid to work, so he and his pet gorilla (Van Horn) prowl the streets, looking for suitable victims.

Why It Sucks

The Ape Man is an embarrassing affair all around. From the guy in the gorilla suit, to Lugosi's "ape man" costume, to the lame trio of comic relief characters. It's often hard to tell if it was intended as a horror film, or a horror film spoof. For the sake of the great Lugosi, I *hope* it's the latter.

Thumbs Down Rating: 🐾🐾🐾🐾

The Crappies

The Special Achievement in the Area of Cinematic Disaster Award goes to . . . William Beaudine, who for the first ten minutes makes viewers think they're in for a fun time with Bela Lugosi in his best over-the-top form. Sadly, that all goes away for the next fifty-five minutes

And the Worst Script Award goes to . . . Barney A. Sarecky for the character of the "spiritualist" Agatha Brewster. This is a film about a guy who turns into an ape-man through the wonders of science. What does a loon who thinks she talks to spirits have to do with anything?

They Really Said It!

Agatha Brewster: Most spirits are honest, gentle, and kind, and only want to bring happiness to humans. But a few are evil and, having been wicked in life, are wicked in death, and only haunt the scenes of desperate crimes, reveling in murder.

Betcha Didn't Know

» Actor Emil Van Horn made a career out of playing gorillas in burlesque performances. Between the years 1941 and 1948, he lent his talents (and ape suit) to eight different movies and matinee serials, including Abbott and Costello's wartime comedy *Keep 'Em Flying.*

» Some film historians have claimed that the script for *The Ape Man* was written as the film's nineteen-day shooting schedule progressed. If true, it certainly explains a lot.

 Trivia Quiz

Which star of *The Ape Man* spent his or her teenage years as a transient?

A: Bela Lugosi

B: Wallace Ford

C: Henry Hall

D: Louise Currie

Answer: B. According to film historian Tom Weaver, Wallace Ford spent several years as a rail-riding hobo. He was born Samuel Jones Grundy but adopted the name Wallace Ford as tribute to a fellow hobo who was killed by a rail car.

BUTTCRACK
Desert Dog Films, 1998

PRODUCER Cindy Geary

WRITER Jim Larsen

DIRECTOR Jim Larsen

STARS Mojo Nixon (*Preacher Man Bob*), Doug Ciskowski (*Brian*), Caleb Kreischer (*Wade "Buttcrack" Jenkins*), Kathy Wittes (*Annie*), Rob Hayward (*Ken*), and Cindy Geary (*Wade's Sister*)

When Brian (Ciskowski) accidentally kills his slobby, repulsive roommate Wade "Buttcrack" (Kreishner), Wade's vengeful sister (Geary) uses witchcraft to bring him back from the dead. But his cursed butt is now a true Crack of Doom: any who gaze upon it are transformed into zombies with melted faces who want to kill Brian.

Why It Sucks
It's a movie about a cursed buttcrack that turns people into zombies. Is there anything else that needs to be said?

Thumbs Down Rating: 👎👎

The Crappies
The One-Shot Wonder Award goes to . . . Just about everyone involved with *Buttcrack.* This is the one and only film credit for most of them, and it's the only starring film role that rocker Mojo Nixon had before his semi-retirement from show business. Most of the cast seem to have been snatched from a nearby community theater and probably returned there directly after production on this turkey wrapped.

And the Making Sure Nothing Falls Through the Crack Award goes to . . . Lloyd Kaufman and everyone else who's taken on films like this one for distribution at Troma Entertainment. (Kaufman and crew have done more for independent filmmakers—especially those who make bad movies—than all other operations combined over the past thirty to forty years.)

They Really Said It!

Preacher Man Bob: Now, God, I done said all I had to say at Brother Wade's first funeral. I just hope you can call him home this time so we don't have to kill him and go through this all over again.

Betcha Didn't Know

» *Buttcrack* is one of hundreds of bizarre low-budget, independently produced films that Lloyd Kaufman of Troma Entertainment has brought to a wide audience over the past four decades.

» Nothing in voodoo or witchcraft lore involves spells that can curse buttcracks. Believe me, I've checked.

 Trivia Quiz

What prompted Mojo Nixon to say that singer Don Henley has "balls the size of church bells"?

A: He saw Don Henley naked.

B: Don Henley beat him up in a parking lot.

C: Don Henley joined him onstage during a performance.

D: Mojo Nixon never said any such thing.

Answer: C. Mojo Nixon, known for being highly critical of the music industry, had written "Don Henley Must Die." He was performing it onstage in Austin when Henley joined him to sing harmony.

CADAVERELLA
Big Atom Productions, 2007

PRODUCER Jennifer Friend

WRITERS Jennifer Friend and Timothy Friend

DIRECTOR Timothy Friend

STARS Megan Goddard (*Cinder*), Ryan Seymour (*Cash/Justin*), Santiago Vasquez (*Baron Samedei*), and Kieran Hunter (*Leonore/Donn*).

When Cinder (Goddard) is murdered the day before her twenty-first birthday—just before she would have gained control of the trust fund her father left her and the power to kick her abusive ex-stripper stepmother and her two freakish stepsisters out of her house—she is restored to life by voodoo god Baron Samedei (Vasquez) so she can take her revenge. But she only has until midnight. . . .

Why It Sucks

Someone should have advised the production team that unnecessary and very badly done computer-generated visual effects only make your movie look worse than it actually is. (Although this was one of the best direct-to-DVD low-budget horror films of 2007. It truly was a sad year for horror movies.)

Thumbs Down Rating: 👎👎

The Crappies

The Special Achievement Award in Misplaced Slapstick Comedy goes to . . . Timothy Friend for sticking some comic relief in his film. We haven't seen humor more out of place since guys in gorilla suits wandered into thrillers during the 1940s.

And the Worst Director Award goes to . . . Timothy Friend for using cheap computer-generated graphics.

They Really Said It!

Baron Samedei: This is a little unusual, isn't it?

Betcha Didn't Know

» Big Atom Productions published a tie-in book that included a Cadaverella novella, the shooting script, and production photos. It was released through the online print-on-demand company Lulu.com.
» As of this writing, Timothy Friend is putting the finishing touches on a film that pits Dracula against Bonnie and Clyde.

 Trivia Quiz
Who is Baron Samedei in voodoo lore?

    A: A powerful spirit affiliated with life, death, and debauchery
    B: A powerful spirit affiliated with unavenged wrongs
    C: The supreme god of the voodoo pantheon
    D: The first human to make contact with voodoo spirits

Answer: A. He has a wide-ranging portfolio, but one of his most important functions is to make sure dead bodies stay in the ground and don't become zombies. Given the rise in zombie popularity, he must be one busy guy.

THE CREEPS

Full Moon Pictures, 1997

PRODUCER Charles Band

WRITER Benjamin Carr

DIRECTOR Charles Band

STARS Rhonda Griffin (*Anna Quarrels*), Bill Moynihan (*Winston Berber*), Justin Lauer (*David Raleigh*), Kristin Norton (*Miss Christina*), Phil Fondacaro (*Dracula*), Jon Simanton (*the Wolfman*), Joe Smith (*the Mummy*), and Thomas Wellington (*Frankenstein's Monster*)

A mad scientist (Moynihan) builds a machine that transports Dracula, the Wolfman, the Mummy, and Frankenstein's Monster into the real world. But interference from a librarian (Griffin) and a wanna-be private detective (Lauer) cause the process to go awry, and the four monsters appear as three-foot-tall midgets. Dracula (Fondacaro) sets about getting the scientist to redo the experiment. . . .

Why It Sucks

How many ways could the filmmakers find to offend audience members? Let's try homophobia. And mocking little people. Not to mention anyone with an ounce of literary knowledge who knows the Mummy and the Wolfman characters were created for films and have no counterparts in classic literature.

Thumbs Down Rating: 👎

The Crappies

The Living the Cliché Special Award goes to . . . Benjamin Carr and director Charles Band for making a film that proves the cliché that no one in Hollywood reads.

And the Most Bizarre Creative Signature Award goes to . . . Charles Band. Hitchcock had his blonds. Bava had his shots of characters reflected in liquid. Tarantino couldn't tell a sequential story if his life depended on it. Band has tiny terrors, be they dimuniative demons, killer puppets, possessed cookies, or classic monsters manifested as dwarfs.

They Really Said It!

Dracula: I recall being somewhat larger.

Betcha Didn't Know

» Dracula has been portrayed in more films than any other fictional character.

» Charles Band has written, directed, and/or produced over 250 movies.

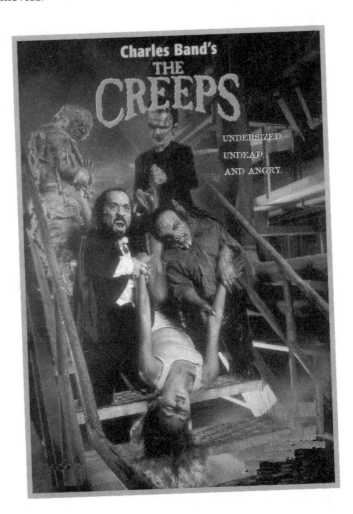

DEAD DUDES IN THE HOUSE (AKA *"THE DEAD COME HOME"* AND *"THE HOUSE ON TOMBSTONE HILL"*)
Troma Entertainment, 1991

PRODUCERS Mark Bladis, Melissa Lawes, and James Riffel

WRITER James Riffel

DIRECTOR James Riffel

STARS Mark Zobian (*Ron*), Naomi Kooker (*Linda*), Douglas Gibson (*Mark/ Old Lady*), James Griffin (*Ricky*), Sarah Newhouse (*Jamie*), Victor Verhaeghe (*Bob*), and Pam Lewis (*voice of the Old Lady*)

A group of twenty-something friends set out to restore a decaying mansion that one of them has bought for an amazingly low price. When one of them maliciously breaks a tombstone in the backyard, he awakens the malevolent spirits that inhabit the house. In the night of terror that follows, our protagonists are stalked and killed. But they don't stay dead for long . . . .

Why It Sucks

Dead Dudes in the House could have been a decent cross between a slasher flick and a haunted house movie . . . if the writers had put some thought into why the ghosts do what they do. It's also rare to find such a collection of annoying noncharacters in a film. (On the other hand, flat characters and ghosts behaving

Independent Oddities

187

inexplicably is a hallmark of the Japanese horror flicks that have gained popularity in recent years, so maybe James Riffel was a genius ahead of his time.)

Thumbs Down Rating: 🦇🦇🦇

The Crappies

The Worst Cross-Dresser Award goes to . . . Douglas Gibson in his role as the Old Lady. You won't find a less convincing old lady outside a school play at a British all-boy boarding school.

And the Worst Director Award goes to . . . James Riffel for staging the film's setup by giving the characters a couple of toolboxes. Hate to break it to you, guy, but renovating a house is going to take a bit more than a hammer.

They Really Said It!

Bob: The main three parts of a carpenter's tools are his hammer, nails, and beer.

Betcha Didn't Know

» In his book *Everything I Need to Know About Filmmaking I Learned from the Toxic Avenger*, Lloyd Kaufman claims Troma Entertainment fans view this movie as an "unsung masterpiece."

» According to Troma Entertainment's publicity material, the title of the film was supposed to evoke an air of hip hop coolness— which is odd because there is no hip hop or coolness in the film.

 Trivia Quiz
Which of the following movies has a ghost in it?

A: *The Amazing Mr. X* (1948)

B: *The Invisible Ghost* (1941)

C: *Hatchet for the Honeymoon* (1970)

D: *The Phantom Creeps* (1939)

Answer: C. Not, as you'd think, *The Invisible Ghost*, but rather *Hatchet for the Honeymoon*.

THE DEMONS OF LUDLOW
Ram Productions, 1983

PRODUCERS Barbara J. Rebane (executive producer) and Bill Rebane (producer)

WRITERS William Arthur (script) and Alan Ross (additional dialogue)

DIRECTOR Bill Rebane

STARS Paul von Hausen (*Preacher*), Stephanie Cushna (*Debra*), Carol Perry (*Ann Schulz*), Michael Accardo (*Andy*), C. Dave Davis (*Mayor*), and Angailica (*Ludlow's daughter*)

A curse that's haunted a small New England town since its founding 200 years ago is brought to horrible life when a piece of its secret history—an upright piano that's described as a harmonium but sounds like a harpsichord (or is that a harpsichord that looks like an upright piano but is called a harmonium?)—resurfaces. Will the town preacher (von Hausen) and a pair of young journalists (Accardo and Cushna) stop the curse, or will they fall victim to it?

Why It Sucks

The ending is so abrupt that it feels as if the real ending got snipped off in the cutting room. I'm *still* trying to figure out if the journalists end up cursed or not. Up to the nonending ending, the film was on track to be one of Bill Rebane's best efforts, but it is all undone in the final few minutes.

Thumbs Down Rating: 👎👎👎

The Crappies

The Worst Research Award goes to . . . Bill Rebane for not being able to tell the difference between a piano, a harmonium, and a harpsichord.

And the Worst Script Award goes to . . . William Arthur and Alan Ross for coming up with dialogue that varies from tinny to nonsensical.

They Really Said It!

Debra: He'll be unstoppable, unless we stop him.

Betcha Didn't Know

» Bill Rebane kept at arm's length from the established film industry for his entire career, and he did the vast majority of his film work in Wisconsin, even establishing a film studio there, the Shooting Ranch.

» Singer Tiny Tim starred as a creepy clown in the Rebane-directed *Marvelous Mervo*.

 Trivia Quiz

What Bill Rebane movie out-performed Robert Redford's *Three Days of the Condor* in some U.S. markets?

A: *The Game* (aka *"The Cold"*) (1984)

B: *The Demons of Ludlow* (1983)

C: *Blood Harvest* (1987)

D: *The Giant Spider Invasion* (1975)

Answer: D. Bolstered by a great poster, *The Giant Spider Invasion*, which cost $250,000 to make, reaped close to $3 million during its theatrical run.

FIST OF FEAR, TOUCH OF DEATH
(AKA *"THE DRAGON AND THE COBRA"*)
Aquarius Releasing, 1980

PRODUCER Terry Levene

WRITERS Ron Harvey (script), Ron Harvey and Matthew Mallinson (story)

DIRECTOR Matthew Mallinson

STARS Adolph Caesar (*himself*), Fred Williamson (*the Hammer*), Bill Louie (*Kato 2*), Aaron Banks (*the Promoter*), and Ron Van Clief (*himself*)

190

When a martial arts competition is held to determine the "successor to Bruce Lee," reporter Adolph Caesar (Caesar) is there to cover the events and relay unknown facts about Lee's life and conspiracy theories about his death.

Why It Sucks

For thirty years it's been marketed as a documentary, but in fact this movie is actually a mockumentary, poking fun at the many sleazy attempts to cash in on Bruce Lee's superstar status in the years following his death. Unfortunately, it's clumsily made with badly re-edited and redubbed clips from early Bruce Lee films and interviews interspersed with footage from a real martial arts competition. Worse, much of the humor of Lee's films has been muted, as the exploitaton genre it mocked has faded into pop culture history.

Thumbs Down Rating: 👎👎👎

The Crappies

The Special Achievement Award in Humorless Nitwittery goes to . . . Countless Internet commentators and web-based movie reviewers. They all seem to have missed the fact that this is a comedy and criticize the movie for making ridiculous claims (Bruce Lee ran away from home to emulate his grandfather, the greatest Chinese samurai ever; Fred Williamson is constantly mistaken for Harry Belafonte, etc.).
And the Worst Director Award goes to . . . Matthew Mallinson for beating just about every joke in the film to death.

They Really Said It!

Bruce Lee: The secret of Karate is power. Internal power. From the ear.

Betcha Didn't Know

» Jackie Chan first rose to stardom as one of numerous Bruce Lee imitators.
» Bill Louie, at the time this film was made, was one of the many martial artists trying to cash in on Bruce Lee's reputation. Louie went onto become a successful martial arts instructor.

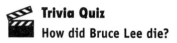

Trivia Quiz
How did Bruce Lee die?

A: Cardiac arrest (heart attack)

B: Drug overdose

C: Stabbed to death by unknown assailants (possibly CIA ninjas)

D: Cerebral edema (swelling of the brain)

GOTHIC
Virgin Vision, 1986

PRODUCERS Al Clarke and Robert Devereux (executive producers), Penny Corke and Robert Fox (producers)

WRITER Stephen Volk

DIRECTOR Ken Russell

STARS Gabriel Byrne (*Lord Byron*), Natasha Richardson (*Mary Wollstonecraft*), Julian Sands (*Percy Shelley*), Myriam Cyr (*Claire Clairmont*), and Timothy Spall (*Dr. Polidori*)

Eccentric poet Lord Byron (Byrne) invites young prodigy Percy Shelley and his fiancée Mary Wollstonecraft (Sands and Richardson), along with her half-sister Claire Clairmont (Cyr) to spend a weekend with him and his personal doctor, Polidori (Spall), at his isolated estate. After an evening of reading ghost stories, drinking wine enhanced with laudanum, and holding an impromptu séance, these outstanding figures of the Romantic Age find themselves trapped in an ever-worsening spiral of confusion and terror.

Why It Sucks

The movie stops making sense about fifteen minutes in. Creepy I'll grant you, but it's also a complete mess, as story threads come briefly together before separating again. Are the events of the film just hallucinations suffered by Mary? Did Shelley and

Independent Oddities

his friends manage to call forth an evil spirit? No one knows the answer, including the filmmakers. This film is all flash (together with puffy shirts and bad hair) but no substance.

Thumbs Down Rating: 👎👎

The Crappies

The Worst Writing Award goes to . . . Stephen Volk, who must have been on something when he wrote this nonsense.

And the Worst Director Award goes to . . . Ken Russell for failing to realize that if he's going to make us sit through a movie full of random nonsense, spooky imagery, and fops being emotionally cruel to each other, he could have at least given us more naked breasts. (I'm sure Charles Band would have given us nudity. He might even have given us some midget sex during the incubus scene.)

They Really Said It!

Byron: And here I had thought you that contradiction in terms: an intelligent woman!

Betcha Didn't Know

» The novel *Frankenstein, A Modern Prometheus* by Mary Shelley was completed when she was just nineteen. The genesis of the idea was actually a nightmare she had shortly after suffering a miscarriage with her first child at the age of eighteen.

» In 2006, almost exactly twenty years after the release of *Gothic*, Julian Sands starred in *The Haunted Airman*, another sexually charged horror film where the lines between reality and nightmare are impossibly blurred.

 Trivia Quiz

Which of the following actresses played Mary Shelley onscreen?

    A: Elsa Lanchester

    B: Holly Hunter

    C: Valerie Hobson

    D: Milla Jovovich

Answer: A. Elsa Lanchester played the author in the prologue for *The Bride of Frankenstein* (1935). Valerie Hobson played Dr. Frankenstein's wife, while Lanchester also portrayed the female created by the doctor as a companion to the Creature.

JESUS CHRIST, VAMPIRE HUNTER
Odessa Filmworks, 2001

PRODUCER Lee Demarbre

WRITER Ian Driscoll

DIRECTOR Lee Demarbre

STARS Phil Caracas (*Jesus Christ*), Maria Moulton (*Mary Magnum*), Jeff Moffet (*El Santo*), Murielle Varhelyi (*Maxine Shreck*), and Josh Grace (*Dr. Praetorious*)

When the evil Dr. Praetorious (Grace) and a cult of vampires threaten to wipe out Ottawa's lesbian community, the Savior Himself, Jesus Christ (Caracas), comes to their rescue with blessings, miracles, and ass-kicking, vampire-busting kung fu (and a little help from masked Mexican wrestler El Santo (Moffet)!

Why It Sucks

Well, for a film with a great title, there's not enough Jesus, vampires, or lesbians to fully live up to the film's promise. (Although maybe there could never be enough of those elements to make this film great.) Demarbre should have been smart enough to leave Jesus's appearance alone, with his beard and long hair and Year Zero Middle Eastern robes.

Thumbs Down Rating: 👎👎

The Crappies

The Special Award for Underacheivement in Costume Design goes to . . . Whoever thought it was a good idea to trade Jesus's robes for jeans and a black T-shirt. Instead of looking like Jesus Christ, he instead spends most of the film looking like actor Phil Caracas. *And the Worst Director Award goes to . . .* Lee Demarbre for failing to properly rehearse and stage the film's fight scenes. In a movie with a kung fu fighting Jesus Christ taking on vampires, the blows should look as if they're at least connecting.

Independent Oddities

They Really Said It!

Jesus: If I'm not back in five minutes, call the pope.

Betcha Didn't Know

» Jeff Moffet is a regular in films directed by Lee Demarbre and has played masked Mexican wrestler El Santo in two other films (*Harry Knuckles and the Treasure of the Aztec Mummy* and *Harry Knuckles and the Pearl Necklace*). Phil Caracas, another Demarbre regular, starred as the title character in both films.

» The New Testament is oddly silent on Jesus Christ's preferred martial arts style when fighting vampires.

 Trivia Quiz

What thriller revolves around a conspiracy to conceal certain facts surrounding Jesus Christ's family?

A: *The Seventh Seal* (1957)

B: *The Prophecy* (1995)

C: *The Da Vinci Code* (2006)

D: *Left Behind* (2000)

Answer: C. *The Da Vinci Code*, based on Dan Brown's mega-bestseller of the same title, involves an effort to conceal the fact that Jesus had a child.

NUDIST COLONY OF THE DEAD
Innate Films/Pirromount Pictures, 1991

PRODUCERS Tom Naygrow and Phil Vigeant (executive producers), Mark Headley (producer)

WRITER Mark Pirro

DIRECTOR Mark Pirro

STARS Deborah Stern (*Shelly Mammarosa*), Rachel Latt (*Mrs. Druple*), Brad Mendelson (*Peter Trickle*), and Forrest J. Ackerman (*Judge Rhinehole*), Dave Robinson (*Reverend Ritz*)

When a judge (Ackerman) orders radical nudists to get dressed and threatens to close their nudist camp they commit ritual suicide. Years later, the former camp is turned into a Bible retreat for troubled youth . . . and the dead nudists rise from their graves, bringing with them murder, mayhem, and song-and-dance numbers.

Why It Sucks

For a movie with a great, whacky premise, it's too slow moving for its own good. It's got funny songs and it's got a "shock twist ending" that's better than what you'll find in any number of serious horror films, but the slow parts are so slow that the payoffs are barely worth it. Still, it does have radical nudists.

Thumbs Down Rating: 👎👎👎

The Crappies

The Special Achievement in Insensitivity Award goes to . . . Writer/director Mark Pirro for including content sure to offend overly sensitive "community organizers" and "spokespeople" of just about any self-described group of "victims," with the elderly, racial minorities, gays, the handicapped, and religious groups all having a few arrows slung their way.

And the Worst Director Award goes to . . . Mark Pirro for failing to realize he needed to pick up the pace. The film sags in the middle almost as badly as the boobs on the old zombie witch (who likes to twirl them during song-and-dance production numbers).

They Really Said It!

Reverend Ritz: The children can't praise the Lord with genitals in their mouths.

Betcha Didn't Know

» In 1995, a stage version adapted from the movie ran for four months in a Hollywood theater.

» Mark Pirro continues to make and market his independently produced movies.

Independent Oddities

POSTAL

Boll KG Productions/Pitchblack Pictures, 2007

PRODUCERS Steve Wik and Vince Desiderio (executive producers), Uwe Boll, Daniel Clarke, and Shawn Williamson (producers)

WRITERS Uwe Boll and Bryan C. Knight

DIRECTOR Uwe Boll

STARS Zack Ward (*the Dude*), Dave Foley (*Uncle Dave*), Chris Coppola (*Richard*), Larry Thomas (*Osama bin Laden*), Michael Benyaer (*Mohammed*), Verne Troyer (*himself*), Jackie Tohn (*Faith*), Uwe Boll (*himselfl*), Rick Hoffman (*Mr. Blither*), and Chris Spencer (*Officer Greg*)

An unemployed factory worker (Ward) teams up with his con-artist uncle (Foley) to steal a shipment of highly collectible dolls and make a fortune selling them. Unfortunately, Osama bin Laden (Thomas) wants to steal the same dolls for far more nefarious purposes.

Why It Sucks

Uwe Boll, being Uwe Boll, has produced a film that's part political satire, part first-person shooter game adaptation, and all stupid. Most of the jokes are gross-out gags that cross the line from funny into heavy-handedly offensive. Boll jammed his film with plots and subplots until nothing got the proper amount of time.

Thumbs Down Rating: 👎 👎 👎

The Crappies

The Worst Actress Award goes to . . . Jackie Tohn, who was given an underwritten part and still managed to do even less than expected. The only thing that isn't flat about her performance is her chest area.

And the Worst Auteur Award goes to . . . Uwe Boll for trying too hard to be offensive, which rapidly becomes tiresome. (The child-molesting-themed Krotchy Dolls are the most painful example.)

Betcha Didn't Know

» The film was slated for theatrical release in the United States on May 24, 2008, but in the months leading up to its release distributors refused to handle it and theater chains refused to screen it. In the end, the film ended up showing in fewer than ten theaters.

» Critics of all stripes like to compare Uwe Boll to Edward D. Wood Jr. The comparison is unfair, as Boll has been more successful than Wood by any standard. His movies also tend to be more entertaining than Wood's films (no matter how much they may suck).

They Really Said It!

Uwe Boll: There are all those rumors out there that my movies are financed with Nazi gold, and what should I say? It's true!

 Trivia Quiz

What 2009 comedy featured a real-world terrorist in a mock interview?

A: *G-Force*

B: *The Proposal*

C: *Delivery Date*

D: *Brüno*

Answer: D. In *Brüno*, Sacha Baron Cohen, posing as the flamboyantly gay fashion critic Bruno, sought out Ayman Abu Aita, a one-time member of the terrorist group Aqsa Martyrs Brigade, and asked that he kidnap Bruno so he could benefit from the publicity.

SATANIC YUPPIES (AKA, *"EVIL AMBITIONS"*)
B+ Productions, 1996

PRODUCERS Jeff Barklage, Denis Roland (executive producers), Mark Burchett and Michael D. Fox (producers)

WRITERS Mark Burchett and Michael D. Fox

DIRECTORS Mark Burchett and Michael D. Fox

STARS Paul Morris (*Pete McGavin*), Amber Newman (*Brittany Drake*), Debbie Rochon *(Madame Natalie)*, Ranae Raos (*Leslie Kellog*), Lucy Frashure (*Julie Swanson*), Randy Rupp (*Satan*), and Rob Calvert (*Lester*)

A reporter struggling to rise above the level of a tabloid writer and return to his glory days (Morris), stumbles upon a Satanic cult in the form of a public relations agency, a cult seeking to give Satan the perfect bride. Will the story be the reporter's path back to the big time, or will it take him straight to Hell?

Why It Sucks

Satanic Yuppies really wants to be television's *Kolchak: The Night Stalker* (1974) but can't quite get there. It gives one of the screen's great Satans (played by Randy Rupp), and Paul Morris makes a good stand-in for Darren McGavin, but most of what surrounds them is half-baked. On the other hand, the idea of a PR agency being a Satanic cult appeals to me.

Thumbs Down Rating: 👎

The Crappies

The Worst Script Award goes to . . . Mark Burchett and Michael D. Fox for undermining an otherwise decent movie with jokes that were trite even in 1996, (such as Rush Limbaugh being a client of the Satanic agency).

And the Worst Actress Award goes to . . . Glori-Anne Gilbert for some of the unsexiest gratuitous nudity during a Satanic ritual I've ever seen. (Her breasts are bigger than her head!)

Independent Oddities

199

They Really Said It!

Brittany Drake: Do you, Julie Swanson, take Satan as your eternally wedded mate? To have and to hold—
Julie Swanson: [Screams into gag]
Brittany Drake: We'll take that as a yes.

Betcha Didn't Know

» For almost as long as they've been making movies, Satan's been in 'em. In 1896, French magician and film-maker Georges Méliès created *House of the Devil*, a two-minute silent film featuring a bat transforming into the devil.

» "Yuppies" is derived from an abbreviation of Young Urban Professionals. It was first used in print in a 1983 column by writer Bob Greene. He did not coin the phrase, and its origins remain murky.

Trivia Quiz

Who wrote the scripts for the Carl Kolchak movies *The Night Stalker* and *The Night Strangler*?

A: Jeff Rice

B: Ray Bradbury

C: Stephen King

D: Richard Matheson

Answer: D. Richard Matheson, author of *I Am Legend*, has written dozens of horror and science fiction short stories. *I Am Legend* has been made into a movie five times.

SKELETON KEY
Darkstone Entertainment, 2006

PRODUCER Rebecca Taylor

WRITERS John Johnson (script), Jimmy Belcher and Neil Wagner (story)

DIRECTOR John Johnson

STARS John Johnson (*Howard*), David Simmons (*Nicopernicus*), Liam Smith (*Neil*), Karthik Srinivasan (*Cornelius*), Chris Jenkins (*Dr. Qubert/*

Mr. Sniffles), Jay Barber (*Dr. Noches*), Denise Shrader (*Sandy*), and Codo the Dog (*himself*)

A tabloid reporter and his photographer (Johnson and Srinivasan) take a cab driven by a Haitian immigrant (Simmons) to the town of Nilbog to discover who's been shipping zombies via parcel post to unsuspecting people. What they find is evil and madness manifested in every conceivably crazy way and a mad scientist (Barber) trying to export this evil to the rest of the world.

Why It Sucks
Skeleton Key is a low-budget film that mocks low-budget amateurish horror films using all the techniques and technical know-how on prominent display in amateurish horror films. Along the way, it takes swipes at the fans of such movies—which include yours truly.

Thumbs Down Rating: 👎

The Crappies
The Too Much of a Good Thing Award goes to . . . Liam Smith for his portrayal of Neil. This movie nerd, who is both a character in the film and watching it as it unfolds, is the center of some really funny breaking-the-fourth-wall humor, but he is so annoying and over the top that the jokes are almost ruined.
And the Worst Best Actor Award goes to . . . John Johnson for playing his character of Howard completely straight and with real restraint while everyone around him is *acting*.

They Really Said It!
Neil: He just got beat up with a penis!

Betcha Didn't Know
» *Skeleton Key* takes place mostly in the town of Nilbog as a tribute to the hideously hilarious cinematic milestone of awfulness that is *Troll 2*.
» John Johnson has helmed two sequels to this movie, one in 2007 and one in 2008.

What classic horror novel inspired John Johnson to write and direct one of the most faithful adaptations ever brought to the screen?

A: *Frankenstein*

B: *Dracula*

C: *The Strange Case of Dr. Jekyll and Mr. Hyde*

D: *Carmilla*

Answer: B. In 2008, Johnson's *Alucard* was released directly to DVD. The film captures the tone of Stoker's novel, keeps to its plot, and includes most of the book's dialogue.

SUBURBAN SASQUATCH
Troubled Moon Films, 2004

PRODUCER Dave Wascavage

WRITER Dave Wascavage

DIRECTOR Dave Wascavage

STARS Sue Lynn Sanchez (*Talla*), Bill Ushler (*Rick Harlan*), and Dave Bonavita (*John Rush/Bigfoot*)

A sasquatch (that's Bigfoot if you're in the American Northwest or Abominable Snowman if you're in the Himalayas) goes on a rampage in a new housing development. Will a young Native American, Talla (Sanchez), equipped with magical arrows and hand axes kill the beast? Or will the handsome tabloid reporter (Ushler) distract her with the promise of romance?

Why It Sucks

Suburban Sasquatch is a campy, low-budget monster flick that revels in its own awfulness. Dave Wascavage makes cheap, awful movies that he knows are cheap and awful. With this film, he creates a homage/spoof of numerous drive-in movie "classics" and a number of B movies from the 1940s and 1950s. His film is every bit as badly plotted and acted as those. Oh yeah, and the Bigfoot costume is a gorilla suit that's received a boob job.

Independent Oddities

Thumbs Down Rating:

The Crappies

The Special Achievement in Bringing Nightmares to Life Award goes to . . . Dan Wascavage for making a movie about a teleporting Sasquatch with strangely hypnotic nipples.

And the Worst Actor Award goes to . . . Bill Ushler for his performance as a whiny, boring romantic hero. This goes even beyond Hayden Christensen in *Attack of the Clones.*

They Really Said It!

Rick: You're going to kill this thing with some bow and arrows?
Talla: Let's move.

Betcha Didn't Know

» Five different actors wore the Bigfoot costume during filming: Dave Bonavita, Juan Fernandez, Wes Miller, David Weldon, and Edward Wascavage. Each also played other parts in the film.

» Wascavage followed this effort with *Fungicide*, a film even more intentionally cheesy and awful than this one. In it, giant mushrooms (created by awful CGI or hilariously bad costumes) attack the residents at a bed and breakfast.

Trivia Quiz

What well-known movie critic believes Sasquatch/Bigfoot is real?

A: Ben Lyons

B: Michael Medved

C: Steven Jay Schneider

D: Robert Ebert

Answer: B. On his nationally syndicated radio show, Michael Medved has frequently spoken of his belief that a giant unknown primate roams the recesses of the North American rainforest in the Pacific Northwest.

THE WITCHES' MOUNTAIN
Azor Films, 1972

PRODUCER Uncredited

WRITERS Raúl Artigot, Juan Cortéz, Félix Fernández, and José Truchado

DIRECTOR Raúl Artigot

STARS John Gaffari (*Mario*), Patty Shepard (*Delia*), Mónica Randall (*Carla*), and Victor Israel (*Inn Keeper*)

A commercial photographer (Gaffari) takes a sexy girl (Shepard)—it *was* the seventies!—to shoot a photo-essay on isolated Witches' Mountain. Weirdnesses and witches haunt them every step of the way.

Why It Sucks

How does the prologue with the evil little girl fit with the film's climax? Was Shepard put in Gaffari's path through magic? Why do witches like to steal the hero's car and break into his house? Why do the rituals performed by the witches make them look like a jazz ballet company rehearsing for a performance? Why, why, why!?! No answers here.

Thumbs Down Rating: 🐾🐾🐾🐾

The Crappies

The Worst Script Award goes to . . . Raúl Artigot, Juan Cortéz, Félix Fernández and José Truchado for writing a story that is incoherent from beginning to end. Maybe they should have shown each other the pages they wrote before shooting began?

And the Strangest Witch Coven Award goes to . . . The witches who perform a ritualistic jazz ballet in the mountains of Spain. (When they aren't stealing cars.)

They Really Said It!

Mario: For a moment there, I thought I had all these voices in my head.

Delia: You must have been dreaming.

Betcha Didn't Know

» American-born Patty Shepard retired from acting in 1988 after a career that spanned two decades and more than forty-five film appearances.

» Victor Israel, who appears as the creepy wall-eyed inn keeper in this film, appeared in over 150 films, ranging from classics like *The Good, the Bad and the Ugly* to drek like *The Witches' Mountain*. He passed away in September 2009.

 Trivia Quiz

In what film does Patty Shepard appear as an immortal witch?

A: *Black Sunday* (1977)

B: *The Witches of Eastwick* (1987)

C: *Burn, Witch, Burn!* (1962)

D: *The Werewolf vs. the Vampire Woman* (1971)

Answer: D. *The Werewolf vs. the Vampire Woman*, in which she plays Countess Wandesa Dárvula de Nádasdy.

CHAPTER THIRTEEN

STRANGE SUPERHEROES

In recent years, comic book adaptations have been big at the box office. Once again, comics are cool, and it's okay for adults to read them. The last time that marketing hook was cast out was in the late 1980s and early 1990s. Well, here are a few comic book movies that may well shock and appall the average fan of Wolverine's cinematic exploits. (For what it's worth, I love comics . . . and I think the first *Iron Man* movie will be remembered as one of the very best films of the past decade.)

DANGER: DIABOLIK

Dino De Laurentiis Cinematographic/Marianne Productions, 1968

PRODUCERS Dino DeLaurentiis and Bruno Toden

WRITERS Mario Bava, Dino Maiuri, Brian Degas, and Tudor Gates (script), Angela Giussani and Luciana Giussani (story and original characters)

DIRECTOR Mario Bava

STARS John Phillip Law (*Diabolik*), Marisa Mell (*Eva Kant*), Michel Piccoli (*Inspector Ginko*), and Aldolfo Celi (*Ralph Valmont*)

The long-standing rivalry between the mysterious super-thief Diabolik (Law) and police inspector Ginko (Piccoli) becomes personal when Ginko forces a top gangster (Celi) to take action against his foe and the love of Diabolik's life, Eva (Mell), is caught in the middle.

Why It Sucks

Although a mostly faithful adaptation of the Italian comic book it is based on, the film fails to capture the relationship between Ginko and Diabolik. And, like so many comic book adaptations, it inadvertently reveals how ridiculous the characters are. Diabolik's mask works fine when it's a drawing. Put it in a live action film, and it's pretty painful.

Thumbs Down Rating: 👎

The Crappies

The Special Achievement in the Area of Not Knowing When to Quit Award goes to . . . Mario Bava. He insists on tacking on one final heist for Diabolik, one that deflates the ending of the movie.
And the Worst Production Design goes to . . . Mario Bava. As excellent as the production designs and cinematography on the film are, Bava on more than one occasion shows off his artistry to the point where it detracts from the film and makes some scenes downright boring.

They Really Said It!

Diabolik: If you didn't see him, he was there.

Betcha Didn't Know

» Mario Bava had access to a budget of $3 million for this movie, but he was so in the habit of working on tiny productions that he made it for around $400,000.

» The film is an adaptation of one of the longest and most popular Italian comic books. It was created by sisters Angela Giussani and Luciana Giussani.

Trivia Quiz

What was the profession of John Phillip Law's father, John Law?

A: Attorney in Washington State

B: Sheriff's deputy in Los Angeles County

C: Second-in-command to a New Jersey Mafia boss

D: Criminal investigator for the United States Navy

Answer: B. John Law was the sheriff's deputy in Los Angeles County.

MY SUPER EX-GIRLFRIEND
New Regency Pictures/Pariah/Regency Enterprises, 2006

PRODUCERS Bill Carraro (executive producer), Arnon Milchan and Gavin Polone (producers)

WRITER Don Payne

DIRECTOR Ivan Reitman

STARS Luke Wilson (*Matt Saunders*), Uma Thurman (*Jenny Johnson/ G-Girl*), Eddie Izzard (*Barry/Professor Bedlam*), Rainn Wilson (*Vaughn Haige*), and Anna Faris (*Hannah Lewis*)

When Matt (Wilson) dumps his superhero girlfriend, G-Girl (Thurman) because she's too jealous, she starts destroying his life and career out of revenge. When her archnemesis and spurned high-school boyfriend, Professor Bedlam (Izzard), approaches him with a scheme to eliminate G-Girl's superpowers, things only get worse.

Why It Sucks

Part superhero spoof, part romantic comedy, this must have seemed like a really good idea to someone. Unfortunately, it's not a particularly funny spoof, and the romance lacks heart and conviction. The characters are shallow and stereotypical and give about as much effort to their parts as the writers gave to the

209

script. You can imagine everyone sighing with relief at the wrap as they collect their paychecks and walk away from this turkey.

Thumbs Down Rating: 👎👎👎

The Crappies

The Worst Script Award goes to . . . Don Payne. Of all the characters, only Professor Bedlam has the tinest bit of texture to him.
And the Worst Actress Award goes to . . . Anna Faris for giving a performance even less interesting and engaging than her character's role in the story.

They Really Said It!

Professor Bedlam: Kill? I didn't say "kill." I said "neutralize." It's a neutral word, like Switzerland.

Betcha Didn't Know

» Although best known for comedies, Ivan Reitman started his career by producing horror films (like David Cronenberg's *Shivers*) and sleazy exploitation films (like *Ilsa: The Tigress of Siberia*).

» Ivan Reitman was the first Canadian convicted under Canada's indecency laws in 1971 for producing an adult comedy titled *The Columbus of Sex*.

Trivia Quiz

Which of the following Ivan Reitman–directed films did not feature Arnold Schwarzenegger?

A: *Junior* (1994)

B: *Father's Day* (1997)

C: *Twins* (1988)

D: *Kindergarten Cop* (1990)

Answer: B. Schwarzenegger starred in three comedies directed by Reitman, but *Father's Day* wasn't one of them.

SGT. KABUKIMAN, N.Y.P.D.

Namco Ltd./Troma Entertainment, 1990

PRODUCERS Tetsu Fujimura and Masaya Nakamura (executive producers), Michael Herz and Lloyd Kaufman (producers)

WRITERS Lloyd Kaufman, Andrew Osborne, and Jeffrey W. Sass (script), Lloyd Kaufman (story), Fumio Furuya and Satoshi Kitahara (original characters)

DIRECTORS Michael Herz and Lloyd Kaufman

STARS Rick Gianasi (*Harry Griswold/Sgt. Kabukiman*), Susan Byun (*Lotus*), Bill Weeden (*Reginald Stuart/the Evil One*), and Thomas Crnkovich (*Rembrandt*)

After he becomes host to an ancient Kabuki spirit, Detective Harry Griswold (Gianasi) finds himself with a new calling in life and even stranger new superpowers. But can the lovely Lotus (Byun) convince Griswold of his new responsibilities before the Evil One (Weeden) brings an ancient prophecy to pass?

Why It Sucks

Sgt. Kabukiman, N.Y.P.D. is split between the usual Troma R-rated off-color humor and a PG-13 approach. But although it's technically one of Lloyd Kaufman's best pictures—he actually had a budget for special effects this time—his attempt to be both mild and spicy means it ends up being mostly bland.

Thumbs Down Rating: 🍗🍗

The Crappies

The Worst Picture Award goes to . . . Michael Herz and Lloyd Kaufman for failing to deliver on what could have been Troma's ticket to a wider audience.

And the Worst Auteur Award goes to . . . Lloyd Kaufman for not having the sense to refrain from including his hallmark head-crushing and off-color humor. It feels forced here, especially during the film's climax.

Fatal Sushi...Lethal Chopsticks...And As American As Apple Pie!

They Really Said It!

Harry Griswold [narrating]: I was depressed, I was confused, and I was turning Japanese!

Betcha Didn't Know

» Although completed in 1990, the film was only shown at film festivals for several years. The distribution deal with investor Namco fell through after the company was unhappy with the final product. No theatrical distributor would take the film until 1996.

» Sgt. Kabukiman has shown up in several other Troma projects, usually portrayed as a miserable alcoholic. The meta-joke is that the difficulties surrounding his movie drove him to depression and drink.

ULTRACHRIST!
LeisureSuit Media, 2003

PRODUCER Jordan Hoffman

WRITERS Kerry Douglas Dye and Jordan Hoffman

DIRECTOR Kerry Douglas Dye

STARS Jonathan C. Green (*Jesus/Ultrachrist*), Jordan Hoffman
(*Archangel Ira*), Celia A. Montgomery (*Molly*), and Samuel Bruce
Campbell (*Parks Commissioner A. C. Meaney*)

Jesus Christ (Green) returns to Earth to resume his ministry but
finds that no one in New York City is willing to pay attention to
his message. After a marketing executive he meets in a bar con-
vinces him he needs a flashier image, he gets a disillusioned
fashion designer (Montgomery) to design and sew a spandex
superhero costume for him. Thus decked out, Jesus hits the
streets to combat sin.

Why It Sucks

It's a very silly movie with a total misfire of an ending that ends
up wiping out what good feelings viewers might have had toward
the film up to that point. The film was going along just fine, with
Jesus facing off against the Anti-Christ's Legion of Ultimate Evil

(consisting of Adolph Hitler, Vlad the Impaler, Richard Nixon, and Jim Morrison of The Doors), and thwarting his Father's plans to embarrass him. But then Dye had to try to poke fun at the old-time movie trope of "let's put on a show to save the day." And at that point *Ultrachrist!* veers from merely silly to ultra-insipid.

Thumbs Down Rating: 👎👎

The Crappies
The Worst Director Award goes to . . . Kerry Douglas Dye for ending the film with an overlong, badly mounted spoof of the Andy Hardy movies.

And the So Fake-Looking It's Probably Real Award goes to . . . The beard sported by Jonathan C. Green in his role as Ultrachrist!

They Really Said It!
Jesus: The crucifix is the symbol of Christianity? I hated the crucifix! Ouch!

Betcha Didn't Know
» Jonathan C. Green was a practicing attorney before becoming an actor.
» When the crew shot scenes in Times Square, no one seemed fazed by a bearded man in cape and a brightly colored spandex costume. Some tourists even asked for Ultrachrist's autograph, assuming he was a local celebrity.

Trivia Quiz
Which of these actors have not portrayed Jesus on film?
- A: Max von Sydow
- B: Jeremy Sisto
- C: Bela Lugosi
- D: James Caviezel

Answer: C. While photos exist of Lugosi in costume as Jesus, he never played the character on film (though he did appear as Jesus in a 1909 Passion play in Hungary).

CHAPTER FOURTEEN
AWFUL ALIENS

For every *Close Encounter of the Third Kind* and *The Day the Earth Stood Still* (original version), there are ten movies like the ones in this chapter. Aliens, according to these movies, are mostly evil, lust after Earth women, and wear really bad costumes—in some cases, so bad that the zipper shows.

ALIEN BLOOD
West Coast Films, 1999

PRODUCERS Michael Herz (executive producer) and Jon Sorensen (producer)

WRITER Jon Sorensen

DIRECTOR Jon Sorensen

STARS Glyn Whiteside (*Michael*) and Francesca Manning (*Alien Mother*)

An alien mother (Manning) on the run with her child takes refuge in a country house where the residents are having a New Year's Eve fancy dress party on the last night of the twentieth century. However, the government agents pursuing her lay siege to the house, and a night of gunfire and gory, psychically induced violence follows. Oh, did I forget to mention the vampires? Yeah, there are also vampires.

Why It Sucks

There is nothing wrong with this movie that a fully developed script wouldn't have fixed. Or maybe just a script. As it stands, nothing in the movie is clear. Is the government chasing the alien mother? Are those vampires in that manor house or are they just dorks in costumes? Why does the alien's powers seem to come and go according to plot dictates? And why does all the dialogue sound like it was ad-libbed? Special-effects guys shouldn't write movies—that's my conclusion.

Thumbs Down Rating: 🦇🦇🦇🦇

The Crappies

The Worst Actor Award goes to . . . Glyn Whiteside for his role as Michael, one of film history's most uninteresting villains, made so both by the weak script and an uninspired performance.

And the Worst Script Award goes to . . . Jon Sorensen for getting around to thinking about narrative only after production had wrapped. And don't get me started on the idea of vampires in a movie about alien mothers being chased by gun-toting morons.

They Really Said It!

The Vampires (in unison): Boo!

Betcha Didn't Know

» Jon Sorensen worked in the visual effects departments on such films as *Alien* (1979), *The Dark Crystal* (1982), *Outland* (1981), and *Time Bandits* (1981).

» "True" tales of alien abductions and landings didn't become common until the late 1940s and into the 1950s when science fiction became a popular genre.

Trivia Quiz

In what British science fiction classic does technology left behind by a long-extinct alien civilization threaten to destroy London?

A: *Quatermass and the Pit* (1967)

B: *Four-Sided Triangle* (1953)

C: *Doctor Who: Dalek Invasion Earth 2150* (1966)

D: *CQk* (1969)

Answer: A. In *Quatermass and the Pit*, a subway construction crew digs up a Martian device, leaving cranky scientist Bernard Quatermass to save London from it.

BAD CHANNELS

Full Moon Entertainmennt, 1992

PRODUCERS Charles Band (executive producer) and Keith S. Payson (producer)

WRITERS Jackson Barr (script) and Charles Band (story)

DIRECTOR Ted Nicolaou

STARS Paul Hipp (*Dan O'Dare*), Martha Quinn (*Lisa Cummings*), Michael Huddleston *(Corky)*, Aaron Lustig (*Vernon Locknut*), Roumel Reaux (*Flip Humble*), and Victor Rogers (*Sheriff Hickman*)

A disk jockey known for crazy on-air stunts (Hipp) becomes the unwitting partner of an alien who has come to Earth to abduct beautiful women via radio waves, otherworldly technology, and rock music.

Why It Sucks

The film is driven almost entirely by its wacky script. The actors showed up for work but not much more than that. The director further dilutes the film's entertainment value by including three full-length songs, wasting entirely too much running time on second-rate filler.

217

Thumbs Down Rating: 👎👎

The Crapples

The Worst Director Award goes to . . . Ted Nicolaou for not having the sense to realize that three full-length music videos were over-kill even for a film about aliens weaponizing rock 'n' roll. We want alien abduction action, not MTV!

And the Worst Actress Award goes to . . . Martha Quinn, who, through her portrayal of frustrated TV reporter Lisa Cummings proved that as an actress she made a darn good VJ. She comes across as so shrill and obnoxious that you'll be praying for the aliens to zap her or infect her with their lethal variant of athlete's foot.

They Really Said It!

Dan O'Dare: Ladies and gentlemen, I know this sounds crazy, but the Super Station studios have been taken over by creatures from another planet.

Betcha Didn't Know

» Martha Quinn was one of the original five VJs when MTV debuted in 1981. She hosted programs on the channel for the next decade.

» When Charles Band used clips from this film in the pseudo-sequel *Dollman vs. Demonic Toys*, he rewrote the ending using dubbing, so that the abducted nurse rather than the high-school student remained miniaturized.

Trivia Quiz

What actor/director directed and narrated a radio play about an alien invasion that caused panic in U.S. towns when it was broadcast in 1938?

A: Orson Welles

B: Alfred Hitchcock

C: Lowell Sherman

D: Leonard Nimoy

Awful Aliens

Answer: A. Orson Welles's Halloween eve broadcast on CBS Radio's Mercury Theater created national hysteria. In Concrete, WA, a power outage knocked out electricity and phone service just after Welles had described the Martian attack. As many as 1.7 million people fled their homes or took up arms during the panic.

KILLER KLOWNS FROM OUTER SPACE
Chiodo Brothers Productions/MGM, 1988

PRODUCERS Paul Mason and Helen Sarlui-Tucker (executive producers), Charles Chiodo, Edward Chiodo, and Stephen Chiodo (producers)

WRITERS Charles Chiodo, Edward Chiodo, and Stephen Chiodo

DIRECTOR Stephen Chiodo

STARS Grant Cramer (*Mike Tobacco*), John Allen Nelson (*Dave Hanson*), Suzanne Snyder (*Debbie Stone*), John Vernon (*Officer Curtis Mooney*), Michael Siegel (*Rich Terenzi*), and Peter Licassi (Paul Terenzi)

Aliens who look and behave like circus clowns invade a small town . . . and turn the citizens into klown kibble.

Why It Sucks
Face it: clowns are just creepy! *Killer Klowns from Outer Space* is a nightmare if you have clownophobia. For the rest of us, it's a supremely goofy movie—albeit with some pacing problems—and a great theme song.

Thumbs Down Rating: 👎👎

The Crappies
The Special Recognition in Underachievement in the Area of Stunt Work Award goes to . . . A weakly done car crash that illustrates what can happen when producers/writers/directors overreach the reality of a meager budget. (According to the Stephen Chiodi, the stunt went wrong, but there was no money in the budget to try it again.)

And the Worst Director Award goes to . . . Stephen Chiodo for the lame, forced happy ending that undermines an emotionally powerful bit of self-sacrifice.

They Really Said It!
Officer Curtis Mooney: I got through Korea; I can get through this bullshit.

Betcha Didn't Know

» *Killer Klowns From Outer Space* features homages to the films of Alfred Hitchcock. The easiest to spot is a shot of water swirling down a drain, with a toilet bowl standing in for a shower drain. Have fun and see if you can spot others!

» In the original cut, Dave perished heroically in order to save everyone else from a giant klown, but an executive at distributor Trans World Entertainment thought the movie needed a happy ending. As a result, Dave survives, thus proving that executives shouldn't have creative input on movies.

 Trivia Quiz

What singer and musician starred in a movie where a clown may or may not be a serial killer?

A: Weird Al Yankovic

B: Tiny Tim

C: Madonna

D: Danny Elfman

Answer: B. In Bill Rebane's 1987 slasher flick *Blood Harvest*, Tiny Tim played Marvelous Mervo.

PLAN 9 FROM OUTER SPACE
Reynolds Pictures, 1959

PRODUCER J. Edward Arnolds (executive producer) and Edward D. Wood Jr. (producer)

WRITER Edward D. Wood Jr.

DIRECTOR Edward D. Wood Jr.

STARS Gregory Walcott (*Jeff Trent*), Mona McKinnon (*Paula Trent*), John Breckinridge (*the Ruler*), Dudley Manlove (*Eros*), Joanna Lee (*Tanna*), Tom Keene (*Col. Tom Edwards*), Criswell (*himself*), Tor Johnson (*Inspector Daniel Clay*), and Lyle Talbot (*General Roberts*)

Aliens from some unnamed planet come to Earth to animate the dead—because that's what Plan 9 calls for. Will a dashing airline pilot and verbose military officers save the world from the aliens and their horde of three zombies?

Why It Sucks

Plan 9 From Outer Space has been called the worst movie ever made, but it is also strangely entertaining. Through its absurd dialogue and technical gaffes, it draws you in. You'll wonder if this movie can possibly get any worse. The answer is invariably "yes," right up to the big showdown between our hero and the dastardly Master of Plan, Eros (played by a fellow named Manlove).

Thumbs Down Rating: 🐾🐾🐾🐾

The Crappies

The Worst Auteur Award goes to . . . Edward D. Wood Jr. for making a movie that's unevenly paced, with dialogue so full of non sequiturs you have to wonder if he's doing it on purpose. The alien civilization is so idiotic and unintentionally hilarious that the movie has become the poster child for an entire genre of bad films.

And the Special Made for Change Found Between the Cushions and Looks Like It Award goes to . . . Edward D. Wood Jr. for a movie with the worst sets you're likely to see outside a grade school stage production, combined with special effects so pathetic even a mother couldn't love them.

They Really Said It!

Criswell: We are all interested in the future, for that is where you and I are going to spend the rest of our lives. And remember, my friends, future events such as these will affect you in the future.

Betcha Didn't Know

» The film was completed in 1956, but it took three years to find a distributor who was willing to pick it up.
» Criswell was a journalist turned professional psychic. It is claimed (by Criswell) that he was accurate 80 percent of the time. His prediction that the world would end in 2001 was among the 20 percent of the incorrect ones.

Trivia Quiz

Which actor appearing in *Plan 9* costarred in films with Ginger Rogers?

A: Bela Lugosi

B: Dudley Manlove

C: Tor Johnson

D: Lyle Talbot

Answer: D. Lyle Talbot costarred in the low-budget mysteries *The Thirteenth Guest* (1932) and *A Shriek in the Night* (1933), both of which costarred Ginger Rogers.

XTRO
Amalgamated Film Enterprises, 1983

PRODUCERS Robert Shay (executive producer) and Mark Forstater (producer)

WRITERS Iain Cassie and Robert Smith (script), Harry Bromley Davenport and Michel Parry (story)

DIRECTOR Harry Bromley Davenport

STARS Bernice Stegers (*Rachael Phillips*), Philip Sayer (*Sam Phillips*), Danny Brainin (*Joe Daniels*), Maryam D'Abo (*Analise Mercier*), and Simon Nash (*Tony Phillips*)

Three years after being abducted by aliens, Sam (Sayer) returns a very different man. And then he passes his newly acquired gooey, gory alien powers on to his young son (Nash).

Why It Sucks

Although creepy at times and downright terrifying at others, the film is overlong. Too much bland acting and too many lazy attempts to cover plot holes. And *waaay* too much Stupid Character Syndrome.

Thumbs Down Rating: 👎 👎 👎

Awful Aliens

The Crappies

The Special Achievement in the Area of Distorted Family Values Award goes to . . . Scriptwriters Iain Cassie and Robert Smith and storywriters Harry Bromley Davenport and Michel Parry for a tale of disturbing perversions of the parent/child relationship.

And the Worst Director Award goes to . . . Harry Bromley Davenport for not knowing when to quit. Why do so many directors insist on milking the hell out of scenes? They just spoil a good thing.

They Really Said It!

Rachael [upon noticing a bloody smear on the front door]: Sam, someone's been here!

Betcha Didn't Know

» *Xtro* was one of seventy-four films on a list drawn up in 1983 by Great Britain's Director of Public Prosecutions as being so perverse and obscene that they might violate British law. (It was later dropped from the list.)

» The movie was followed by two sequels, neither of which have anything to do with the plot of this film or each other.

 Trivia Quiz

In what James Bond movie did Maryam d'Abo appear?

A: *A View to a Kill* (1985)

B: *Golden Eye* (1995)

C: *The Living Daylights* (1987)

D: *Octopussy* (1983)

Answer: C. In *The Living Daylights* d'Abo played Kara Milovy, a professional cellist who moonlights as a sniper.

CHAPTER FIFTEEN

TEST YOUR STAMINA

I've been hardened by decades of bad-movie watching. But even I almost could not sit through the movies in this chapter. (In fact, I am not too proud to admit that *Oasis of the Zombies* almost got the best of me.) So test your mettle. Watch all the films in this chapter. If you get through them, you'll be able to count yourself among the best of those who love the worst. You'll also have some genuine benchmarks to evaluate the accuracy of that most-often-misapplied label "worst movie ever."

ALONE IN THE DARK
Boll KG Productions/Herold Productions/Brightlight Pictures, 2005

PRODUCERS Uwe Boll and Wolfgang Herold (executive producers), Shawn Williamson (producer)

WRITERS Elan Mastai, Michael Roesch, and Peter Scheerer

DIRECTOR Uwe Boll

STARS Christian Slater (*Edward Carnby*), Stephen Dorff (*Richard Burke*), and Tara Reid (*Aline Cedrac*)

Edward Carnby (Slater) is a paranormal investigator trying to unlock a mystery in his past that is somehow tied to a mysterious prehistoric culture. He is on the verge of finding his answers when a series of events involving invisible monsters, his girlfriend (Reid), symbiot-infected government agents, and a bitter coworker (Dorff) from the government's paranormal research branch erupt.

Why It Sucks

This movie starts with one of the dullest bits of exposition to ever open a big-budget horror film and it doesn't get much better. There's no character development, no logic, and the plot is so half-baked it doesn't even feel as if they stuck it in the oven. For extra suck, the creatures look exactly like what they are: computer-generated animations.

Thumbs Down Rating: 👎👎👎👎

The Crappies

The Worst Script Award goes to . . . Elan Mastai, Michael Roesch, and Peter Scheerer for creating the most incompetent monster-fighting government agency ever. The creatures in the film are vulnerable to light. Private citizens can rent portable light towers with gas or battery-powered generators. But the hi-tech, paramilitary Department 713 can't find any. I dunno. Maybe Haliburton was in charge of their procurement process.

Test Your Stamina

225

And the Worst Special-Effects Award goes to . . . Peter Giliberti, lead animator, for computer-generated critters and effects so badly done that most of the $10 million-plus that was spent on them must have gone to hookers and blow.

They Really Said It!

Edward Carnby: Fear is what protects you from the things you don't believe in.

Betcha Didn't Know

» Director Uwe Boll blames the failure of this movie on actress Tara Reid. He has been quoted in interviews saying that he regrets not firing her and replacing her with an unknown actress.

» Boll stated that this film taught the importance of starting with a good script when making a movie. His films since show no sign that he took this lesson to heart.

 Trivia Quiz

What unusual publicity stunt did Uwe Boll orchestrate during production of his 2008 comedy *Postal*?

A: He placed a bounty on Osama bin Laden.

B: He challenged film critics who have slammed his films to face him in a boxing ring.

C: He joined peace protests in Seattle, Washington.

D: He attempted to stow away on Air Force One.

Answer: B. Boll challenged his harshest critics to face him in a Las Vegas boxing match. It was originally stated the resulting footage of Boll beating the crap out of his critics would be included in *Postal* (2008), but it ultimately ended up only as a bonus feature on the DVD release.

AN AMERICAN CAROL
Mpower Pictures, 2008

226

PRODUCERS Diane Hendricks and Myrna Sokoloff (executive producers), Stephen McEveety, John Shepherd, and David Zucker (producers)

WRITERS David Zucker, Lewis Friedman, and Myrna Sokoloff

DIRECTOR David Zucker

STARS Kevin Farley (*Michael Malone*), Kelsey Grammer (*General Patton*), Robert Davi (*Aziz*), Geoffrey Arend (*Mohammed*), Serdar Kalsin (*Ahmed*), Chriss Anglin (*John F. Kennedy*), Trace Adkins (*Death*), and Jon Voigt (*George Washington*)

Left-wing, America-hating, self-absorbed filmmaker Michael Malone (Farley) starts a movement to outlaw the Fourth of July. He attracts the attention of Taliban terrorist leader Aziz (Davi), who under the pretense of funding Malone's first feature film, wants to use him to stage a massive Fourth of July suicide bombing attack. The spirits of great American leaders General George S. Patton (Grammer), George Washington (Voigt), and John F. Kennedy (Anglin) visit him in dreams in an attempt to change his heart toward love of his country.

Why It Sucks

David Zucker and his co-creators got so wrapped up in this diatribe against liberal Hollywood that they forgot to take their script past the draft. The film consists of little more than half-baked insults directed at Michael Moore and other left-wingers that are passed off as jokes. The script doesn't even adhere to the structure of *A Christmas Carol*, (something pretty big in a film titled *An American Carol*). Unlike Scrooge, who had a change of heart and started using his wealth and power for good once he returned firmly to the real world, Malone apparently remains in the dreamworld of truth-revealing ghosts, making his transformation meaningless.

The Crappies

The Worst Script Award goes to . . . David Zucker, Lewis Friedman, and Myrna Sokoloff for either being so lazy or incompetent that they couldn't figure out how to properly template their film with *A Christmas Carol.*

And the Worst Actor Award goes to . . . Dennis Hopper for his cameo role as a gun-toting, judge-fighting, mindless ACLU zombie. His performance is so flat and uninspired that he makes the already bad dialogue seem even worse.

They Really Said It!

Mohammed: It is getting harder to recruit suicide bombers, and all the really good ones are gone.

Betcha Didn't Know

» In an article on the *Los Angeles Times* website the day the film opened, David Zucker was quoted as saying the producers chose not to have the film screened for critics since it wouldn't get a fair shake because of its political message.

» The working title of the film was *Big Fat Important Movie*.

 Trivia Quiz

Who Wrote *A Christmas Carol*, the literary classic this film is sloppily modeled after?

A: Bram Stoker

B: Mark Twain

C: Charles Dickens

D: Emily Brontë

Answer: C. Charles Dickens's classic tale was published in 1843.

THE ASTRO-ZOMBIES (AKA *"THE SPACE VAMPIRES"*)
Ram Ltd., 1968

PRODUCERS Kenneth Altose and Wayne Rogers (executive producers), Ted V. Mikels (producer)

WRITERS Wayne Rogers and Ted V. Mikels

DIRECTOR Ted V. Mikels

STARS Wendell Corey (*Holman*), John Carradine (*Dr. DeMarco*), Joan Patrick (*Janine Norwalk*), Tura Satana (*Satana*), and Rafael Campos (*Juan*)

A disgraced NASA researcher (Carradine) trying to create the perfect astronaut uses dead bodies, hi-tech, and radio waves. He also employs the brain of a homicidal maniac for one of this cre-

Test Your Stamina

ations, and (surprise!) it runs amok. A sinister Mexican spy ring dispatches sultry psycho Satana (Satana) to secure the zombie for their use as a super-soldier. Meanwhile, the Astro-Zombie is stalking a beautiful nurse (Patrick) . . . .

Why It Sucks

The Astro-Zombies mixes all sorts of genres into a wild B movie stew. It offers action, spy versus spy intrigue, blood and guts . . . everything but competent filmmaking. A weak script, bland camerawork, flat direction, and an excess of padding make this film excruciating, despite all the plots and subplots and characters crammed into it.

Carradine putters around his lab for what seems like hours. There are long stretches of badly delivered expository dialogue. And then we're back to Carradine puttering.

Thumbs Down: 🎀 🎀 🎀 🎀

The Crappies

The Worst Auteur Award goes to . . . Ted V. Mikels for not having the sense to make a movie that fit the length of the material. Nothing sends an already borderline effort into the Suck Zone like stretching it to fit a particular running time.

And the Worst Title Design Award goes to . . . Ted V. Mikels for the not-so-thrilling opening credits sequence. Battling toy robots. I mean, come on!

They Really Said It!

Satana: There's a certain look men get just before they die.

Betcha Didn't Know

» Cowriter and executive producer Wayne Rogers starred as Trapper John on the television series *M.A.S.H.*

» Ted V. Mikels wrote and directed a sequel to *The Astro-Zombies* in 2002 titled *Mark of the Astro-Zombies*. This sequel is *not* an improvement on the original.

Trivia Quiz

Who played Dr. DeMarco in *Mark of the Astro-Zombies* (2002)?

A: John Carradine

B: Wayne Rogers

C: Ted V. Mikels

D: Robert James Taylor

Answer: D. Robert James Taylor took over the role originally played by John Carradine. The latter had died in 1988. Taylor actually attempted to imitate Carradine's voice, which was remarkably unsuccessful.

BACK FROM HELL (AKA *"DEMON APOCALYPSE"*)

Kashmir Motion Pictures, 1993

PRODUCERS Brian E. Morey (executive producer) and Matt Jaissle (producer)

WRITER Matt Jaissle

DIRECTOR Matt Jaissle

STARS Shawn Scarbrough (*Father Aaron*), Larry DuBois (*Jack*), Don Ruem (*Satan*), and Matt Hundley (*Azzagras, High Priest of Satan*)

Jack (DuBois), an actor who sold his soul for Hollywood stardom, renegs on the deal with Satan (Ruem) and finds himself under the effects of a terrible curse. He turns to his childhood friend, Aaron (Scarbrough), now a priest, hoping not only to free himself from the curse, but also to stop the coming demonic conquest of the world.

Why It Sucks

Back From Hell features a good idea—an actor who is cursed to inspire homicidal rage in anyone who looks into his eyes—but that's watered down by the addition of an insipid "demons are going to conquer the world" storyline. And then there's the badly written dialogue delivered by actors who are outstanding in their lack of talent. Larry DuBois would barely be believable as a porn star, let alone a Hollywood leading man. The music sounds like it was stolen from the garbage cans outside John Carpenter's office.

Thumbs Down: 🐕🐕🐕🐕🐕

The Crappies

The Worst Cinematography Award goes to . . . Matt Jaissle for failing to realize that camera angles are important when filming stage fighting. As it is, the actors look like they're eleven-year-olds playing in the backyard.

And the Worst Sound Editing Award goes to . . . Matt Jaissle for such poor Foley work and mixing that he might have set a new low for filmmaking, surpassing even *Heaven's Gate*.

They Really Said It!

Father Aaron: Tell Satan I said, "Kiss my black ass!"

Betcha Didn't Know

» In 1997, Matt Jaissle won the Film of the Year Award from the Miami Horror Film Festival for *The Necro Files*. That appears to be the only year there *was* a Miami Horror Film Festival.

» This is the only film (at least the only one I can find) in which a priest is literally touched by the Bible. A demonic hand comes out of it and grabs Father Aaron's crotch.

 Trivia Quiz

What does a Foley artist do?

A: Designs the lighting of movie sets

B: Loads film into cameras

C: Creates special makeup effects

D: Engineers many of the common sounds heard in movies, such as doors opening and closing.

Answer: D. The name "Foley" comes from Jack Foley, a pioneering sound engineer who helped Universal Pictures make a hugely successful transition from silent films to talkies.

THE CASTLE OF FU MANCHU
(AKA *"ASSIGNMENT ISTANBUL"* AND *"THE TORTURE CHAMBER OF FU MANCHU"*)
Balcázar Producciones, 1969

PRODUCERS Harry Alan Towers and Jaime Jesús Balcázar

WRITERS Manfred Barthel (script and story), Peter Welbeck (dialogue, English version), and Jaime Jesús Balcázar (dialogue, Spanish version)

DIRECTOR Jess Franco

STARS Richard Greene (*Nayland Smith*), Christopher Lee (*Fu Manchu*), Howard Marion-Crawford (*Dr. Petrie*), and Tsai Chin (*Lin Tang*)

The immortal Dr. Fu Manchu (Lee) launches yet another nefarious scheme—this one involving a chemical weapon that will freeze the world's oceans solid—and only Sir Dennis Nayland Smith (Greene) can stop him. But will Sir Dennis save the audience from dying of boredom?

Why It Sucks

There's about twenty minutes worth of plot in this movie . . . and another hour of dull filler, not to mention stock footage grabbed from a couple of far better movies.

The only decent thing about it is Christopher Lee's Fu Manchu makeup and costumes. Franco was smart enough not to mess with something that worked, even if he couldn't pull off anything decent when it came to the new material.

Thumbs Down Rating: 🦃🦃🦃🦃🦃

The Crappies

The Worst Director Award goes to . . . Jess Franco for not even bothering to add sound effects to the fight scenes in post-production. The lack of meaty thwacks or sound of bodies falling to the ground emphasize the fact that it's just a bunch of grown men swinging at thin air.

And the Worst Actress Award goes to . . . Tsai Ching as Fu Manchu's daughter Lin Tang. The character's supposed to sexy, dammit! With Tsai's performance we get a sensuality-free portrayal of the character that could pass muster with the Family Research Council.

They Really Said It!

Lin Tang: Even Nayland Smith cannot touch you now, father.
Fu Manchu: I wish that he would try.

Betcha Didn't Know

» Jess Franco has directed, produced, or written films under sixty-five different confirmed pseudonyms.
» Jess Franco's two Fu Manchu films were the final serious movies to feature Sax Rohmer's creation.

 Trivia Quiz

Who was Arthur Sarsfield Ward?

A: Fu Manchu's most dedicated adversary after Dennis Nayland Smith

B: The creator of Fu Manchu

C: The first actor to portray Fu Manchu on film

D: The first victim killed by Fu Manchu in the novel *The Trail of Fu Manchu*

Answer: B. Ward was a prolific British author who wrote under the name Sax Rohmer.

THE DEAD TALK BACK
Headliner Productions, 1993

PRODUCER Merle S. Gould

WRITER Merle S. Gould

DIRECTOR Merle S. Gould

STARS Aldo Farnese (*Henry Krasker*), Scott Douglas (*Lt. Lewis*), and Laura Brock (*Renee Coliveil*)

When a young woman (Brock) is murdered by a stalker with a crossbow, Lt. Lewis of Homicide (Douglas) turns to unorthodox criminologist/psychic researcher/creepy science dweeb Henry Krasker (Farnese) for help in cracking the case. How will the Boy Wonder do it? With his radio set that picks up signals from the Afterlife, of course!

Why It Sucks
A rooming house full of bizarre possible suspects, an unusual detective, and a suitably twisted solution to the case . . . *The Dead Talk Back* could have been a fun, quirky mystery film. But then it went in for bad acting, inept direction, shoddy camera-work, badly done lighting, and horrendous editing. Even a second draft on the script would have helped.

Thumbs Down Rating: 👎 👎 👎 👎

The Crappies
The Worst Script Award goes to . . . Merle S. Gould for his attempts to infuse the film with a "hardboiled detective" that are so overblown they ruin what could have been a cool murder scene.
And the You Made James Randi Cry Award goes to . . . Merle S. Gould for conceiving an experiment in otherworldly communication that involves a speaker, some wire, a wineglass, and a razor blade.

They Really Said It!
Renee: Oh shut up, you potentate of righteousness.

Betcha Didn't Know

» Although completed in 1957, this film wasn't seen by the public until 1993 when Sinister Cinema acquired the rights to distribute the film on home video from Headliner Productions.

» *Ghost Whisperer*, a popular television drama in which Jennifer Love Hewitt talks to dead people, employs real-world psychics as consultants.

 Trivia Quiz

What was Aldo Farnese best known for?

A: Inventing television

B: Producing and hosting children's television programming

C: Investigating the death of Marilyn Monroe

D: Creating a real-life, highly successful paranormal research institute

Answer: B. During the 1960s, Farnese created, produced, and hosted children's programming that was broadcast in the Philadelphia and Boston areas.

THE EVIL BRAIN FROM OUTER SPACE
Fuji Eiga/Shintoho, 1965

PRODUCERS Kazuya Hamana, Yashushi Kotani (executive producers), Takashige Ichise (producer)

WRITER Ichiro Miyagawa

DIRECTORS Koreyoshi Akasaka, Akira Mitsuwa, and Teruo Ishii

STARS Ken Utusi (*Starman*), Junko Ikeuchi (*Minako Yamada*), Shoji Nakayama (*Kan Hayashi*), and Minoru Takada (*Utako Mitsuya*)

Starman (the Japanese answer to Superman) defends Earth from the disembodied alien brain of Balazar, his murderous mutant minions, and an omniscient narrator who tells viewers what's about to happen in the scene that's coming up.

Test Your Stamina

Why It Sucks

Yaaaaawwwwn! Repetitive, overlong, tedious—are there any other words like that? What potential excitement isn't leeched away by the lame fight scenes is destroyed by the narrator who time and again tells us what we're about to watch until you want to jump through the screen and throttle him.

Thumbs Down Rating: 👎👎👎👎

The Crappies

The Worst Costume Design goes to . . . Whoever decided everyone in the movie should wear sinister hats and trenchcoats, whether they are plain-clothes police or the evil mutants!

And the Worst Script Award goes to . . . Ichiro Miyagawa and/or the anonymous translator who outfitted the film with a narrator who spoils any plot twists or drama.

They Really Said It!

Omniscient Narrator: So powerful was Balazar's genius that as he lay dying, his brain ordered built a mechanism, which would keep it alive even though his body was destroyed. And now Balazar's Brain seeks universal conquest!

Betcha Didn't Know

» Starman's Japanese name translates into English as Super Giant. (Good thing he got renamed, because he's not particularly super nor is he much of a giant.)

» Ken Utusi has been appearing on television and in movies for over fifty years. He hated the role as Starman, and refuses to talk about it to this day.

 Trivia Quiz

From what does Starman get many of his amazing powers?

A: The Aerometer, the fin on his hood that lets him fly, transmit thoughts telepathically, and receive TV transmissions

B: The Globemeter, the watch on his wrist that lets him fly through space, detect radioactivity, and comprehend all languages on Earth

C: The Galactic Capelette that lets him fly through space, gives him invulnerability, and lets him impersonate any one of the Three Musketeers at will

D: Boots of the Stars, which give him invulnerability and the ability to literally leap from planet to planet (or just tall buildings in a single bound).

Answer: B. The Globemeter is almost as good as the Latest Smart Phone!

FREDDY GOT FINGERED
Regency Enterprises, 2001

PRODUCERS Arnon Milchan (executive producer), Larry Brezner, Howard Lapides, and Lauren Lloyd (producers)

WRITERS Tom Green and Derek Harvie

DIRECTOR Tom Green

STARS Tom Green (*Gordy Brody*) Marisa Coughlan (*Betty*), Rip Torn (*Jim Brody*), and Eddie Kaye Thomas (*Freddy Brody*)

Gordy (Green) is forced to move back in with his parents after losing his job. When his parents demand he leave to find new work, he starts spreading rumors that his father (Torn) sexually abused his brother Freddy.

Why It Sucks

Ambush comedian Tom Green succeeded in making an entirely unfunny comedy. It's hard to say what anyone involved in this cinematic cow pat was thinking . . . if they were. The attempt to stretch brief sketch ideas where Green tormented his real parents for amusement results in a film about a completely unlikeable character who destroys his family with false accusations for no reason other than he's a jerk. The supporting cast isn't much better, although one can admire Rip Torn's character for not simply murdering his son to spare himself and the world anymore misery.

Thumbs Down Rating: 🦃 🦃 🦃 🦃 🦃

The Crappies

The Worst Directing Award goes to . . . Tom Green, for proving, yet again, that a comedy sketch can't bear the weight of a feature film.

And the Worst Acting Award goes to . . . Tom Green for his obnoxious signature character who is onscreen for virtually the entire eighty-seven-minute running time of the picture.

They Really Said It!

Betty: You got a problem with my legs?

Jim: No, you got a problem with your legs. It's that or you're just lazy.

Betcha Didn't Know

» With a production budget of $15 million, *Freddy Got Fingered* barely managed to break even during it U.S. theatrical run.

» The film was originally rated NC-17, and Green had to go back to the editing room to tone it down to get an R rating.

 Trivia Quiz

What star of *Freddy Got Fingered* sued Dennis Hopper for defamation of character and won?

A: Tom Green

B: Marisa Coughlan

C: Eddie Kaye Thomas

D: Rip Torn

Answer: D. Hopper claimed, in an appearance on *The Tonight Show*, that Torn had pulled a knife on him during preproduction of *Easy Rider*. Torn sued, won, and Hopper was ordered to pay $1.5 million.

FUTURE FORCE
Action International Pictures, 1989

PRODUCER Kimberley Casey

WRITERS Thomas Baldwin and David A. Prior

DIRECTOR David A. Prior

STARS David Carradine (*John Tucker*), Anna Rapagna (*Marion Sims*), D. C. Douglas (*Billy Parke*), William Zipp (*Jason Adams*), and Robert Tessier (*Becker*)

In the near future, John Tucker (Carradine) is the top officer of C.O.P.S, a privatized police force that's little more than an elaborate bounty-hunting service. When he refuses to kill a television reporter who claims she can expose corruption within the police force (Rapagna), he is targeted for death by his boss (Zipp).

Why It Sucks

The film was conceived and shot in 1989, but the future looks like 1978. The one exception to that is the dippy self-propelled flying robotic gauntlet that fires laser beams and is kept in a remote-controlled toolbox in the back of David Carradine's car.

Thumbs Down Rating: 🦃🦃🦃🦃

The Crappies

The Most Incompetent Futurist Award goes to . . . Thomas Baldwin and David A. Prior for conceiving something so illogical as the flying, laser-beam shooting gauntlet (and the remotely activated toolbox it is kept in).

And the Worst Costume Design Award goes to . . . The anonymous person (possibly Erica Nedly) who decided police uniforms of the future are jeans and jean vests.

They Really Said It!

John Tucker: You have committed a crime. You are presumed guilty until proven innocent. You have the right to die. If you

Test Your Stamina

choose to relinquish that right, you will be placed under arrest and imprisoned.

Betcha Didn't Know

» David Carradine died in a Bangkok hotel room in 2009, the victim of auto-erotic aphyxiation gone bad or assassination by a shadowy cult of martial artists protecting their secrets. (Seriously. I can't make stuff like this up.)

» This film was successful enough to spawn a sequel (*Future Zone*) that features time travel and is even more illogical than this one.

Trivia Quiz

John Tucker sports a red hand on the back of his vest and his house robe. What other character portrayed by David Carradine wore that same symbol?

A: Bill (in *Kill Bill*)

B: Kwai Chang Caine (in *Kung Fu*)

C: Frankenstein (in *Death Race 2000*)

D: Rawley Wilkes (in *Lone Wolf McQuade*)

Answer: B. Carradine played the wandering kung fu master and restless man of peace in two television series and two made-for-TV movies.

GRAVEYARD OF HORROR (AKA *"NECROPHAGUS"* AND *"THE BUTCHER OF BINBROOK"*)
FISA, 1971

PRODUCER Tony Recoder

WRITER Michael Skaife (aka Miguel Madrid)

DIRECTOR Michael Skaife (aka Miguel Madrid)

STARS Bill Curran (*Michael Sherrington*), Frank Braña (*Dr. Lexter*), Titania Clement (*Lilith*), and Beatriz Lacy (*Margaret*)

When Michael (Curran) sets out to uncover the mystery surrounding the death of his wife, he comes into conflict with her evil, crazy sisters, a bizarre grave-robbing cult, and the lizard-monster they serve.

Why It Sucks

It's a mishmash of badly connected plot-threads that add up to incoherent nonsense. Like all bad movies you'll keep watching it to see whether it can get any worse. In that respect, *Graveyard of Horror* doesn't disappoint. It goes from a limp gothic horror to a lame monster movie at a rapid pace.

Thumbs Down Rating: 👎 👎 👎 👎

The Crappies

The Worst Movie Monster Award goes to . . . The rubber-faced, gratuitous lizard creature, which serves next to no purpose in the overall story (except to have a movie with a lizard creature).
And the Worst Director Award goes to . . . Miguel Madrid for a five-minute montage of flashback clips that serves no purpose other than to remind us what a great director he is . . . or maybe just pad out the running time.

They Really Said It!

Lilith: I think I'll take a bath in perfume.

Betcha Didn't Know

» Bill Curran left the movie business at the end of the 1970s but resurfaced in 2005, playing the part of a dead body in the sci-fi thriller *Into the Maelstrom*.
» "Necrophagus" describes a creature that feeds on carrion.

 Trivia Quiz
Who was cinema's first mad scientist?
A: Dr. Jekyll
B: Dr. Frankenstein
C: Dr. Caligari
D: Dr. Kildare

Test Your Stamina

Answer: B. Dr. Frankenstein first appeared in the 1910 silent adaptation of Mary Shelley's novel.

HOBGOBLINS

Rick Sloane Productions, 1988

PRODUCER Rick Sloane

WRITER Rick Sloane

DIRECTOR Rick Sloane

STARS Tom Bartlett (*Kevin*), Paige Sullivan (*Amy*), and Jeffrey Culver (*McCreedy*)

When the world's most incompetent night watchman allows a group of diminutive, furry aliens to escape from the film vault of a bankrupt studio, it's up to security guard trainee Kevin (Bartlett) to capture or kill the creatures before the sun rises and they kill everyone in the city.

Why It Sucks

The only thing worse than the lame puppetry of the creatures is the performances of the actors. In the 1980s, *Gremlins* started a trend of "small killer creatures" (continued in the Chucky movies). Maybe the makers of this film thought they were spoofing those movies. Or maybe this was an honest attempt at making a humorous horror movie. In either case, *Hobgoblins* fails completely.

Thumbs Down Rating: 👎👎👎👎👎

The Crappies

The Special Edward D Wood Jr. Memorial Award goes to . . . Rick Sloan for using so much stock footage in the picture that one might think it was a demo reel.

And the Worst Actor Award goes to . . . Tim Bartlett for his role as Kevin, which he played with about the same degree of animation as one of the puppets.

They Really Said It!

McCreedy: All my work! Thirty years I have tried to prevent this from happening!

Betcha Didn't Know

» Since the turn of the century, two different DVD editions of *Hobgoblins* have been issued, one of them a twentieth anniversary special edition of the film.

» Rick Sloane's sequel to this film was released in 2009. He once again wrote, produced, and directed and demonstrated that his filmmaking skills haven't improved in twenty years.

 Trivia Quiz

What prolific B movie director/producer has made tiny terrors a signature element of his movies?

A: Roger Corman

B: Charles Band

C: Val Lewton

D: William Castle

Answer: B. If you've been reading this book carefully, you know it's Charles Band. Starting with *Dolls*, he's made dozens of movies featuring small creatures creating big mayhem.

THE ISLE OF THE SNAKE PEOPLE (AKA *"SNAKE PEOPLE"* AND *"ISLAND OF THE DEAD"*)
Azteca Films/Columbia Pictures, 1971

PRODUCERS Juan Ibáñez and Henry Verg

WRITER Jack Hill

DIRECTORS Juan Ibáñez and Jack Hill

STARS Ralph Bertrand (*Capt. Pierre Labesch*), Charles East (*Lt. Andrew Wilhelm*), Boris Karloff (*Carl van Molder*), Julissa (*Anabella Vandenberg*), Santanón (*Dwarf*), and Tongolele (*Kalea*)

When a new police captain (Bertrand) arrives on a small Caribbean island, he vows to break up the local voodoo cult. Can one honest cop hope to defeat a cult specializing in zombie sluts and

Test Your Stamina

244

led by a crazed, top-hat-wearing dwarf (Santanón), a voodoo priestess who looks like an exotic dancer (Tongolele), and a mysterious masked man who can't *possibly* be the eccentric plantation owner, Van Molder (Karloff)?

Why It Sucks

Even the great Boris Karloff—who ended a long career on this embarrassing note—can't make this movie work. The scantily clad belly-dancer voodoo priestess might have helped if she had acted with a bag over her head, because it would have hidden her vacant, burned-out sex-worker expression. But none of that saves any scene, even the most frightening, from fizzling. No one involved with the production seems to have known how to properly *end* a scene.

Thumbs Down Rating: 👎👎👎👎

The Crappies

The Worst Picture Award goes to . . . Producers Juan Ibáñez and Henry Verg. If they'd trimmed the film by about twenty-five minutes and titled it *Night of the Flesh-Eating Zombie Sluts*, they might have had a hit on their hands.

And the Worst Actress Award goes to . . . Tongolele for infusing her portrayal of a voodoo priestess with a vacant "I've been in this business too long and it's sucked out my soul" stripper/sex industry worker attitude.

They Really Said It!

Anabella: Modern science has shown that alcohol is responsible for ninety-nine point two percent of all the world's sins.

Betcha Didn't Know

» Although filmed primarily in Mexico, all of Boris Karloff's scenes were shot on sets in Los Angeles.
» Jack Hill, director of the scenes filmed in America, worked on several pictures directed by Roger Corman.

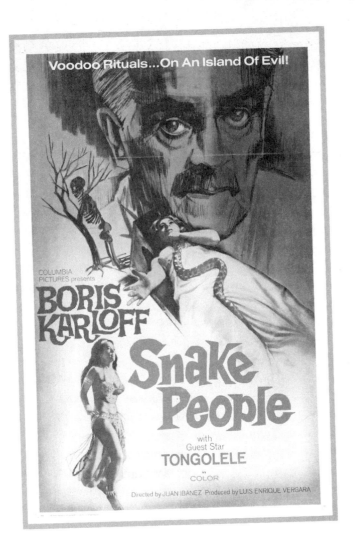

 Trivia Quiz

What celebrated actor did Jack Hill label as "terrible" after working with him on a film?

A: William Powell

B: Jack Nicholson

C: Boris Karloff

D: Cary Grant

Answer: B. Hill has stated that he was underwhelmed by Nicholson's performance in Roger Corman's *The Terror*. He later re-evaluated his opinion.

THE KILLER EYE
Full Moon Entertainment, 1999

PRODUCER Charles Band (executive producer) and Richard Chasen (producer)

WRITERS Benjamin Carr, Rolf Kanefsky, and Matthew Jason Walsh

DIRECTOR Richard Chasen

STARS Jonathan Norman (*Dr. Jordan Grady*), Jacqueline Lovell (*Rita Grady*), Costas Koromilas (*Morton*), Blake Bailey (*Creepy Bill*), Dave Oren Ward (*Tom*), and Nanette Bianchi (*Jane*)

Dr. Grady (Norman) has discovered a way to look into the Eighth Dimension using eye drops and a special inter-dimensional microscope. Unfortunately, a creature from that nightmarish realm has crossed into our world, possessed the eyeball of a male prostitute, and grown it to gigantic size . . . and it is now roaming Dr. Grady's building, seeking women to hypnotize and fondle with its tentacles (and what, you may ask, is a giant eyeball doing with tentacles? You've got me).

Why It Sucks

Well, the cameraman kept each shot in focus. I suppose that's one positive thing about the movie. For the rest, it's an unsexy soft-core porn flick, an unscary horror film, and an unfunny comedy. Nothing works in this picture, from the poorly structured story to the sparsely decorated sets. Even the actors suck in comparison to performances they gave in *Head of the Family* and *Hideous!*

Thumbs Down Rating: 🖓🖓🖓🖓🖓

The Crappies

The Worst Director Award goes to . . . Richard Chasen. Why film nude scenes if you're going to be a prude about it?

And the Worst Monster Award goes to . . . The Killer Eye, which looks like a beach ball that someone took a paint brush to. Unconfirmed rumors hold that the eye went onto co-star with Ben Stein in commercials for Clear Eyes-brand eye drops.

They Really Said It!

Tom: You killed my friend, you stupid bitch!

Betcha Didn't Know

» Richard Chasen is a pseudonym of David DeCoteau, and Robert Talbot is once again the name assumed by Charles Band.

» This was the last film role for actor Blake Bailey.

 Trivia Quiz

Who starred in the American remake of a Japanese horror movie about an eyeball possessed by the powers of evil?

A: Jennifer Love Hewitt

B: Sarah Michelle Gellar

C: Jessica Alba

D: Lindsay Lohan

Answer: C. Alba's *The Eye* (2008) was a remake of a 2002 Japanese horror film that has, to date, spawned two sequels. There must be a lot of evil eyeballs out there.

LASER MISSION (AKA *"SOLDIER OF FORTUNE"*)
Azimuth, 1989

PRODUCER Hans Kühle

WRITERS David A. Frank and Phillip Gutteridge

DIRECTOR Beau Davis

STARS Brandon Lee (*Michael Gold*), Ernest Borgnine (*Dr. Braun*), Debi Monahan (*Alissa*), and Graham Clarke (*Col. Kalishnakov*)

It's the final decade of the Cold War. Michael (Lee) is hired by the CIA to extract a brilliant scientist (Borgnine) from a facility being guarded by incompetent Cubans in Angola. At stake: Laser weapons that can tip the balance of power.

Test Your Stamina

Why It Sucks

How many viewers remember that Cuba had a significant military presence in Angola during the Cold War? How many care? The action scenes are lame, and the "humor" would embarrass a group of fourth graders.

Thumbs Down Rating: 🐟🐟🐟🐟

The Crappies

The Worst Stunt Coordinator Award goes to . . . Paul Siebert for the fight scenes. Kids playing Cops and Robbers would seem more convincing.

And the Worst Director Award goes to . . . Beau Davis for casting Ernest Borgnine as a brilliant Russian scientist. *Ernest Borgnine?!* Please!

They Really Said It!

Michael Gold: I never put price tags on women. It's much more fun taking them off.

Betcha Didn't Know

» Ernest Borgnine won a Best Actor Academy Award in 1955 for his starring role in *Marty.*

» Director Beau Davis (better known as BJ Davis) is a lifetime Boy Scout, having earned forty-three merit badgets. He has also worked extensiely in movies as a stuntman, stunt coordinator, director, and producer.

 Trivia Quiz

How did Brandon Lee die?

A: He was shot by jealous girlfriend.

B: He was in an accident while filming his last movie.

C: He overdosed.

D: He was in a plane crash.

Test Your Stamina

Answer: B. Lee was shot in the back while filming *The Crow* after the crew misloaded a prop gun because they failed to consult the film's weapons coordinator.

MANIAC (AKA *"SEX MANIAC"*)

Roadshow Attractions, 1934

PRODUCERS Dwain Esper, Louis Sonney, and Hildegarde Stadie

WRITERS Hildegarde Stadie (script), Edgar Allan Poe (original story)

DIRECTOR Dwain Esper

STARS Bill Woods (*Don Maxwell*), Horace B. Carpenter (*Dr. Meirschultz*), Ted Edwards (*Buckley*), Phyllis Diller (*Mrs. Buckley*), and Thea Ramsey (*Alice Maxwell*)

Don (Woods), an actor turned mad doctor's assistant, kills his boss (Carpenter) and then impersonates the doctor to cover up the crime. Things get weirder from there, including eyeball eating and zombie rape.

Why It Sucks

Here's another film supposedly based on Edgar Allan Poe's "The Black Cat" that bears next to no resemblence to the source material—except perhaps in showing a man's descent into madness. It's been more than seventy-five years since this film was unleashed upon an unsuspecting audience, and parts of it still remain startling and appalling. Of course, Esper was looking for an excuse to show the girls in their undies. The film exists to shock and outrage. It's what Esper and his creative and marital partner did with their movies.

Thumbs Down Rating: 🖓🖓🖓🖓

The Crappies

The Worst Picture Award goes to . . . Dwaine Esper and Hildegards Stadie for making a movie that just wants to provoke an extreme reaction. That was Esper's specialty, and he went no-holds barred for this one. The eyeball eating and zombie rape is as gross and pointless now as it was in 1934.

The Worst Actor Award goes to . . . Bill Woods, who gives hams a bad name.

Test Your Stamina

They Really Said It!

Don Maxwell: I think too much of Satan to use cats as experiments.

Betcha Didn't Know

» Dwain Esper handled the distribution of this picture himself, personally taking prints from town to town, theater to theater. He used this same method when he acquired the distribution rights to MGM's controversial 1932 horror film *Freaks*, helping to earn it its legendary reputation and possibly saving it from oblivion.

» Dwain Esper and Hildegarde Stadie married in 1920. They remained faithful to each other until his death in 1982 and raised two children together. This goes to show that one can't make judgments about the people behind the movies based solely on their movies.

 Trivia Quiz

Which of the following was not a movie produced by Dwain Esper?

A: *Reefer Madness*

B: *Sex Madness*

C: *How to Take a Bath*

D: *The Nun's Habit*

Answer: D. Surprisingly, no one seems to have made a movie titled *The Nun's Habit*. I can think of three or four awful films that are lurking behind a title like that.

MONSTER A-GO-GO
BI & L Releasing Corp., 1965

PRODUCERS Sheldon S. Seymore and Bill Rebane

WRITERS Jeff Smith, Dok Stanford, and Bill Rebane

DIRECTORS Bill Rebane and Herschell Gordon Lewis

STARS Phil Morton (*Col. Steve Connors*), June Travis (*Ruth*), and Henry Hite (*Frank Douglas/the Monster*)

In the wake of a space mission gone wrong, an astronaut (Hite) transforms into a ten-foot-tall rampaging beast that menaces a freeway underpass and an apparently deserted countryside. Or does he?

Why It Sucks

Schlock movie producer Herschell Gordon Lewis bought an unfinished, failed movie and finished it with almost inconceivable incompetence. He stuck in a narrator who either explains the blindingly obvious or rambles incoherently; characters who vanish halfway through the film because the cast couldn't be reassembled; and an ending that is so astoundingly lame that it renders this already crappy movie the textbook definition of pointless.

"THIS PICTURE COULD SET OUR SPACE PROGRAM BACK AT LEAST FIFTY YEARS!"
—N.A.S.A.

MONSTER A GO-GO!

(the picture that comes complete with a 10-foot-tall monster, to give you the wim-wams!)

starring
PHIL MORTON
JUNE TRAVIS

AN ASTRONAUT WENT UP—
A "GUESS-WHAT"
CAME DOWN!

RELEASED BY B I & L RELEASING CORP.

Thumbs Down Rating: 🎀🎀🎀🎀🎀

The Crappies

The Lifetime Achievement Award for Awful Writing goes to . . .
Whoever came up with the movie's ending, most likely Herschell
Gordon Lewis. It either relegates everything that went before to
the status of a hallucination or suggests that an exact duplicate of
the astronaut was the rampaging monster. On the whole, the hallucination makes a bit more sense.

And the Rock and a Hard Place Award goes to . . . Herschell Gordon Lewis for finding the worse possible solution to the problem
of finishing a movie after the cast has moved on and there is no
money to hire them back.

They Really Said It!

Narrator: With the telegram, one cloud lifts and another descends.

Betcha Didn't Know

» This was the directorial debut of Bill Rebane, a filmmaker who
  spent the majority of his career making movies in Wisconsin
  and Minnesota.
» Herschell Gordon Lewis leaped safely from the film industry
  as it crashed onto financial rocks during the 1970s, going on
  to a successful career in advertising. He has in recent years
  returned to script writing and directing, with *Grim Fairy Tale*
  in 2010.

 Trivia Quiz

**When Lewis was able to get back one of the original actors
in the film in order to finish it, the man had changed his
physical appearance. Lewis dealt with this by:**

A: Making the actor undergo plastic surgery to restore his original
looks

B: Immediately firing the actor and hiring someone else to take
his place

C: Having the actor play the brother of his initial character

D: Shooting the actor entirely from behind

Test Your Stamina

Answer: C. Since Lewis was into saving money at all costs, it seemed the easiest way to go.

NIGHT CRAWLERS

Intercoast Productions/Polonia Bros. Entertainment, 1996

PRODUCER Albert Z. White

WRITER Charles Hank

DIRECTORS Mark Polonia and John Polonia

STARS Mark Polonia (*Tom*), Maria Russo (*May*), and Armond Sposto (*Adam*)

A young couple (Polonia and Russo) buys a fully furnished house for a ludicrously low price. Shortly after they move in, they discover why: monsters are tunneling into the town's basements and eating the occupants.

Why It Sucks

Watching this movie you can feel the earnestness of the people involved. Everyone really, *really* wanted to make a great movie. However . . .

The monster is so badly made that it's obvious that its claws are coat hangers, its body is a football, and its head is a papier-mâché blob with egg-carton eyes and magic-marker-drawn pupils. And then the Brothers Polonia treat the audience to long, loving scenes of their badly made and badly animated creature.

Thumbs Down Rating: 👎👎👎👎👎

The Crappies

The Worst Directors Award goes to . . . Mark Polonia and John Polonia for this, their third feature, which might have earned a high schooler a low C if it had been a class project.

And the Worst Special-Effects Award goes to . . . Phil Ogden and Joel Torris for the supposed tunnel dug in the wall by the Night Crawler—it's a piece of cardboard with a badly painted "hole" on it.

They Really Said It!

The Night Crawler: [Unintelligible]. (Given the level of dialogue in the rest of the film, it's a blessing.)

Test Your Stamina

Betcha Didn't Know

» This was the fifth film directed by Mark Polonia, so he had no excuse.

» Mark and John Polonia were twin brothers who worked together on some twenty low-budget films between 1987 and 2008.

 Trivia Quiz

Who gave the Polonia brothers an Independent Film Lifetime Achievement Award?

A: Director Bill Rebane

B: Actress Jacqueline Lovell

C: Director Jess Franco

D: Actor Brice Kennedy

Answer: D. Kennedy acted in nine of the brothers' films and gave them a special award during a surprise birthday party. If passion translated to talent, they and Ed Wood would be as celebrated as Orson Welles.

THE NIGHT EVELYN CAME OUT OF THE GRAVE
Phoenix Cinematografica, 1971

PRODUCER Antonio Sarno

WRITERS Massimo Felisatti, Fabio Pittorru, and Emilio Miraglia

DIRECTOR Emilio Miraglia

STARS Anthony Steffen (*Lord Alan Cunningham*), Marina Malfatti (*Gladys Cunningham*), Erika Blanc (*Susie*), and Giacomo Rossi-Stuart (*Dr. Richard Timberlane*)

A nobleman (Steffen) is released from an insane asylum . . . only to find himself haunted by the ghost of his dead wife. Will he end up back in the booby-hatch, or will the secret behind her restless spirit be uncovered in time to save him?

Why It Sucks

The protagonist of the film, Lord Cunningham, is a wealthy, masochistic serial killer who gets his rocks off by picking up hookers and torturing them to death in his estate. The creators of this travesty obviously think the viewer should feel sympathy for this reptile. Worse, the "surprising twist" about the ghost was a tired cliché forty years ago.

Thumbs Down Rating: 🖓 🖓 🖓 🖓

The Crappies

The Worst Director Award goes to . . . Emilio Miraglia for making a movie about which nothing positive can be said except "Erika Blanc is easy on the eyes."

And the Worst Writer Award goes to . . . Massimo Felisatti, Fabio Pittorru, and Emilio Miraglia for creating a collection of completely unlikeable characters and for ending their story with attempts at twists that are so lame and goofy that one has to wonder if anyone bothered to read the finished script.

Betcha Didn't Know

» This Z-grade picture spawned a highly acclaimed poster.

» Emilio Miraglia worked on roughly a dozen Italian films in a variety of behind-the-camera jobs before leaving the business in the mid-1970s. This film and *The Red Queen Kills Seven Times* were his biggest successes.

They Really Said It!

Lord Cunningham: It's not unusual for a man to do strange things for kicks.

 Trivia Quiz

Critics and fans refer to violent mystery films like *The Night Evelyn Came Out of the Grave* as "giallo pictures." Where did the term originate?

A: With the first director who made such a film, Mario Giallo

B: A series of cheap paperback mystery novel adaptations which served as the beginning of the subgenre these films represent, books that were known for their yellow cover designs. *Giallo* is Italian for "yellow"

C: The title of an early violent Italian mystery movie

D: American film critic Roger Ebert, describing his squeamishness for movie violence to an Italian newspaper, in which he stated "I'm yellow . . . giallo"

Answer: B. These books were first published in 1929, but the term was used of a certain kind of mystery movie starting in the early 1960s.

NINJA PHANTOM HEROES (AKA *"NINJA EMPIRE"*)
Filmark International, 1987

PRODUCERS Godfrey Ho and Thomas Tang

WRITER Duncan Bauer

DIRECTOR Bruce Lambert

STARS Glen Carson (Ford), George Dickson (George), Bruce Lambert (Bruce), Dinny Yip (Alan), and Christine Wells (Christine)

A Hong Kong crime syndicate and an Evil Ninja Cult become embroiled in a turf war over who gets to sell illegal arms to the Arabs. A Good Ninja (Carson) and his girl sidekick (Wells), in the employ of the CIA, are tasked with putting a stop to all the arms-dealing shenanigans.

Why It Sucks

Ninja Phantom Heroes is an incoherent patchwork of a movie, cobbled together from scenes of a boring gangster/romance film and footage of grown men embarrassing themselves in ninja outfits. This is the worst of Godfrey Ho's efforts. The plotline involving two American ninjas, once good friends but now deadly enemies, is lame even by Ho standards.

Thumbs Down Rating: 🦃🦃🦃🦃

Test Your Stamina

The Crappies

The Worst Film Award goes to . . . Godrey Ho for taking a dead project with too many characters in its story and adding a bunch of ninja nonsense.

And the Worst Acting Award goes to . . . Everyone who dubbed voices for this picture. It's rare to hear voices acting as devoid of talent as we experience here.

They Really Said It!

Glen: Now that we've exposed ourselves, we must be extra careful.

Betcha Didn't Know

» "Bruce Lambert" is one of forty different confirmed pseudonyms used by producer/director Godfrey Ho. The Bruce Lambert actor who appears in this film may be the *real* Bruce Lambert, however.

» Actor Richard Harrison blames Godfrey Ho for ruining his career after he "starred" in several Ho films via outtakes and cut scenes that originally came from other films.

 Trivia Quiz

What is the origin of the black outfits worn by many ninja?

A: Kabuki theater performances

B: Like everything else about ninja, it is shrouded in mystery

C: Uniform commissioned by Oda Nobunaga in AD 1581

D: A Japanese costume designer who worked on the 1962 film *Godzilla vs. the Ninjabots*

Answer: A. After gaining fame as scouts, spies, and assassins in sixteenth-century Japan, the ninja entered the realm of popular imagination and began appearing as characters in Kabuki theater.

OASIS OF THE ZOMBIES
(AKA *"BLOODSUCKING NAZI ZOMBIES"*)
Eurociné, 1981

PRODUCER Marius Lesoeur

WRITER A. L. Mariaux

DIRECTOR A. M. Frank

STARS Manuel Gélin (*Robert*), France Lomay (*Erika*), Henry Lambert (*Kurt*), Myriam Landson (*Kurt's wife*), and Caroline Audret (*Sylvie*)

Two rival groups head to a distant oasis in search of Nazi gold. There they are set upon by Nazi zombies who are guarding the treasure for who-knows-what-reason.

Why It Sucks

Jess Franco, in his second effort worthy of this chapter—hiding behind the pseudonyms A. M. Frank (for direction) and A. L. Mariaux (for the script, together with producer Marius Lesoeur)—managed to make a movie about sexually perverted Nazi zombies that is almost completely unwatchable. From its nonexistent story (nothing is explained and no characters are interesting or developed in the slightest) to its badly written dialogue, to its overblown musical score, bad makeup effects on the zombies, a near-criminal lack of gore and nudity, this is truly one of the worst movies included in this book.

Thumbs Down Rating: 🦃🦃🦃🦃🦃

The Crappies

The Mysogonistic Sex Pervert Award goes to . . . Jess Franco for making a film where the zombies tend to fondle a female's genitals while attacking her.

And the Worst Picture Award goes to . . . Jess Franco and Marius Lesoeur for not even being able to pull off the idiot-proof concept of a horror film wth Nazi zombies.

They Really Said It!

Col. Meitzell: Did you find what you were looking for?

Robert: Mainly I found myself.

Betcha Didn't Know

» The World War II battle scenes in the film were lifted from *Heroes Without Glory* (1971).

» Two nearly identical vesions of this film were made, one intended for the French market and the other for international release.

Trivia Quiz

What classic horror novel formed the basis for one of Jess Franco's best films?

A: *Frankenstein*

B: *Herbert West: Re-Animator*

C: *The Strange Case of Dr. Jekyll and Mr. Hyde*

D: *Dracula*

Answer: D. With a cast that included Christopher Lee, Herbert Lom, and Klaus Kinski, in 1970 Franco managed to make one of his best movies.

RING OF TERROR
Playstar, 1962

PRODUCER Alfeo Bocchicchio

WRITERS Lewis Simeon and G. J. Zinnerman

DIRECTOR Clark L. Paylow

STARS George E. Mather (*Lewis Moffitt*), Jospeh Conway (*R. J. Dobson*), Esther Furst (*Betty Crawford*), Norman Ollstead (*Lewis's roommate*), Lomax Study (*Professor Rayburn*), Pamela Raymond (*Alice Lund*), and Ollie O'Toole (*Dr. Walsh*)

260   A dippy graveyard caretaker (Conway) relates a deadly, dull tale of a medical student (Mather) who experiences the ultimate terror . . . and tries to bore the viewers to death.

Why It Sucks

From its cast of "college students" (played by actors in their late thirties or early forties) to the goofy plot, there's not much to recommend here. It's as if a group of actors whose starring roles had been in health education films wrote a script outline on a napkin from the strip-club they were working at, rented a camera, and ad-libbed the whole thing. No exaggeration.

Thumbs Down Rating: 🦃🦃🦃🦃🦃

The Crappies

The Worst Director Award goes to . . . Clark L. Paylow. Maybe he liked this film, but I can't find anybody else who did.

And the Special Achievement in Discouraging Teenage Sexual Activity Award goes to . . . The lover's lane make-out scene between the actors who are all twenty years' older than they're playing. It is so awkward and painful and embarrassing to watch that it will cool all but the hottest of jets.

They Really Said It!

Dobson: All monuments, from the simplest to the most elaborate, stand erect on the closed books of the lives of our dearly departed.

Betcha Didn't Know

» Clark Paylow's career in film spanned forty years. Among his many credits is producer on Steven Spielberg's sci-fi hit *Close Encounters of the Third Kind* (1977).

» George Mather worked as a production supervisor on the original *Star Wars* (1977), overseeing the miniature effects.

 Trivia Quiz

What other project did scripters Lewis Simeon and G. J. Zinnerman contribute to?

A: *Close Encounters of the Third Kind* (1977)

B: *Battle Star Galactica* (1978 pilot)

C: *Buck Rogers in the 25th Century* (1979 pilot)

D: None of the above.

Answer: D. *Ring of Terror* was the only script credit for either writer.

ROCKABILLY VAMPIRE (AKA *"BURNIN' LOVE"*)
Garage Rock Pictures, 1996

PRODUCER Stacy Haber Hofberg

WRITERS Lee Bennett Sobel and Paul Gambino

DIRECTOR Lee Bennett Sobel

STARS Stephen Blackehart (*Wrecks Vincent*), Margaret Lancaster (*Iris Dougherty*), Paul Stevenson (*Eddie Vincent*), Wendy Walker (*Emma Cross*), and Dennis Davies (*Benny Lawalski*)

An Elvis-obsessed writer (Lancaster) falls in love with a vampire who bears a passing resemblance to the King when he was young (Stevenson).

Why It Sucks

Some people just shouldn't try to make comedies. *Rockabilly Vampire* is unfunny and badly executed with pathetically weak horror overtones, with attempts to make the characters endearing through stereotypically dorky behavior and making the villains menacing using techniques that schoolyard bullies might be ashamed of. There isn't a scene in the film that doesn't go on for far too long. Worse, the characters are universally uninteresting. Great title, though!

Thumbs Down Rating: 🐾🐾🐾🐾🐾

The Crappies

The Worst Editing Award goes to . . . Dennis Chomininsky for cutting every single scene and shot in the movie so languidly that you'd think he was on Valium.

And the Worst Director Award goes to . . . Lee Bennett Sobel, who didn't have the sense to know when to end scenes. In fact, sometimes characters repeat themselves as if the editors had left several takes of the same scene in the film.

Test Your Stamina

They Really Said It!

Wrecks: God, huh? Well, you better hope the Devil doesn't jump up and bite you in the ass.

Betcha Didn't Know

» This film was completed in 1995, but sat on the shelf until 2001 when it was released by Troma as part of a vampire-themed multifilm DVD set. Even the Troma team knew what a dog this film is.

» Stephen Blackehart, who plays the evil vampire Wrecks, has enjoyed a busy career playing bit parts on television and larger roles in low-budget horror flicks from the likes of Full Moon Features, Troma Films, and the Asylum.

Trivia Quiz

What real-world mythological creature could well be a "rockabilly vampire"?

A: Banshee

B: Gaki

C: Poltergeist

D: Kraken

Answer: B. According to Japanese beliefs, a gaki is the restless spirit of someone who died in a state of envy and spends the afterlife trying to obtain in death what it could not in life.

SCREAM BLOODY MURDER (AKA *"MATTHEW," "CLAW OF TERROR,"* AND *"THE CAPTIVE WOMAN"*)

Alan Roberts Productions/First American Films, 1973

PRODUCERS Alan Roberts (executive producer) and Marc B. Ray (producer)

WRITERS Larry Alexander and Marc B. Ray

DIRECTOR Marc B. Ray

STARS Fred Holbert (*Matthew*), Leigh Mitchell (*Vera/Daisy Parsons*), and Angus Scrimm (*Dr. Epstein*)

A demented freak (Holbert) with an Oedipus complex that extends to every couple (or hooker and john) he meets, goes on a killing spree.

Why It Sucks

I suppose if you're into pointless sadistic mysogynism, this will pretty much be your cup of tea. The main character is repulsive, and there's not much to like about most of his victims. Although the fact that the killer's hand has been replaced with a murderous hook does give this a strange surreality.

Thumbs Down Rating: 👎 👎 👎 👎 👎

The Crappies

The Worst Actor Award goes to . . . Fred Holbert for his somnambulistic portrayal of a serial killer. You've got a hook for a hand, guy! Enjoy it!

And the Worst Director Award goes to . . . Marc B. Ray for a sense of pacing that stops with knowing how to say, "Cut!"

They Really Said It!

Matthew: Eat, or I'll cut your tongue out.

Betcha Didn't Know

» The soundtrack was composed by Rockwell (born Kennedy Gordy), the son of Motown founder Berry Gordy. Rockwell had a small number of hit songs during the 1980s, the biggest of these being "Somebody's Watching Me."

» This was the first and only credited film role for actor Fred Holbert.

 Trivia Quiz

Who is the only actor appearing in *Scream Bloody Murder* with more than one or two film credits?

A: Leigh Mitchell

B: Angus Scrimm

C: Robert Knox

D: Gloria Earl

Test Your Stamina

Answer: B. Angus Scrimm is best known for his portrayal of the monstrous undertaker in the Phantasm series.

SIN, YOU SINNERS!
Farno Productions, 1963

PRODUCER Arnold Panken

WRITER Joseph W. Sarno

DIRECTORS Joseph W. Sarno and Anthony Farrar

STARS June Colburne (*Bobbi*), Dian Lloyd (*Julie*), Derek Murcott (*Dave*), and Beverly Nazarow (*Gloria*)

An aging stripper (Colburne) keeps her youthful looks (sort of) and energy thanks to a voodoo amulet and enchantments powered by a moon goddess. Between shows, she tells fortunes and brews love potions with a method that involves putting her daughter (Lloyd) through magically induced orgasms until she passes out. Until someone steals her amulet . . . .

Why It Sucks

Sin, You Sinners! was made by filmmakers with no talent and features actors only slightly more able. But there's an interesting idea here. Of course, there's the fact that the majority of the film seems to have been shot in the same tiny room, rearranging the furniture for different scenes. The cameraman tried to get around this by filming as much of the movie as possible in close up, which gives us a weird feeling of claustrophobia.

Thumbs Down Rating: 👎👎👎👎

The Crappies

The Worst Script Award goes to . . . Joseph W. Sarno for his inability to properly exploit the fertile voodoo angle he put into the story (although as director, he did do a nice job with the magic orgasm potion brewing scene).

And the Worst Producer Award goes to . . . Arnold Panken for not being able to raise enough funds to rent a second room to film in.

They Really Said It!

Julie: Mama, how long? I mean, how long are you going to go on like this? I mean, your dirty act, taking off your clothes in front of a bunch of filthy drunks. You can't do it forever.

Betcha Didn't Know

» Reportedly, only one single, damaged print of the film remained when the DVD version was made for Alpha Video.

» Joseph W. Sarno helped create the sexploitation genre in the 1960s.

 Trivia Quiz

Whom among the stars of *Sin, You Sinners!* had an honest-to-God acting career?

A: June Colburne

B: Dian Lloyd

C: Derek Murcott

D: Beverly Nazarow

Answer: C. Derek Murcott started in the late 1950s and continued to work through the mid-1980s. His final role was in the pilot for the television show *The Equalizer.*

SEE NO EVIL
WWE Films/Lions Gate Entertainment, 2006

PRODUCERS Peter Block, Matt Carroll, Vince McMohan (executive producers), Joel Simon (producer)

WRITER Dan Madigan

DIRECTOR Gregory Dark

STARS Glen "Kane" Jacobs (*Jacob Goodnight*), Samantha Noble (*Kira*), Christina Vidal (*Christine*), Luke Pegler (*Michael*), and Steven Vidler (*Williams*)

Eight juvenile offenders trade a weekend of cleaning up at a historical landmark for a month off their sentence. Unfortunately, an insane killer with a love for plucking his victims' eyes out (Jacobs) is hiding inside the landmark, and he starts killing them, one by one.

Why It Sucks

The director and producers of this film were so focused on grossing out viewers with disgusting and sadistic violence that they didn't bother to hire decent actors or to commission a real script. (In fairness the girls seem to have been hired for their ability to scream.)

Thumbs Down Rating: 👎👎👎

The Crappies

The Worst Script Award goes to . . . Dan Madigan for coming up with a film that's little more than a string of slasher-movie clichés. *And the Worst Acting Award goes to* . . . Glen Jacobs who was more intimidating back when he wore a black duster and wide-brimmed hat and played The Undertaker, a wrestler backed by Dark Supernatural Powers, back when the WWE was known as the WWF.

They Really Said It!

Kira: This is not what God wants!

Betcha Didn't Know

» The villain's name, Jacob Goodnight, is never mentioned in the film and can only be gleaned from the credits.
» A room has walls that are papered with dollar bills, each and everyone has its eyes cut out. It's the creepiest sight in the whole thing.

 Trivia Quiz
Why did the World Wrestling Federation (WWF) change its name to World Wrestling Entertainment (WWE)?

A: They were sued for trademark infringement by the World Wide Fund for Nature (WWF)

B: WWF is an abbreviation for necropheliac bestiality in eastern European nations.

C: Founder Vince McMohan wanted a new name for the company for the new century.

D: WWF and WWE have always been two seperate professional wrestling circuits.

SKELETON MAN
Martini Film/Nu Image/Two Sticks Productions, 2004

PRODUCERS Boaz Davidson, Danny Dimbort, Avi Lerner, and Trevor Short (executive producers), Charles Arthur Berg, Johnny Martin, David E. Ornston, and Richard Salvatore (producers)

WRITER Frederick Bailey

DIRECTOR Johnny Martin

STARS Michael Rooker (*Capt. Leary*), Casper Van Dien (*Staff Sgt. Oberron*), Sarah Ann Schultz (*Lt. Scott*), Jerry Trimble (*Staff Sgt. Lawrence*), Noa Tishby (*Sgt. Davis*), Jackie Debatin (*Sgt. Cordero*), and Eric Etebari (*Lt. York*)

Captain Leary (Rooker) leads a team of military specialists into the forests of the Northwest to hunt a killer who has already taken out some of best the U.S. military has to offer—as well as some civilians. Unfortunately, the soldiers are fighting the awakened spirit of a homicidal maniac bent on killing everything and anything he comes across.

Why It Sucks

Skeleton Man is a tepid, disorganized slasher flick. Elements are tossed in at random, with no attempt to resolve anything. *Why* is Skeleton Man killing? *Why* is his spirit roaming? You'd think the writers would at least be interested in these questions.

Thumbs Down Rating: 🐾🐾🐾🐾🐾

The Crappies

The Worst Costume Design goes to . . . Erica Englehardt and Kristen Evenson, who created the look of Skeleton Man out of a mask bought at Wal-Mart and some blackout curtains.

Test Your Stamina

And the Worst Director Award goes to . . . Johnny Martin for either not noticing or not caring that his monster and the horse it rides on changed appearances from scene to scene.

They Really Said It!
Sgt. Cordero: If you can see it, I can shoot it.

Betcha Didn't Know
» Since 1986, Michael Rooker has appeared in almost 100 movies and television series, and as of this writing he has more than ten projects under way.
» The German-market DVD edition of this film identified it not as a horror movie but as a comedy, invoking the name of Edward D. Wood Jr. in the sell-copy on the cover.

 Trivia Quiz
Which of the behind-the-camera people who worked on *Skeleton Man* is an accomplished stuntman and stunt coordinator, having worked on over 150 movies and television series (including *Killer Klowns From Outer Space*)?

A: Johnny Martin

B: Trevor Short

C: Danny Dimbort

D: Kristen Evenson

Answer: A. And he makes one helluva stuntman.

THE ST. FRANCISVILLE EXPERIMENT
Kushner-Locke Company, 2000

PRODUCERS Charles Band (executive producer), Paul Salamoff, Dana Scanlon, and Gary Schmoeller (producers)

WRITER Uncredited

DIRECTOR Ted Nicolaou

STARS Tim Baldini (*Videorapher/Film Student*), Madison Charap (*Psychic*), Paul James Palmer (*Team Leader*), Troy Taylor (*Ghost Historian*), and Ryan Larson (*History Student*)

A psychic and three college students agree to spend the night in a reputedly haunted house in order to prove the existence of the supernatural.

Why It Sucks

The tagline for this film was "Everything You've Heard Is True." If you've heard that *The St. Francisville Experiment* is a steaming pile of crap, then . . . well . . . this is one of an endless stream of films that have attempted to recapture the success of *The Blair Witch Project*. I doubt I will ever see another movie that fails so spectacularly at doing what it set out to do.

The movie starts pretending to be a documentary, but the filmmakers quickly abandon that conceit, thus undercutting the whole premise of the movie. If all their "evidence" of supernatural hauntings were true, it would have been all over CNN.

Thumbs Down Rating: 🖓🖓🖓🖓

The Crappies

The Worst Picture Award goes to . . . Everyone involved in the production and post-produciton of this film. How could they have screwed up a "reality-based" film as badly as this?

And the Worst Animation Award goes to . . . John R. Ellis for some of the worst fake poltergeist activity ever captured on film, not to mention some of the most out-of-place CGI ever. (It might not be his fault . . . the producers might have thought they needed to "sex up" this deadly dull movie, and they may have decided that everything is better with computer-animated ghosties!)

They Really Said It!

Tim: It was me. I farted.

Betcha Didn't Know

» Troy Taylor is an author of nonfiction works about and an organizer of tours of haunted places. He reportedly did not know he was taking part in a project of pure fiction.

» Director Ted Nicolaou has worked with Charles Band in many capacities since the 1980s, serving as editor and/or director on many of his productions, including Leapin' Leprechauns.

(Maybe this film would have been better with leprechauns instead of ghosts.)

Trivia Quiz

What monster movie franchise did writer/director Ted Nicolaou helm, making the series uniquely his own in the process?

A: *Mandroid*

B: *Puppet Master*

C: *Subspecies*

D: *Trancers*

Answer: C. During the 1990s, Nicolaou wrote and directed four entries in the *Subspecies* series, plus the loosely affiliated spinoff *The Vampire Diaries*.

TRACK OF THE MOON BEAST
Brandon Films/Lizard Productions, 1976

PRODUCERS Frank J. Desiderio (executive producer) and Ralph T. Desiderio (producer)

WRITERS William Finger and Charles Sinclair

DIRECTOR Dick Ashe

STARS Chase Cordell (*Paul Carlson*), Donna Leigh Drake (*Kathy Nolan*), and Gregorio Sala (*Professor Johnny "Longbow" Salinas*)

When a meteor crashes near where archaeologist Paul Carlson (Cordell) is stargazing with his free-lovin' honey, Kathy (Drake), a tiny space-rock fragment is lodged in his brain. Now, whenever the moon is in the sky, he transforms into a hideous, reptilian creature. To make matters worse, his body is becoming "molecularly unstable"! Will his American-Indian colleague, Johnny "Longbow" Salinas (Sala) be able to use science and Ancient Native Wisdom to save or slay Paul before he blows up?

Why It Sucks

The acting is universally wooden, the dialogue atrociously written, and the camerawork and other production values are barely

Test Your Stamina

competent. In some cases they aren't even that, such as during the painfully bad time-lapse photography sequence of Paul transforming into the Moon Beast. Or maybe when one changes from a human to a giant, humanoid reptile, an extra set of eyes and a second nose appear and disappear as part of the process.

Thumbs Down Rating: 🎭🎭🎭🎭🎭

The Crappies
The Worst Cinematography Award goes to . . . R. Kent Evans (hiding behind the pseudonym E. Scott Wood) for stop-motion photography so bad that even grade schoolers would have been embarrassed to show their efforts in public.
And the Worst Writing Award goes to . . . Bill Finger. Why, Bill, why? You wrote so many great comic book scripts!

They Really Said It!
Johnny Longbow: My guess is that there is some unusual element in this fragment that synchronizes with that larger mass over there and it produces some kind of energy reaction!

Betcha Didn't Know
» Although completed in 1972, this film wasn't released until 1976 due to problems finding a distributor willing to take it on.
» This was the last (or only) film project for Richard Ashe, Bill Finger, R. Kent Evans, Charles Sinclair, and Gregorio Sala. It's not hard to see why.

 Trivia Quiz
What famous comic book hero did *Track of the Moon Beast* writer William Finger co-create in 1939?
A: The Spirit
B: Superman
C: Batman
D: Spider-Man

Test Your Stamina

TRANSYLMANIA
Film Rock/Hill & Brand Entertainment, 2009

PRODUCERS Nicolas Bonavia, Aaron L. Gilbert, Edward Jarzobski, Michael Long, Scott Nell (executive producers), Sandford Hampton, and Viorel Sergovici (producers)

WRITERS Patrick Casey and Worm Miller

DIRECTORS David Hillenbrand and Scott Hillenbrand

STARS Oren Skoog (*Rusty/Radu*), Jennifer Lyons (*Lynne*), Tony Denman (*Newmar*), Patrick Cavanaugh (*Pete*), Paul H. Kim (*Wang*), Musetta Vander (*Teodora Van Sloan*), Natalie Garza (*Lia*), Nicole Garza (*Danni*), David Steinberg (*Dean Floca*), James DeBello (*Cliff*), and Irena A. Hoffman (*Draguta Floca*)

A group of American college students travel to a remote Transylvanian university for a semester of studying and partying abroad. Will the partying or the vampires kill them first?

Why It Sucks
The humor is more stupidly offensive than funny, and the acting universally weak. The story features numerous characters who do nothing and clutter up the film and story. In the hands of competent writers who understood how to streamline a story (not to mention write funny jokes) and with some better actors, this could have been a really good movie. Oh, well.

Thumbs Down Rating: 👎👎👎👎

The Crappies
The Underachievement in Marketing Award goes to . . . Distribution and production company Hill & Brand Entertainment for thinking that their film could ride the coattails of the *Twilight*-type teen vampire movies even though they're spoofing a completely different area of the the horror genre. (The film was completed in 2007 but not released until 2009.)

And the Worst Directors Award goes to . . . David Hillenbrand and Scott Hillenbrand for crossing a stoner comedy with a spoof of

Test Your Stamina

classic horror movies and still not being able to come up with anything that inspires more than a chuckle.

They Really Said It!

Cliff: I've got the perfect way to pick up girls. I tell them I'm a vampire hunter.

Betcha Didn't Know

» *Transylmania* died harder at the box office than a vampire venturing outside at high noon. It opened on roughly 1,000 screens and only brought in around $400,000.

» Before teaming with his brother to direct stoner comedies, David Hillenbrand worked as a conductor and music coordinator on a number of different television series, including *Mighty Morphin' Power Rangers*.

 Trivia Quiz

What was the first movie to feature vampires and mad scientists in the same story?

A: *House of Dracula*

B: *House of Frankenstein*

C: *Son of Dracula*

D: *Nosferatu*

Answer: B. *House of Frankenstein* featured John Carradine as Dracula and Boris Karloff as a mad scientist. It also included Frankenstein's Creature and the Wolfman.

UFO: TARGET EARTH
Jed Productions, 1974

PRODUCER Michael A. DeGaetano

WRITER Michael A. DeGaetano

DIRECTOR Michael A. DeGaetano

STARS Nick Plakias (*Alan Grimes*), Cynthia Cline (*Vivian*), and Ed Lynch (*University Professor*)

Alan (Plakias) and his psychic sidekick (Cline) search for evidence that a UFO has crashed in a remote, backcountry lake, and of a possible government cover-up.

Why It Sucks

Even before it's clear just how bad the script for this film is, viewers will recognize what a lack of vision and focus can accomplish for a director. Among the disjointed, ineptly filmed, amateurishly acted scenes we are also treated to a couple of pointless references to *2001* and 1970s occult culture. And they present it in the most turgid and mind-numbingly dull fashion—at least to those of us who aren't high on 'shrooms and whatever else might be handy. I'm sure the filmmakers thought they were being artsy, but the film appears to have been made in the outer reaches of the No Talent Zone.

Thumbs Down Rating: 👎👎👎👎👎

The Crappies

The Special Achievement in Helping the Cover-up Award goes to . . . Cinematic jack-of-trades Michael A. DeGaetano. Listen to late-night talk radio or even watch an episode of the Fox series *Lie to Me*, and you'll discover how the government is covering up UFOs. Watch this movie, and you'll be so bored with the topic, you won't care if the truth is here, out there, or anywhere.

And the Worst Actor Award goes to . . . Nick Plakias, who performs in this film with no changes in facial expressions or vocal inflections; every line is delivered with the vacant tone of a heavily medicated mental patient.

They Really Said It!

Alan: Something is bothering me. Partly, it's a scientific curiosity. Partly it's just curiosity.
University professor: Do you understand the difference?
Allen: Does anyone?

Betcha Didn't Know

» This is the one and only film appearance for the stars of this movie. In fact, the most accomplished cast members in the flick—some of the bit players—appeared in small roles in as many as three other films.

» Nick Plakias went onto a career as a stage actor and a folk-singer. In 2002 he also had a small part on an episode of *Law & Order: Criminal Intent*.

 Trivia Quiz

Which actor's break-through role saw him playing an alien visitor to the planet Earth?

A: John Wayne

B: Ray Walston

C: Robin Williams

D: Orson Welles

Answer: C. In 1978 Williams guest starred on television's *Happy Days* as Mork, a visitor from the planet Ork. The character was such a hit that Mork was given his own show, *Mork and Mindy*, which ran from 1978 to 1982.

THE UNDERTAKER AND HIS PALS
Eola Pictures, 1966

PRODUCERS David C. Graham (executive producer) and Alex Grattan (producer)

WRITER T. L. P. Swicegood

DIRECTOR T. L. P. Swicegood

STARS Rad Fulton (*Harry Glass*), Ray Dannis (*The Undertaker*), Rick Cooper (*Spike*), Marty Friedman *(Doc)*, and Warrene Ott (*Thursday* and *Friday*)

A crooked undertaker (Dannis) and his café-owning psychotic friends (Cooper and Friedman) murder beautiful young women so that the cooks can serve part of the bodies in their restaurant, while the undertaker overcharges the families for burying the remaining remains. The scheme is working perfectly until they target twin sexpots Thursday and Friday (Ott) and draw the attention of a gallant private eye (Fulton).

Why It Sucks

It's a failed attempt to make a dark comedy that spoofs horror films and detective films, but you need to have the sense of humor of a ten-year-old boy to appreciate what few decent gags are present. While the ending does offer something unexpected (and is far better than anything that leads up to it), to get there you'll suffer through bad acting and even worse dialogue.

Thumbs Down Rating:

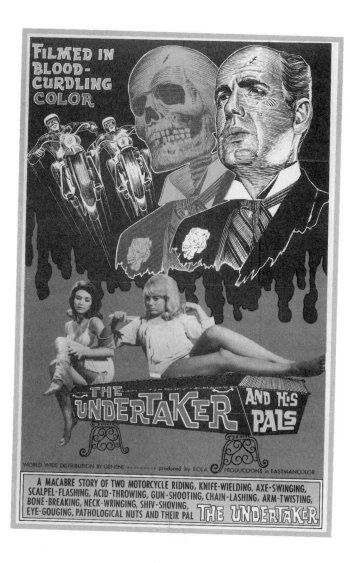

The Crappies

The Worst Editing Award goes to . . . Whoever butchered this film in response to demands from censors. The violent and gory scenes are sloppily and obviously edited in ways not consistent with the rest of the film, and are invariably missing anything resembling a "money shot."

And the Worst Cinematic Sleight-of-Hand Award goes to . . . T. L. P. Swicegood for his clumsy attempt to create the illusion of a tall building by showing actors running up the same flight of stairs over and over.

They Really Said It!

The Undertaker: We specifically agreed that I could bury Doc's mistakes!

Betcha Didn't Know

» Reportedly, the film was recut and many gory scenes removed after being banned in several American cities upon its original release. No prints of the original film are known to survive.

» Actress Warrene Ott appeared in over a dozen movies and on numerous television series in small roles. She started her show business career as a toddler.

Trivia Quiz

How did Rad Fulton (also known as James Westmoreland) make a living after his semi-retirement from acting in the early 1970s?

A: Motorcycle racer

B: Professional golfer

C: Professional surfer

D: Drama coach

Answer: B. He was a professional golfer and later an inventor. Another James Westmoreland, British and born in 1988, races motorcycles.

MOVIE INDEX

279

GENERAL INDEX

General Index

287

Timberlake, Justin, 99–100
Tishby, Noa, 268–69
Toden, Bruno, 207–9
Tohn, Jackie, 197–98
Torn, Rip, 98–99, 238–39
Tostevin, Carl, 73–75
Towers, Harry Alan, 232–34
Toyoshima, Izumi, 161–63
Travis, June, 251–53
Travolta, John, 1–3
Tremblay, Pierre, 171–73
Trimble, Jerry, 268–69
Troyer, Verne, 99–100, 197–98
Truchado, José, 204–5
Tsai Chin, 232–34
Tucker Jonathan, 59–60
Turkel, Ann, 132–33

Ulmer, Edgar G., 104–6
Urecal, Minerva, 179–81
Ushler, Bill, 202–3
Uslan, Michael E., 25–26, 95–98
Utusi, Ken, 236–38

Vaillancourt, Marc, 65–66
Van Clief, Ron, 190–92
Vander, Musetta, 273–74
Van Dien, Casper, 268–69
Van Hawley, Norman, 138–40
Van Horn, Emil, 179–81
Varhelyi, Murielle, 194–95
Vasquez, Santiago, 183–84
Vega, Paz, 25–26
Vere-Jones, Peter, 77–79
Verg, Henry, 244–46
Verhaeghe, Victor, 187–88
Vernon, John, 219–20
VeSota, Bruno, 114–16
Vickers, Yvette, 114–16
Vidal, Christina, 266–68
Vidler, Steven, 266–68
Vidor, Charles, 31–33
Vigeant, Phil, 195–97
Vitti, Monica, 108–9
Voigt, Jon, 226–28
Von Hausen, Paul, 189–90

Wah Yuen, 169–71
Walcott, Gregory, 220–22
Walken, Christopher, 16–17
Walker, Clint, 146–47
Walker, Wendy, 262–63
Wallerstein, Herb, 146–47
Walters, Luana, 41–42
Walters, Toddy, 81–83
Walton, Fred, 67–69
Wang, Joey, 163–64
Wang, Zhonglei, 169–71
Ward, Dave Oren, 247–48
Ward, Zack, 197–98
Ware, Irene, 112–13
Wascavage, Dave, 202–3
Washburn, Richard R., 85–86
Washburn, Rick, 85–86
Watanabe, Noriko, 161–63
Waterston, Sam, 16–17
Watkin, Ian, 51–52
Watson, Barry, 122–23
Watts, Robert, 101–2
Wayne, John, 14–15
Webster, Nicholas, 71–73
Weeden, Bill, 211–13
Weidoff, David, 127–29
Weiner, Paul, 140–41
Weintraub, Cindy, 132–33
Welles, Mel, 44–46
Wellington, Thomas, 185–87
Wells, Christine, 257–58
Wells, Jacqueline, 104–6
Wells, Julian, 120–21
Weng Weng, 166–67
Werner, Michael J., 149–50
West, Beth, 140–41
West, Dan, 140–41
Whitaker, Forest, 1–3
White, Albert Z., 254–55
White, Steve, 39–41
Whiteman, Paul, 44–46
Whiteside, Glyn, 215–17
Wik, Steve, 197–98
Williams, Treat, 91–93
Williamson, Fred, 190–92
Williamson, Shawn, 197–98, 225–26
Willis, Bruce, 19–20
Wilson, George, 118–20

Wilson, Lambert, 22–24
Wilson, Luke, 209–10
Wilson, Michael G., 109–10
Wilson, Rainn, 209–10
Wilson, Thomas F., 67–69
Winnick, Katheryn, 73–75
Wittes, Kathy, 182–83
Wong, Casanova, 89–90
Wong, Jing, 163–64
Wong, Michael, 163–64
Wood, Edward D., Jr., 3–5, 220–22
Woods, Bill, 250–51
Woods, Ella, 43–44
Woronov, Mary, 75–76
Wren, Doug, 77–79
Wright, Jason, 9–11

Yamada, Goichi, 61–62
Yamaguchi, Kazuhiko, 176–78
Yashiro, Minase, 55–57
Yau, Chingmy, 163–64
Yellen, Mark, 39–41
Yen-Ping Chu, 165–66
Yi-Jung Hua, 137–38
Yip, Dinny, 257–58
Yorke, Carl Gabriel, 47–49
Yoshimine, Kineo, 176–78
Yu, Jimmy Wang, 165–66
Yuasa, Noriaki, 159–61, 168–69
Yuka, 175–76
Yunza, Brian, 57–59, 106–7

Zabalza, José María, 129–30
Zadora, Pia, 71–73
Zahn, Steve, 22–24
Zemeckis, Robert, 102–3
Zien, Chip, 17–19
Zimmern, Terri, 138–40
Zinni, Karl, 54–55
Zipp, William, 240–41
Zobian, Mark, 187–88
Zucker, David, 226–28

DAILY BENDER

Want Some More?

Hit up our humor blog, The Daily Bender, to get your fill of all things funny—be it subversive, odd, offbeat, or just plain mean. The Bender editors are there to get you through the day and on your way to happy hour. Whether we're linking to the latest video that made us laugh or calling out (or bullshit on) whatever's happening, we've got what you need for a good laugh.

If you like our book, you'll love our blog. (And if you hated it, "man up" and tell us why.) Visit The Daily Bender for a shot of humor that'll serve you until the bartender can.

Sign up for our newsletter at
www.adamsmedia.com/blog/humor
and download our Top Ten Maxims No Man Should Live Without.